D1617554

The CLANDESTINE

Building of

Libya's Chemical

Weapons Factory

*A Study in
International
Collusion*

Thomas C. Wiegele

Southern Illinois University Press
Carbondale and Edwardsville

Edited by Jill Butler

Designed by Kyle L. Lake

Production supervised by Natalia Nadraga

95 94 93 92   4 3 2 1

Library of Congress Cataloging-in-Publication Data

Wiegele, Thomas C.
    The clandestine building of Libya's chemical weapons factory : a
study in international collusion / Thomas C. Wiegele.
        p.   cm.
    Includes bibliographical references and index.
    1. Chemical arms control.   2. Chemical weapons—
Libya.   3. Weapons industry—Political aspects—Libya.   I. Title.
JX5133.C5W54   1992
341.7'35—dc20   91-32975
ISBN 0-8093-1775-3   CIP

To
Katharine Lindsey
Jordan Mary
Jonathan Taylor
Thomas Nieman
David Edward
Timothy Garrett

CONTENTS

Acknowledgments   ix

1. Introduction   1

2. The Development of a Critical International Situation   12

3. The Aftermath of the Charge, 1   24

4. The Aftermath of the Charge, 2   35

5. The Paris Chemical Weapons Conference   56

6. The Explosion of Events in West Germany   70

7. Satisfaction and Disenchantment   113

8. An Operational Assessment of the Rabta Episode   124

9. Deception, Lies, and Secrecy in an Act of Proliferation   137

10. Some Policy-making Considerations   154

Notes   169

References   187

Index   193

ACKNOWLEDGMENTS

Few books are written without considerable help from others, and this volume is no exception. Primary financial support was provided by the United States Institute of Peace, grant number USIP-015-2-90. I also employed funds from my appointment as a Presidential Research Professor at Northern Illinois University. I appreciate the support of the Institute of Peace as well as the confidence placed in me by President John E. La Tourette and Vice President for Research Jerrold H. Zar, both of Northern Illinois University.

Several graduate research assistants helped considerably in locating the source materials utilized in constructing this study. Chief among these was Yong Xing, who did the initial spade work with great diligence and professional acumen. James David Ivers provided assistance for the chapter on deception, and on short notice, Kenneth Biswell and Miriam Levitt sought numerous documents to fill various cracks.

A number of individuals read portions of the manuscript, and their invaluable comments not only cleared up factual difficulties but also helped me think through numerous judgments. My valued colleague at Northern Illinois University, Professor Manfred W. Wenner, read substantial portions of the manuscript and provided numerous useful suggestions from the point of view of a Middle Eastern scholar. Ambassador Lynn M. Hansen's extensive reflections on the Paris Chemical Weapons Conference gave me a much clearer sense of what actually happened there. Two British readers, J. P. Perry Robinson of the University of Sussex and Edward M. Spiers of the University of Leeds, were meticulous and thorough in their critique of an early draft. Raymond A. Zilinskas of the University of Maryland, Baltimore County, not only read the core chapters but also sent me numerous items of information that proved important in documenting certain aspects of the case. Milton Leitenberg of the University of Maryland and Michael Brzoska of Hamburg University very kindly answered several key questions and steered me to a number of useful resources.

My secretary, Carolyn Cradduck, performed her usual magic in word processing the manuscript, which went through numerous drafts. Her careful work over many years has been invaluable to me. I salute her for her good cheer and professional abilities.

I also owe a word of thanks to Dr. S. Bhaskaran, chairperson of the Department of Political Science at Annamalai University, India, who very kindly provided me with office facilities to complete the final draft of the manuscript, when I served there as a Fulbright professor during the spring of 1991.

This book is dedicated to my grandchildren. I pray that they may never have to experience the horrors of chemical warfare and that they will grow up in a world in which the creation of chemical arsenals is impossible and such conflict is irrevocably banned for all time.

I alone am responsible for any errors of fact or judgment this volume might contain.

The CLANDESTINE Building of Libya's Chemical Weapons Factory

1

Introduction

The purpose of this study is to develop an understanding of how a third world nation could engage in a decade-long effort to clandestinely extract chemicals and chemical processing equipment from an international system that was presumably predisposed to halting the proliferation of chemical weapons capabilities. From around 1980 through 1989, Libya succeeded in acquiring the necessary ingredients to construct an elaborate chemical weapons production facility within its borders. This was done in spite of the strong opposition of several nations, including one of the superpowers, the United States. Libya's successful quest was supported by several of her Middle Eastern neighbors, although the primary physical assistance came from high technology industrialized powers that willingly allowed their products to be assembled into a facility to produce chemical weapons. In this, firms of the Federal Republic of Germany became the major suppliers. The main body of this study focuses on the many details of Libya's success in this effort in which conventional wisdom might easily have predicted a failure.

A major aim of the study is to provide for a broad spectrum of specialists information about the operational anatomy of a case of chemical weapons proliferation. This information should be of particular importance to foreign policy decision makers and their staffs, who have the political responsibility to deal with questions relating to the spread of chemical weapons. The work is also addressed to political scientists and students of science and technology policy, who often deal with the uncomfortable issue of chemical weaponry. These latter individuals produce the literature on chemical weapons proliferation that is at times utilized by the policy-making community. A detailed examination of this important case will throw considerable light on general questions of chemical weapons.

When I first became interested in the Libyan effort, I viewed it as a case of successful antiproliferation. The United States publicly raised the issue of the Libyan chemical weapons factory. That issue

1

remained on the front pages of many newspapers for many months, and a major international conference was called to deal with chemical weapons. Over several months, however, my initial views were gradually transformed into a disappointing reversal. Not only had Libya built a chemical weapons production facility, but it was most unlikely that it would be deterred from proceeding with its further development. Thus, this became a case of successful chemical weapons proliferation, as many nations in the international community watched with concern.

As implied above, this is not a general study on the problems of chemical weapons. Many fine works on this topic already exist, and readers would do well to consult, for example, the writings of Valerie Adams, Julian Perry Robinson, and Edward M. Spiers.[1] However, it is important to note that the international community has yet to approve a convention to control and/or unconditionally prohibit the use of chemical weapons.[2] Much discussion and many meetings of diplomats have been devoted to this topic, so far without success. As technology in this area unfolds, the topic is becoming more complex and seemingly more resistant to a diplomatic solution.

That no international convention on chemical weapons presently exists is an important consideration in the Libyan case. Libya's public dialogue with the international community has been strongly influenced by this fact. Indeed, the case for chemical weapons activities on the part of a number of nations is considerably stronger because of the lack of a convention. Nevertheless, this study should make a contribution to our general knowledge of the proliferation of chemical weapons.

A Definition of Chemical Weapons

A 1969 United Nations document defined chemical weapons as "chemical substances whether gaseous, liquid, or solid, which might be employed because of their direct toxic effects on man, animals, or plants."[3] "Chemical warfare," according to Adams, "is the use against an enemy of chemical weapons. These are weapons which achieve their effect primarily or mainly by the dispersal of a toxic agent derived from chemical substances. They may be used directly to cause casualties, or to deny the use of terrain to an enemy by contaminating it, or to harass the enemy, undermining his operational efficiency by imposing the need for protection."[4] Chemical warfare agents differ from harmful biological agents in that the latter are living materials that can infect other living things and cause disease or death by multiplying in the organism being attacked. Chemicals inflict damage by poisoning organisms.

Chemical weapons, along with nuclear and biological weapons, are usually referred to as instruments of "mass destruction." The capability to harm large numbers of human beings with relative "efficiency" makes chemical weapons universally feared. Their use is considered abhorrent by most observers.

A number of criteria must be met for toxic substances to be of military value. As cataloged by Spiers, these criteria are:

1. "Highly toxic substances must be able to be produced from available raw materials in the quantity required for military purposes."
2. "They must also be stable in storage during the period between production and use."
3. "They must be capable of dissemination from a practical military device in sufficient concentration to produce the desired effect on the target."
4. "They should be capable of being produced easily from [an] existing commercial plant and of being handled and transported safely."
5. "They should have little or no corrosive effects on munitions or containers during storage."
6. "They should be difficult to detect by field armies before the onset of their physiological and/or psychological effects."
7. "They should be difficult for potential enemies to protect against."
8. "The agents' mechanism of action and their requirements in protection and medical treatment should be understood by those proposing to use them."[5]

One problem in controlling the development and proliferation of chemical weapons is that the substances or precursors that initiate the production process that ultimately results in a chemical weapon are readily available through common commercial channels. Numerous chemical weapons precursors have legitimate nonmilitary uses, and they could be acquired for seemingly innocuous and easily justifiable purposes, such as pharmaceutical, fertilizer, petrochemical, or pesticide production. Unfortunately, once acquired, these precursors can be utilized to produce chemical weapons.

Over the past quarter century, a considerable amount of diplomatic attention has been directed to chemical and biological weapons.[6] Conventional diplomatic practice has divided these two weap-

ons areas into distinct political regimes. In 1975 the Convention on
The Prohibition of the Development, Production, and Stockpiling
of Bacteriological (Biological) and Toxin Weapons and on Their
Destruction, commonly referred to as the Biological and Toxin
Weapons Convention (BWC), entered into force, essentially attempting to control the development, stockpiling, and spread of
biological weapons. Acquiring international agreement for a chemical weapons convention, however, has proven much more difficult.

Since 1972 negotiations for a chemical weapons convention
have been held in Geneva under the auspices of the Conference on
Disarmament. In 1984 the United States presented a draft treaty on
chemical weapons disarmament, which was appended to what has
become known as the "rolling text" because it has undergone virtually continuous modification through proposals from various nations. The "rolling text" is now over 100 pages long, and it calls
for the complete elimination of production capacity and chemical
weapons within ten years of entering into force. An important point
to repeat, and one that has critical implications for Libyan diplomacy, is that no ban on chemical weapons has yet been approved
by the international community.

Both the BWC and the proposed chemical weapons convention,
however, are being challenged by new technical developments that
may blur distinctions between biological and chemical weapons. For
example, advances in biotechnology, or genetic engineering, now
make it possible to synthetically produce new toxic substances and
chemicals, increase their pathogenicity, and manufacture them with
enhanced efficiency. The resulting "biochemicals" are not easily
classified diplomatically under the BWC or the proposed chemical
convention, even though chemists consider all chemicals, no matter
how produced, to be chemicals. Statesmen will have to address these
emerging technical realities in future diplomatic negotiations.

Technology, International Relations, and Crazy States

This study can be classified appropriately under the general
area of science, technology, and international relations. It leans
heavily on the insightful work of Dennis Pirages, which emphasizes
the unfolding importance of scientific advancement and technological progress in the international community. Pirages refers to this
phenomenon as "global technopolitics," which he defines as "the
dynamics of an emerging post-industrial international system in-

4

creasingly driven by the imperatives of technology."[7] The emphasis on science and its application in technology has shifted the attention of states "away from gain by conquest to gain through technological domination and resource manipulation."[8] This has created a situation in which the industrialized world finds itself with enormous technological advantages over third world societies, thus forcing developing nations to occasionally choose deceptive strategies to overcome technological backwardness. This is especially the case if such nations view technological advance as a precondition of national security.[9]

Coupled with the importance of science and technology in international relations is Yehezkel Dror's 1971 reconceptualization of the behavior of some states. Dror argues that traditional conceptualizations of state behavior have to be adjusted to take into account what he calls "crazy states" and their emerging influence in the international system. In general, crazy states are those nations that do not conform to normal patterns of behavior but rather adopt behavioral repertoires that counter customary expectations. Dror lays out "five basic dimensions" that define craziness. They are:

1. "Goals . . . are very aggressive against others
2. "[A] deep and intense commitment to these goals, with readiness to pay a high price for their achievement, including a propensity to accept high risks"
3. "[A] sense of superiority towards conventional morals and accepted rules of international behavior, with willingness to be very immoral and illegal in the name of 'higher values'"
4. "[A] capacity to behave logically within the aforementioned paradigms, in the sense of picking means and tools which are instrumental-rational for achieving the 'crazy' goals . . ."
5. "External-action capabilities which permit the crazy state to achieve actual impact on reality including through symbols and threats."[10]

Dror emphasizes that he is not using the concept of craziness in a pejorative way. Rather, states are crazy if they are willing to risk behaving in an unconventional, but rational, manner. Moreover, it is helpful in achieving their objectives for crazy states to engage in acts of deception. "As long as a crazy state is expecting possible counteraction by other multi-actors to its crazy features, before it is ready to absorb them, efforts to hide craziness are preferable" to exposure.[11] Some crazy states, however, may intentionally display their craziness to take advantage of the unwillingness of others to oppose it.

The concept of craziness within an international system that is increasingly structured and organized for the purpose of acquiring the fruits of technology, especially those that relate to national security, forms a backdrop for this study. I have not used the details of Dror's crazy state conceptualization in constructing this case study, but I believe that his general perspective is most useful.

Methodological Considerations

The Libyan chemical weapons factory episode is an awkward case because we are dealing with a clandestine international activity. By their very nature, such activities are carefully guarded by the governments that engage in them. As a result, the amount of information available to researchers is relatively small. I anticipated that I would have a difficult time acquiring a satisfactory base of information upon which to examine a case of successful chemical weapons proliferation. In one respect this was true, but in another it was not.

Most certainly I did not have access to classified documents from any of the nations discussed. The United States, as the chief antagonist against Libyan undertakings, was curiously loathe to provide detailed public information regarding Libya's quest. This is unusual because one would expect the nation making the charges to provide as much public evidence as possible to verify the correctness of its position. Instead, U.S. public charges were often devoid of detail and concrete evidence, thereby allowing critics to insist that the United States had little substantive information implicating Libya. Presumably, the United States transmitted hard evidence to friendly foreign ministries such as those of Great Britain and the Federal Republic of Germany, but this allowed critics of U.S. policy to assert that there was no real case against Libya.

Libya too provided no definitive information, but this should not be surprising since Libya insisted that it was not building a chemical weapons production facility. Nations do not normally have to demonstrate virtue to critics who charge malice. Thus, the Libyans provided little official information regarding their clandestine activities. It should be borne in mind, however, that by their very nature clandestine undertakings related to national security will bring forth policies of stringent secrecy. As a result, the Libyans behaved in customary international ways in constructing a chemical weapons factory.

West Germany and its commercial firms were also major players in the Libyan case. However, though the Germans initially with-held information, they eventually became the most important source of material. This was true both unofficially, in the press, and offi-cially, in documentation eventually released.

Primary sources of information for this project consisted of periodical and press reports. Because international commercial activ-ities regarding chemicals and chemical processing equipment are widespread, and because chemical manufacturers are most sensitive to negative publicity resulting from the misuse of chemicals, com-mercial periodicals frequently carried information about Libyan ac-tivities. Because Libyan undertakings were commercial—since the resources for the production of chemical weapons had to be pur-chased in the international marketplace—commercial literature proved to be valuable in piecing together the network that Tripoli had established.

The *New York Times* was a special source of information because American statesmen chose to use it as a vehicle of public communication to both Libya and the Federal Republic of Germany. Beyond this, I made considerable use of the Foreign Broadcast Infor-mation Service *Daily Reports* (FBIS *Daily Reports*). Without ques-tion, the FBIS *Daily Reports* are a major source of foreign policy information for researchers. The *Daily Reports*, distributed by the National Technical Information Service in Springfield, Virginia, is indexed monthly and contains a wealth of information regarding news agency dispatches, newspaper stories, and periodical articles, as well as television and radio broadcasts. All of this information is translated into English and can be easily accessed through either hard copy paper form or microfiche.[12] I used the *Daily Reports* to track Libyan television, radio, and press reports documenting government views on the chemical factory episode. This involved positions emanating from Tripoli as well as Libyan activities at the United Nations. Since the public information outlets in Libya are government controlled, I am confident that I have provided an accu-rate description and appraisal of Libyan positions.

The situation in West Germany is more complex. A free press in that country provides a variety of viewpoints and engages in considerable scrutiny and criticism of the government. Through articles in the *Daily Reports*, I have shown changes in press views toward the Libyan situation, and to describe and assess the activities of the German government and commercial firms, I have examined a vast amount of information from newspapers, magazines, and press agency reports. Moreover, I have utilized extensively a lengthy and crucial report on Libya issued by the government, and I have used the FBIS *Daily Reports* to document the spirited debate in the Bundestag regarding the Libyan factory.

I am well aware that everything to be known about the Libyan case is not available. Furthermore, it is unlikely ever to be publicly available, because it involves critical questions of national security for a number of nations. However, the spread of chemical weapons is such a serious political issue that any contribution to an understanding of clandestine proliferation should be welcomed.

Readers will note that I treat this Libyan case as a critical international situation and not as a crisis. The concept of international crisis has a special and constricted meaning for international relations scholars, even though that meaning has been subjected to considerable debate.[13] I do not believe that the Libyan episode can properly be categorized as a true crisis, even though press accounts and statesmen have referred to it as such. Thus, it is more appropriate to consider Libya's quest for a chemical weapons production facility as a critical international situation that, though it spanned a period of ten years, had no immediate effect on power distributions in the international community, no direct challenge to the security of any individual nation, and no requirement for immediate action leading to long-term consequences. However, there were real possibilities for violent action. The spread of chemical weapons to Libya, a nation often charged with supporting terrorism and other unconventional foreign policy activities, could ultimately have major destabilizing effects in the Middle East and perhaps elsewhere.

I am quite aware that there may be important connections, both operational and theoretical, between the Libyan episode and the events in Iraq that eventually resulted in the outbreak of war in the Middle East during January 1991. It is important to repeat that this is the study of only a single significant example of chemical weapons proliferation. The Iraqi case is much more complex because it represented a massive buildup of numerous weapons systems including a chemical weapons capability. However, as I will explain in the concluding chapter, Iraq's activities in acquiring military power may have convincingly demonstrated to Libya that it would encounter no international resistance if it attempted to acquire a chemical weapons production facility.

Readers should note that I have not presented material in a strict chronological order. One aim of this study is to contribute to an understanding of how a nation acquires resources from the international system to produce chemical weapons. A strict chronological treatment is therefore not necessary or even desirable. Instead, although I often follow chronological sequences, I frequently depart from this format to extract substantive topics for a sustained examination. This results in occasional overlapping of information, but these are held to a minimum, and when they do occur, they contribute to a more thorough understanding of the topic at hand.

After discussing some background issues that provide a context for the U.S. charge that Libya was building a chemical weapons factory, I analyze the situation both prior to and after the charge. Of course, if we had perfect knowledge, we would begin at the true beginning—the decision by Libya to seek a chemical weapons production capability. The U.S. charge occurred at least eight years after Libya made this decision.

Translations from Arabic are often rendered differently by various translators. The word *Qadhafi* is spelled in a variety of ways, but I have utilized the most common and simplest way in English, *Qadhafi*, for this study. Rabta, the town in which the chemical weapons factory was charged to be located, is often spelled *Al-Rabitah*. Again, I have used the simple *Rabta* for convenience. However, readers may expect to find various spellings of these two words in the references cited.

Because this case took place at a time when East and West Germany were separate juridical entities, I have maintained that distinction throughout the study. Indeed, it is important to do so because a number of important distinctions flow from that division. For stylistic reasons I use *Federal Republic of Germany* (FRG) and *West Germany* interchangeably.

The Chapters Ahead

In the remaining chapters I examine the anatomy of a case of successful chemical weapons proliferation. It is a complex undertaking composed of many details. Indeed, a comprehensive understanding of how an "act" of proliferation can take place requires acknowledgment of the multiple details, both diplomatic and technical, that comprise what is often described as a singular act. Without an understanding of these details, the international community will be ill-prepared to deal with future questions of chemical weapons proliferation.

Chapter 2 describes the origins of the hostile relationship that existed from the mid-1980s between the United States and Libya.

This provides a backdrop for the public U.S. charge that Libya was in the process of building a chemical weapons production facility within its territory. This charge marks the beginning of what I have called a critical international situation.

In Chapter 3 I examine the aftermath of the U.S. charge, which resulted in a deepening and sharper hostility between the United States and Libya. More details about Libya's chemical activities began to emerge in the public domain. President Reagan indicated on television that he was considering a possible military attack on Libya, and Colonel Qadhafi's vociferous reaction to the president's statement is examined for its future policy implications.

An introduction to the West German-Libyan commercial relationship is provided in Chapter 4. Details about this relationship began emerging in official U.S. statements, which in late 1988 took on a much more accusatory tone toward the Germans. The German government expressed harsh concern over the statements of its alliance partners. The ensuing public debate between foreign ministries is analyzed carefully. As the debate between the United States and the Federal Republic of Germany was intensifying, Libya began to sculpture a comprehensive public position regarding the U.S. charge. That position was multifaceted and served to suggest what might be referred to as a model position for any nation wishing to acquire a weapons system, the use of which was prohibited by an international convention.

Chapter 5 is devoted exclusively to an analysis of the 1989 Paris Chemical Weapons Conference. As viewed by the United States, this conference was to serve as an element of public pressure on Libya to halt its chemical weapons activities. Since Libya continued with its undertaking, the conference must be judged as something short of complete success.

The complex series of events in West Germany during 1989 is examined in Chapter 6. The elaborate scheme to funnel chemical processing equipment from western Europe to Libya is analyzed partly from press revelations and partly from a lengthy report issued by the Kohl government. The latter report is a key document of the Libyan situation, and it revealed German knowledge of Libyan chemical weapons activities through information generated by Bonn's own intelligence and diplomatic agencies.

The end of the critical Libyan situation is described in Chapter 7, and a conceptual framework to deal with this ending is proposed. Further developments in Libya—a fire at the production facility—and in West Germany—the prosecution of a key business person—

are used to complete the factual record, which extends to the end of 1990 for this case.

Chapter 8 provides an operational assessment of the Libyan chemical weapons factory episode. It analyzes the situation through conclusions organized around the interests of the United States, Libya, and West Germany. Illustrated here are some of the problems of analyzing a clandestine international undertaking. But such analyses must proceed, in spite of difficulties, if we are to make progress in our knowledge of the spread of chemical weapons.

Because much, if not all, of the international activity related to the clandestine acquisition of a chemical or biological weapons capability involves the use of deception, Chapter 9 explores the concept of deception and lying in human affairs. I believe that it is critical for students of international relations to develop a better literature and understanding about the concept of deception. It is likely that deception will play an increasingly important role in the high technology orientation that characterizes present-day international relations.

In Chapter 10 the study concludes with some general reflections for policymakers who must deal with questions of chemical weapons proliferation. These reflections are, of course, based on the Libyan experience, but it is hoped that they may have some applicability beyond it.

2

The Development of a Critical
International Situation

This chapter discusses the unfolding of a critical international situation that approached becoming a crisis in the Middle East region. It ultimately involved individual nation states both in the Middle East and elsewhere, international organizations, international conferences, individual business firms in several nations, and above all, the threat of war. After beginning with the chemical weapons context during the late 1980s, the chapter moves on to examine U.S. sensitivity to the spread of chemical weapons. As a counterpoint to American policy, the Libyan orientation to the United States is briefly examined. All of these topics are preliminary to the main body of the chapter, which focuses on the details of confrontations between the United States, Libya, and the international community regarding the discovery of what was charged to be a Libyan chemical weapons production facility.

The Chemical Weapons Context

In the three years preceding the December 1987 U.S. charge that Libya was building a chemical weapons factory, relatively little attention was paid to chemical weapons. For the most part, the attention of military establishments and arms control bodies was focused on nuclear weapons and, to a lesser but still significant extent, on conventional forces. This orientation was reflected in the formal speeches and statements in which heads of state and other officials addressed arms control questions. It is probably safe to say that chemical weapons represented an isolated afterthought when the statesmen of the world discussed military questions.

This was true in spite of the fact that there had been some use of chemical weapons during the Iran-Iraq War. Indeed, a United Nations appraisal team had concluded that Iraq had been using chemical weapons since 1984.[1] These chemicals included mustard gas and the nerve gas Tabun. By the end of 1985, five thousand Iranians were estimated to have perished from battlefield use of poison gas.[2] Moreover, there were strong suspicions that chemical weapons were proliferating in the Middle East. Numerous press reports mentioned Egypt, Israel, Libya, and Syria as nations suspected of having or developing chemical weapons.

Although the United States, the Soviet Union, and France were known to possess significant arsenals of chemical weapons, little press or academic attention was directed toward these stores.[3] For the most part, these three nations adopted the attitude that their possession of chemical weapons was responsible and defensive, and that their use of them was not anticipated. Furthermore, any discussion of the chemical weapons capabilities of these three powers was relatively unimportant because each of them possessed nuclear weapons, which were thought to be far more dangerous and challenging to world peace and stability.

In addition to the Iran-Iraq War, there had been other alleged or confirmed uses of chemicals in conflict situations in the modern era. These included use by Egypt in Yemen in the 1962–68 civil war, the United States during the Vietnam War, the North Vietnamese against Laotian tribesmen, and the Soviets against the mujahadeen in Afghanistan. Because of the relatively frequent use of chemicals, especially during the Iran-Iraq War, it is surprising how little public concern was directed toward them. The general mind-set seemed to be that chemical weapons did not represent a major threat to the international community, and that the key proliferation problem, at least as far as the Soviet Union and the United States were concerned, remained nuclear weapons. Although most individuals consider the use of chemical and biological weapons to be especially frightening and abhorrent, recognition of the dangers of such weapons did not come to the forefront of public consciousness during this period. Nevertheless, the Conference on Disarmament had been dealing with chemical weapons issues since 1984.[4]

American Activities with Regard to Chemical Weapons and Libya

During this preliminary period, relations between the United States and Libya were hostile and strained. The basis of this hostility grew out of American and West European perceptions that Libya was a major sponsor of terrorist activity. On 27 December 1985, these perceptions were reinforced by a terrorist attack on the Rome and Vienna international airports in which an eleven-year-old American girl, Natasha Simpson, was killed. It was widely thought that Abu Nidal, who presumably received support and sanctuary from Libya, organized these attacks. Indeed, Libya's leader, Colonel M. Qadhafi, praised the attacks as "heroic actions."[5] Moreover, in January 1986, the U.S. Department of State issued a report that provided a host of details regarding terrorist activities allegedly sponsored by Libya.[6]

As a result of the death of an American during the airport attacks, President Reagan issued Executive Order 12543 on 7 January 1986, an order that virtually cut off all intercourse between the United States and Libya. The basis for this action was the administration's finding "that the policies and actions of the Government of Libya constitute an unusual and extraordinary threat to the national security of the United States." The president declared a "national emergency to deal with [the] threat." A number of concrete actions were taken, and they deserve quotation at length. The following items were prohibited:

(a) The import into the United States of any goods or services of Libyan origin, other than publications and materials imported for news publications or news broadcast dissemination;

(b) The export to Libya of any goods, technology (including technical data or other information), or services from the United States, except publications and donations of articles intended to relieve human suffering, such as food, clothing, medicine and medical supplies intended strictly for medical purposes;

(c) Any transaction by a United States person relating to transportation to or from Libya; the provision of transportation to or from the United States by any Libyan person or any vessel or aircraft of Libyan registration; or the sale in the United States by any person holding authority under the Federal Aviation Act of any transportation by air which includes any stop in Libya;

(d) The purchase by any United States person of goods for export from Libya to any country;

(e) The performance by any United States person of any contract in support of an industrial or other commercial or governmental project in Libya;

(f) The grant or extension of credits or loans by any United States person to the Government of Libya, its instrumentalities and controlled entities;

(g) Any transaction by a United States person relating to travel by any United States citizen or permanent resident alien to Libya, or to activities by any such person within Libya, after the date of this Order, other than transactions necessary to effect such person's departure from Libya, to perform acts permitted until February 1, 1986, by Section 3 of this Order, or travel for journalistic activity by persons regularly employed in such capacity by a newsgathering organization; and

(h) Any transaction by any United States person which evades or avoids, or has the purpose of evading or avoiding, any of the prohibitions set forth in this Order.[7]

This represented a virtual total embargo on goods, services, credits, and loans from the United States to Libya. It prevented U.S. firms from purchasing Libyan goods for sale anywhere, and it even prohibited the travel of Americans to Libya. On the following day, 8 January 1986, the president issued still another executive order (#12544), which blocked the Libyan government from holding property in the United States and U.S. persons from holding Libyan property.[8] The one exception to this almost complete break in contact, an important exception, is listed in section (b) above. "Publications and donations of articles intended to relieve human suffering, such as food, clothing, medicine and medical supplies intended strictly for medical purposes" could legally be exported to Libya.

However, the actions described in the executive orders do not capture the emotional flavor that existed in Washington. In the opening remarks of his press conference on 7 January 1986, the president described the airport attacks as "criminal outrages by an outlaw regime." Libya, the president asserted, "has engaged in armed aggression against the United States . . . just as if . . . [it] had used its own armed forces." Indeed, "Qadhafi deserves to be treated as a pariah in the world community."[9]

Three months later, the United States attacked Libya in a complex nighttime bombing raid on five Libyan targets, including the home of Col. Moammar Qadhafi. Twenty-three attacking planes were launched both from U.S. aircraft carriers in the Mediterranean Sea and from U.S. facilities in Great Britain.[10] In describing this attack to a national U.S. television audience, President Reagan asserted that the United States was retaliating against Libya for a "reign of terror" that ten days earlier, in a terrorist attack on a West Berlin discotheque frequented by U.S. military personnel, had resulted in the death of an American serviceman and a Turkish woman. Mr. Reagan charged that the United States had intelligence information that directly linked Libya to the attack. The rhetoric of the president's speech was especially harsh.

15

Beyond this, in mid-1987 the United States expanded export controls to a total of eight chemicals that could be used to produce weapons. License requirements were imposed for these chemicals "to curb the supply of chemicals . . . being sought by Iran, Iraq, and Syria for their respective chemical weapons programs" and "to insure that American chemicals do not contribute to the manufacture of chemical weapons which are subsequently used in the Iran-Iraq War."[11] Coupled with the embargo on goods to Libya, these export controls presented a picture of U.S. interest in and concern about chemical weapons in the Middle East.

However, these policies for the Middle East did not interfere with U.S. development of its own chemical munitions program. On 29 July 1986 the president certified that specific congressional requirements had been met as a condition of the release of chemical weapons modernization funds.[12] With the release, which eventually ran into considerable congressional difficulty, updating the stockpile of chemical weapons with binary munitions could proceed. At the same time, the administration asserted that until a ban on chemical weapons was adopted by the international community the United States would maintain a credible chemical retaliatory capability. The administration viewed the chemical threat to U.S. forces as worldwide.

Other International Activities and Libya

West European nations were sensitive to the growing public revulsion toward terrorist activities. Of particular importance was the large number of Libyan nationals who were employed in a variety of occupations on the European continent. It was assumed that such individuals might contribute to the effectiveness of terrorist activities.

In the spring of 1986, the foreign ministers of the European Community (EC), meeting in Luxembourg, agreed to impose a set of restrictions on the movement of Libyans in Western Europe.[13] They agreed to significantly reduce the number of Libyan diplomatic personnel within the EC nations, to allow Libyan diplomats to travel only to capital and mission cities, and to expel from Western Europe all Libyans suspected of terrorist activities. In addition the ministers agreed to study the presence and numbers of Libyans employed in trade offices and airlines. Beyond this, the foreign ministers agreed to reduce the number of EC diplomats in Libya. At virtually the same time, the EC Commission removed Libya from the list of nations eligible to receive surplus milk powder and butter.[14] All of these were serious, concrete acts by the EC and were designed to place considerable diplomatic pressure on Libya.

Libyan and other Arab diplomats viewed the activities of the Reagan administration and the EC as highly provocative. Arab ambassadors in the EC nations issued a joint statement declaring that an act of force against one Arab nation is an act against all Arab nations.[15] The United States was described as a rabid terrorist nation; an imperialist nation; an enemy of the people, one who lusts to annihilate others; and a carrier of the banner of sabotage. Although the process of withdrawing diplomats began almost immediately, little invective was directed at Western Europe by Libya. At least one nation that had close ties to the United States supported Libya. Japan's foreign minister declared to his parliament that Japan did not support the United States in its aggression against Libya. He declared Libya to be a peace-loving and antiterrorist nation.[16]

The Diplomatic Context

On the eve of the U.S. charge that Libya was building a chemical weapons production facility, the international political status of chemical weapons was familiar and routine. Two major diplomatic instruments had been in place for some years.

In the aftermath of World War I, and as a reaction to the use of chemical agents and gas in that conflict, the "Protocol for the Prohibition of the Use in War of Asphyxiating, Poisonous or Other Gases, and of Bacteriological Methods of Warfare" was drawn up at Geneva in 1925. From 1928 through 1980, most of the nations of the world, including the United States and the Soviet Union, had accepted the provisions of the Protocol. The Protocol asserts that the use in war of asphyxiating, poisonous, or other gases, and of all analogous liquids, materials, or devices, has been justly condemned by the general opinion of the civilized world."[17] The signatories "accept this prohibition" on the use of poisonous gases and "agree to extend this prohibition to the use of bacteriological methods of warfare."

Of the 140 nations that signed the Protocol, including Libya and the Federal Republic of Germany, forty-five have attached some type of reservation to their acceptance. The vast majority of reserving nations state that their commitments to the Protocol are binding only with regard to other signatories. Moreover, these same nations declared that they will not be bound by the Protocol when other nations do not observe the provisions. In effect, signatories of this document are usually viewed as having made little more than a "no first use" pledge.

The 1925 Geneva Protocol has a major flaw common to many diplomatic instruments. It contains no enforcement provisions against violators. There are also no provisions against the research, development, and stockpiling of gaseous or other biological warfare agents. Prohibitions are directed only against the use of such agents. As such, the Protocol must be considered a weak, although not insignificant, document.

The second major diplomatic instrument, growing out of the spirit of détente during the early 1970s, is the "Convention on the Prohibition of the Development, Production, and Stockpiling of Bacteriological (Biological) and Toxin Weapons and on their Destruction."[18] It was signed simultaneously in Washington, D.C., London, and Moscow on 10 April 1972 and entered into force during 1975, after numerous national ratification procedures. The United States and the Soviet Union were among the first 46 signatories. Libya acceded to the convention in 1982, and the Federal Republic of Germany ratified in 1983. This convention is frequently referred to as the Biological and Toxin Weapons Convention or BTW Convention.

Article 1 is the centerpiece of the BTW Convention, and it deserves to be cited in its entirety.

> Each State Party to this Convention undertakes never in any circumstances to develop, produce, stockpile, or otherwise acquire or retain:
> (1) Microbial or other biological agents, or toxins whatever their origin or method of production, of types and in quantities that have no justification for prophylactic, protective, or other peaceful purposes;
> (2) Weapons, equipment, or means of delivery designed to use such agents or toxins for hostile purposes or in armed conflict.

Article 2 obliges signatories ". . . to destroy, or to divert to peaceful purposes, as soon as possible but not later than nine months after the entry into force of the Convention, all agents, toxins, weapons, equipment, and means of delivery." Taken together, articles 1 and 2 represent an outright ban on the possession of biological and toxin weapons and on their means of delivery.

Beyond these two critical provisions is article 3 in which states

18

pledged "not to transfer to any recipient whatsoever, directly or indirectly, and not in any way to assist, encourage, or induce any State, group of States or international organizations to manufacture or otherwise acquire any of the agents, toxins, weapons, equipment or means of delivery." Biological weapons are defined as living organisms that cause disease in humans, animals, and plants when utilized for conflict purposes. Toxins are poisonous substances produced by living organisms (for example, snake venom). It is generally thought that the BTW Convention deals with biological (sometimes called bacteriological) and toxin weapons and not with chemical weapons. Not only does the convention not define chemical weapons, but it has a provision in its preamble that recognizes the BTW Convention as "a first possible step toward the achievement of agreement on effective measures also for the prohibition of the development, production, and stockpiling of chemical weapons."

All of this seems to imply that chemical weapons represent a category of weapons distinct from the biological and toxin varieties. However, new technical developments have created considerable ambiguity regarding this point. Adams writes, for example, that toxins occupy "a curious middle ground between biological and chemical warfare." She also indicates, quoting Geissler, that although Western governments consider toxins as part of biological weaponry, Warsaw Pact nations describe them as "unequivocally . . . types of chemical warfare."[19] Moreover, toxins can be synthesized in the laboratory through the processes of biotechnology. It is not diplomatically clear whether these artificial toxins are true toxins and whether this distinction has any meaning under the terms of the BTW Convention. For example, we do know that using genetic manipulation to produce a pathogenic life form is covered by the convention. However, is a nonliving, artificially created toxin also covered because it was produced through genetic manipulation? If it is, then certain types of chemical weapons, that is, toxins, might be included under the convention. As will be described later, this unstable reasoning has not been widely accepted by the international community. Instead, there has been broad movement toward a distinct convention banning chemical weapons.

The Pre–Chemical Weapons Factory Episode

In the two to three years prior to the chemical weapons factory episode, the world witnessed an increase in hostility between the

United States, and to some extent Western Europe, and Libya. The suspicion that Libya was engaged in terrorist activities, especially in the airport and other attacks, encouraged the United States to place a virtual embargo on all commercial contacts with that country as well as to initiate efforts to diplomatically isolate it. The one exception to the embargo was the provision to allow the shipment of food and medical supplies to Libya. West Europeans, acting through the EC, also attempted to exert political pressure on Libya by scaling down diplomatic contacts. The U.S. air raid on the Tripoli and Benghazi areas was a startling, concrete illustration of the level of tension in U.S. Libyan relations. The two diplomatic instruments addressing gas and biological weaponry had been in place for years. Some rethinking of the BTW Convention was underway, especially as it related to the emerging capabilities in biotechnology. On balance, this was a period of considerable political tension regarding Libya, the United States, Western Europe, and the broader question of terrorism emanating from Middle Eastern nations.

The Opening Charge

The hostile relationship between the United States and its Western allies and Libya provided a background to U.S. sensitivity regarding chemical weapons and other arms control issues. Early in 1987, in a speech before the Conference on Disarmament in Geneva, Kenneth Adelman, then director of the U.S. Arms Control and Disarmament Agency, laid out an especially detailed explanation of American policies toward chemical weapons. In a wide-ranging examination of numerous arms control issues, Adelman indicated that the United States "considers the negotiations on achieving a comprehensive and effective verifiable global ban on chemical weapons to have the highest priority."[20] Although much of Adelman's emphasis was on the Soviet Union's lack of openness about its development of a chemical weapons arsenal, he described a number of specific U.S. concerns. For example, he remarked that until a verifiable ban on chemical weapons was in place, the United States would maintain its own stocks of such weapons. He emphasized that chemical weapons are especially difficult to contain, because their components are similar to those in legitimate nonmilitary uses (pesticidal, for example). Moreover, concealment of the chemicals themselves is quite easy. Adelman indicated that although the use of chemical weapons is considered illegal by most of the nations of the international community, their manufacture is not illegal.

A Critical International Situation

U.S. sensitivity to the proliferation of chemical weapons exploded on 24 December 1987, in a front page story in the *New York Times*.[21] The story marks the public beginning of the rapid emergence of a critical international situation based on a U.S. charge that Libya was in the process of constructing a factory to produce chemical weapons. The author, Michael R. Gordon, had apparently talked to (or been summoned to talk to) a number of U.S. government officials who spoke about the Libyan activities with considerable accuracy and detail. Also, the article was laden with direct quotations, a sign that the administration was willing to tolerate precise descriptions of its thinking. However, names of individual officials were not used. It is likely that the administration chose to make its charges through a newspaper account not only because there were a number of uncertainties regarding the charges but also because there were sensitivities on the part of the United States with respect to certain of its allies.

In the newspaper story, the Reagan administration charged that Libya was building a factory that U.S. officials strongly suspected, based on intelligence reports, would be employed to produce chemical weapons. One "senior administration official" was quoted as saying that there is "considerable evidence" that a plant is under construction and that "our suspicion is that it will be used for chemical weapons." Curiously, even though officials identified that plant as Libyan, they declined to provide details as to its exact location. Another official stated that the Libyans were well into the construction of the plant, and that it might even have been completed. Other officials expressed doubts as to its completion. Beyond this, some officials indicated that it was "not cut and dry" as to whether the plant was operational. Nevertheless, whether it was producing chemical weapons or not in December 1987, the plant was described as being some distance from populated areas, which would seem to indicate that it was designed to handle highly toxic substances.

In addition to the charges concerning the production facility, the newspaper article mentions reports that Libya had used poison gas in its war with Chad, and that Libya and Iran had a trade relationship in chemical arms. These developments, of course, pointed to a new case of the proliferation of chemical weapons, a development the administration strongly opposed.

Beyond the existence of a production facility, there remained a question of engineering and/or acquiring the processing equipment itself. As one observer familiar with Libya's technical capabilities described it, "the Libyans have some good theoretical scientists, but their engineers are hopeless. . . . I doubt whether they will be able to get any mustard gas out of the plant without killing all of their employees."[22]

Engineering weaknesses, of course, require remedies. Gordon's news story hinted that U.S. intelligence about the plant had been shared with some allies, and that non-Libyan firms had somehow assisted in the construction of the facility. The United States, it was reported, was reluctant to identify the nations involved because the factory was not yet operational. Apparently, the United States was following a strategy of quiet diplomacy to determine with some accuracy just how foreign firms may have assisted Libya in creating a chemical weapons production capability. In all likelihood officials must have felt that attacking one's friends publicly without incontrovertible evidence was both foolhardy and dangerous.

The points made by the administration in its opening charge can be summarized as follows:

Items known with certainty:
1. A factory is under construction in Libya
2. The factory is some distance from populated areas
3. Libya has a record of interest in poison gas
4. Libya's internal engineering capabilities are weak
5. U.S. intelligence information about the factory has been shared with some allies

Items revealed with less than certainty:
1. The factory could be used to produce chemical weapons
2. The factory building may be completed
3. There is doubt as to whether the factory is operational
4. It is doubtful that Libya could have produced its own chemical processing equipment
5. Non-Libyan firms may have assisted in the construction of the factory

Several other items regarding this site were eventually reported after interviews with workers. Apparently a larger technology center with multiple buildings was under construction at the site known as Pharma 150. Confusingly, the purported chemical plant within the larger technology center also carried the designation Pharma 150. The West German publication *Der Spiegel* described the site in the following terms:

Workers . . . contracted out . . . for the supposed technology center report that the construction site for Libya's Pharma 150, located at a distance from the other buildings, was strictly guarded. Unauthorized persons were not admitted. The Libyan "technical center" does not even remotely resemble a place for basic research. Building 2 has a door that is almost 80 feet by 20 feet. The floor is made of steel plates more than three-quarters of an inch thick. A moving crane can handle 500 tons. And why would a pharmaceutical plant be surrounded by an earthen wall and kept under observation by video cameras? Why would containers from Europe be covered with camouflage nets? The radar equipment and the anti aircraft missiles also do not look very peaceful. The production building has acid-resistant tiles. At every connection, there are alarm devices for escaping gas and sensors that warn of leaks.[23]

Summary

This, then, was the origin of the critical international situation that existed at the end of December 1987. After two years of hostility, the United States publicly accused Libya of clandestinely constructing a factory to produce chemical weapons that could have major destabilizing consequences in the highly volatile arena of Middle Eastern politics. It is to the aftermath of this charge that we now turn.

3

The Aftermath of the Charge, 1

This chapter addresses events during the immediate aftermath of the U.S. charge that Libya was in the process of developing a chemical weapons production facility. It begins by examining Libyan reactions to U.S. policy. From this point on, the chapter examines the increasing U.S. diplomatic pressure on Libya in a number of differing environments, and it ends with an examination of Libyan policy themes.

Libyan Reactions

Given the preceding two years of hostile relations between the United States and Libya, it should not be surprising that Libyan spokespersons reacted with fury to the chemical weapons plant charge. On 27 January 1988, the Jamahiriyah News Agency of Libya (JANA) condemned what it described as the Reagan administration's ban of the sale of medical supplies and medicines to Libya. Medical supplies and medicine were included in the one exclusion in the administration's embargo. However, JANA's political affairs editor stated that "Reagan's ban on medicines and medical supplies to Libya is both uncivilized and inhumane, apart from showing prejudice and racism. . . . This ban represents a declaration of hostile war waged by a state like the U.S. against small nations that reject its hegemony."[1]

In order to replace its "lack" of some medicines, Libya apparently requested assistance from the World Health Organization (WHO). That agency was reported to have approved the purchase of several medicines on behalf of Libya. Included in this group was an anticancer drug manufactured only in the United States.

Libya's initial reaction was interesting on two counts. First, its announcement that a state of war existed between the United States and Libya was the mirror image of President Reagan's earlier statement. Second, Libya's charge that the United States had embargoed medicines to their nation, a distortion of U.S. policy, established a rationale for the existence of the Pharma 150 facility. The Libyans could now argue that they had little choice but to construct a factory to produce pharmaceuticals and medicines.[2]

Increasing U.S. Pressure

During the spring of 1988, the United States became very assert-ive regarding chemical weapons. L. Paul Bremer III, ambassador at large for counter-terrorism, appeared before a congressional com-mittee and provided a comprehensive statement regarding U.S. inter-est in high technology terrorism. Bremer indicated that although terrorists have generally preferred the use of simple technologies, "one of the ironies we face is that successful protection of more and more targets may drive terrorists to use higher technologies."[3] He went on to indicate that while nuclear terrorism represents consider-able technical constraints, the acquisition and use of chemical and biological weapons provides far fewer difficulties, primarily because the raw materials for such weapons are readily available. Toxic chemicals can be easily manufactured or stolen. Various toxic sub-stances are routinely transported across national boundaries for legitimate purposes. And medicines and fruits have been clandes-tinely poisoned, although it is doubtful whether these were acts of political terrorism.

The Reagan administration, Bremer indicated, had designated the Department of State the lead agency in its antiterrorism cam-paign, and the Inter-Departmental Group on Terrorism (IG/T) had been formed. The IG/T had the responsibility to coordinate the U.S. response to nuclear, chemical, and biological terrorist threats. With funds from the Department of State, it also established an external program for researching such threats.

By early 1988 the IG/T had approached several nations with plans to coordinate research of high technology terrorism. Ap-proaches were made to the Federal Republic of Germany, Japan, the United Kingdom, and Canada.[4] Part of this effort was directed at determining new methods for detecting chemical and biological substances that might be used in terrorist activities. Bremer implied that the United States saw the situation as a race between terrorists that might use chemical and biological weapons and the develop-ment of antiterrorist measures.

Secretary of State George Shultz, in an address before the third

UN General Assembly Special Session on Disarmament in June 1988, specified a three point process to be followed when evidence is available regarding suspected involvement with chemical weapons. The three points are:

1. "Bringing political pressure and moral suasion to bear on offending states,"
2. "States with chemical manufacturing capabilities have a special responsibility to work against proliferation,"
3. "Stringent export controls for the chemicals needed to make these weapons [must be inaugurated],"[5]

Coming shortly after the U.S. charge against Libya, Shultz's prescription had to have the situation in Libya in mind. These three points were clearly the core of U.S. policy regarding the chemical weapons production facility. Each became a major policy thrust applied to both Libya and America's allies.

In an announcement that moved beyond the initial charge against Libya, the United States stated in September 1988 that Libya appeared to be nearing "full scale production" of chemical weapons.[6] Of course, this announcement implied that the United States was engaged in continuous monitoring of the Libyan facility, and that it was willing to provide the international community with periodic reports on the situation. Such reports represented a modicum of diplomatic pressure on Libya.

Japan and Libya

During 1987 a storm of protest arose in the United States when the Toshiba Corporation sold high technology milling machines to the Soviet Union for the production of quiet running submarine engines. Some penalties were imposed on Toshiba, and this represented a major embarrassment to the Japanese government. Thus, in the fall of 1988, when the United States charged that the Japanese firm Nihon Seikojo, or Japan Steel Works, was assisting Libya in developing a chemical weapons posture, Tokyo officials investigated immediately. The United States had asserted that, although the firm was not directly involved in the chemical weapons factory, it was assisting Libya in building a nearby metallurgical complex that could be used to make containers or other components for chemical weapons.[7]

Japan's Ministry of International Trade and Industry (MITI)

conducted the investigation. According to Japanese news reports, Japan Steel Works admitted exporting steel and machines to Libya but stated that it believed those products were to be used for repairing desalinization facilities. However, the firm indicated that the ten engineers it had sent to Libya did not visit other buildings in the technical complex, and therefore they had no direct knowledge of chemical weapons production.[8]

Later and more precise press reports established that MITI had authorized the export of three plastic injection molding machines and a metal processing machine. Some members of the U.S. Congress reportedly charged that plastic injection molding machines were to be utilized in the production of chemical artillery shell parts, and that Japan Steel Works was quite aware of this usage. The firm's response to these charges was that it was exporting general purpose equipment as authorized by MITI, and that it had not violated any regulations of the Coordinating Committee for Export Controls (COCOM). However, it deserves to be pointed out that, as one of Japan's defense contractors, Japan Steel Works manufactures specially clad rustproof and anticorrosion steel plate as well as artillery pieces and tank weapons. Apparently it does not produce artillery shells.[9]

The U.S. tête-à-tête with Japan was inconclusive. No doubt American officials felt that the Japanese government should have been attentive to the possibility that it might have been aiding the proliferation of chemical weapons. Yet the Japanese rigidly maintained the position that the exported equipment and expertise were in no way prohibited by existing diplomatic commitments. In any case, this episode was minor compared to the major international events emerging from West Germany's commercial involvement with Libya.

Continuing International Pressures

Following Secretary of State Shultz's three pronged strategy of pressure on Libya, the United States continued, through various international channels, to try to prevent the proliferation and use of chemical weapons. These activities amplified U.S. concerns about proliferation, projected such concerns forcefully into the international arena, and by implication, drew attention to the Libyan chemical weapons factory.

For example, in mid-September the United States charged that

Libya was "on the verge of full-scale production" of chemical weapons.[10] Department of State spokesman Charles E. Redman asserted that the United States wanted the international community to take "vigorous action" in "a very concerted effort" to prevent the spread of chemical weapons to third world nations. Redman refused to say which nations might have supplied equipment to Libya to produce chemical weapons. Although there was some indication that West Germany was involved, administration officials refused to be drawn into speculation regarding what was at the time a highly sensitive diplomatic issue.

In late September 1988, the United States began consulting several major states on the possibility of a future conference on chemical weaponry.[11] Such a conference would have attempted to halt the proliferation of chemical weapons among third world nations but would not have been a substitute for the forty-nation chemical weapon disarmament conference in Geneva. In his farewell address to the United Nations, President Reagan concentrated on the issue of chemical weapons. He stated that "it is incumbent upon all civilized nations to ban, once and for all, and on a verifiable and global basis, the use of chemical and gas warfare." Confirming earlier activities, the president formally proposed a conference on chemical weapons. Referring to the 1925 Protocol, which he saw as being violated by recent developments, he said, "I call upon the signatories to that protocol, as well as other concerned states, to convene a conference to consider actions that we can take together to reverse the serious erosion of this treaty."[12] This proposal was the only new initiative that emerged from President Reagan's address.

Soviet Foreign Minister Eduard Shevardnadze endorsed the proposal, but the six foreign ministers of the Persian Gulf states were unenthusiastic. They criticized the United States for focusing on the Middle East, maintaining that the chemical weapons problem was international and not limited solely to a single region. In their view, any enforcement provisions that might emerge from the proposed conference could appear to be aimed directly at Middle Eastern nations and thus be quite limited, with perhaps Iran, Iraq, and Libya as the intended targets. Indeed, U.S. officials admitted that the president's proposal was a stopgap measure designed "to focus attention on the use of weapons as almost an emergency."[13] Although many analysts might have viewed the use of chemical weapons in the Iran-Iraq War as the obvious "emergency," a strong case could be made for the Libyan situation as the driving force.

Much to the surprise and satisfaction of the Reagan administration, just a few days after the president's proposal was publicly advanced, French President Francois Mitterrand endorsed it in a speech before the UN General Assembly.[14] At Reagan's request, President Mitterrand agreed to host the conference, although at this time no date or place was established. Eventually, a White House Statement announced that 7 to 11 January 1989 had been agreed upon for a conference to be held in Paris.[15]

In his speech, Mitterrand called for an embargo against states using chemical weapons, asking that no arms or any other products be furnished to them. He followed this call with the sentence "I appeal to the supplier countries in this respect."[16] As will be described later, Mitterrand's emphasis on suppliers of chemical weapons and perhaps processing equipment was well taken. He may have been informed by the United States about forthcoming public charges regarding Libya's success in assembling the components of a chemical weapons factory. At any rate, this was an important, though not fully appreciated, comment.

Through the end of 1988, various U.S. government spokespersons, reports, and speeches emphasized Libya's interests in chemical weapons. Illustrative of these efforts was a statement to a congressional subcommittee by Richard W. Murphy, assistant secretary of state for Near East and South Asian Affairs. In appraising the political situation in the Middle East, Murphy paid special heed to chemical weapons and Libya, continuing the diplomatic pressure on that nation.

> We have drawn public attention to Libyan efforts to acquire a capability to produce chemical warfare agents. In view of reports that Libya used chemical weapons against Chad, as well as Libya's general irresponsibility, we have called on all countries to refrain from supplying Libya with any assistance in developing a chemical weapons capability. . . . Unfortunately, the spread of chemical weapons is difficult to control. The technology required to manufacture chemical warfare agents is within the reach of many countries. The necessary equipment closely resembles that used for legitimate chemical industries, and can be acquired piecemeal from a large number of commercial suppliers, often without any knowledge or involvement by the exporting country's government. Nonetheless, we are committed to continue our efforts to stem the chemical weapons threat.[17]

Murphy's statement is of interest for several reasons. Although months earlier the United States had instituted its own embargo on

29

all commodities except medicines, it reiterated that it wanted the entire international community to "refrain from supplying Libya with any assistance in developing a chemical weapons capability." The observation that a nation can acquire a chemical weapons capability from multiple suppliers and without the knowledge of the exporting country's government appears to foreshadow the forth-coming public debate over the involvement of West German firms.[18] Moreover, Murphy's sensitivity to the clandestine character of such efforts is noteworthy since the West German issue had not yet fully entered the public arena.

One of the more striking developments during this period was a speech by the director of the Central Intelligence Agency (CIA), William H. Webster, who disclosed that Libya was building the largest chemical weapons facility that the CIA had detected any-where in the world.[19] Predicting that chemical warfare would be-come one of the most serious threats to peace in the future, Webster pointed out that, given the spread of chemical weapons in the Middle East, virtually all of the region's major cities could be vulnerable to chemical attack. He further indicated that the quest for chemical weapons among the smaller powers may be an attempt on their part to balance the acknowledged strength of the major powers. Stating the CIA estimate that twenty nations appeared to be attempting to develop a chemical warfare capability, Webster admitted it is extremely difficult to detect chemical weapons efforts because they can easily be disguised as such legitimate activities as producing fertilizers.

By late 1988 U.S. and Israeli analysts were reported to have ascertained that the Libyan government was creating a "staggering" manufacturing complex to produce chemical weapons. The complex was identified as located 35–50 miles south of Tripoli, at a desolate site near the town of Rabta. Further speculation emerged regarding assistance that Libya might have received from "nearly a dozen East and West European and Japanese firms."[20] As Libyan activity at Rabta progressed, it became clear that Libya, if it so desired, could supply toxic chemical substances to a variety of terrorist groups. Moreover, although the nuclear powers seemed to have some control over the development and proliferation of nuclear weapons, the major powers of the world seemed to be losing their ability to influence the course of chemical weapons development. As it pro-gressed, therefore, the Rabta complex became an increasingly salient challenge to the arms control process.

The Threat of an Attack on Rabta

Turning up the diplomatic pressure on Libya, President Reagan stated in a television interview that the United States was considering some type of military attack on the chemical weapons factory. Given the air raid on Libya in 1986, such comments by the president were highly credible. When asked by the ABC interviewer whether the bombing of Libya was a possibility, the president responded, "Well, let me say that's a decision that has not been made yet, we're in communication with our allies and with NATO forces and all, and we're watching very closely that situation." A senior administration official was quoted as saying, "The thrust of our consultations [with our allies] is to establish what we know about this plant and to raise the issue as a menace to world peace and to make this a major item of consideration at the . . . [Paris chemical weapons] conference." He went on to state, "It's also true that we are not ruling out a military option."[21] President-elect George Bush also publicly supported the administration's position on a possible military attack. At a news conference he stated that "one shouldn't give up trying to turn around the Libyan regime. But what happens beyond that, if there is a direct refusal to do that, then we'll consider options . . ."[22]

Whether the United States could get its NATO partners to support a joint military assault on Libya, however, was doubtful. Several West European firms were deeply involved in supplying the chemical weapons complex, and some European governments, with the exception of Great Britain, had refused to allow U.S. fighter-bombers to overfly their territories in the 1986 American attack on Libya. Moreover, such an attack would have been difficult to stage because the site was heavily defended by Soviet built surface-to-air missiles. Thus, it was not unreasonable to assume that an attack on the Rabta facility would have to be a unilateral U.S. effort.

U.S. public discussion about a possible military response was noted with some concern in Tripoli. Within a week, Col. Qadhafi sent a message through Italian Foreign Minister Giulio Andreotti, offering to allow a onetime international inspection of the Rabta plant. The American reaction to this offer was an immediate rejection. Phyllis Oakley, Department of State spokesperson, asserted that "a one-time inspection could not be conclusive in this regard. A CW [chemical warfare] plant could easily be modified to appear as a legitimate industrial chemical plant such as a pharmaceutical or fertilizer facility." She added that "all traces of chemical weapons production could be erased from a plant on extremely short no-tice."[23] Needed for this type of facility is some form of continuous monitoring and/or a surprise inspection capability. Libya has never expressed an interest in allaying international fears by accepting such a process.

The Libyan Response to U.S. Pressures

After the United States charged, in late 1987, that Libya was developing a major chemical weapons complex, the Libyan govern-ment reacted vociferously and consistently in a variety of interna-tional forums, including bilateral diplomatic contacts, international organizations, interviews with key officials, and a steady flow of press releases. In all of this verbal, communicative activity, Libya claimed that the technical complex at Rabta was a pharmaceutical facility designed to produce medicines for the alleviation of sickness and disease. It never wavered from this assertion, and it is instructive to look at the specific dimensions of Libyan positions.

Illustrative of the Libyan viewpoint is a Tripoli Domestic Ser-vice news dispatch that reports on an official government statement regarding chemical weapons.

> First, U.S. officials' repetitious statements on the creation of chemical weapons factories in the Jamahiriyah [Libya] are totally unfounded. The People's Bureau for Foreign Liaison stresses that the Jamahiriyah has no intention whatsoever of producing this type of weapon.
>
> Second, the Great Jamahiriyah's interest in chemical industries is no greater than the interest displayed by any other state in the peaceful benefits of these industries, such as medicines and agriculture and similar things.
>
> Third, such hostile statements by U.S. Administration officials are nothing new. For some time they have been part of this administra-tion's policy toward the Jamahiriyah. Because the accusations of terrorism made against the Jamahiriyah failed under this policy new accusations have been made about the Jamahiriyah producing chemi-cal arms.
>
> Fourth, we wonder whether it would not be better for a superpower like the United States to try to destroy its factories and arsenal of such totally destructive weapons. Why does the United States ignore the Zionist enemy which has a nuclear capability and chemical arms. Furthermore the United States signs agreements with the Zionist enemy and aids its development in these fields.

Fifth, the Great Jamahiriyah previously announced its adherence to international charters on weapons of total destruction. It reiterates its total adherence to these charters.

Finally, we have no explanation for the renewal of this hostile U.S. campaign other than considering it as preparation for a new aggression against the Jamahiriyah using new pretexts.[24]

This statement captures the core of Libyan policy themes on Rabta, which consisted of claims that the charges against Libya were without substance; that Libya's interest in chemical industries was legitimate and peaceful, that there was no evidence that Libya was a terrorist nation; that rather than concentrating on Libya, the United States should have destroyed its own weapons of mass destruction; that the United States was helping Israel acquire nuclear and chemical arms; that Libya endorsed the 1925 Protocol and the 1972 BTW Convention; and that the United States was planning to attack Libya.

It is important to understand the deeply held, emotional views behind these pronouncements. In a CBS interview, Col. Qadhafi asserted that "the United States of America is not a policeman in this world for it to ask about these things [chemical factories] or monitor them, and it is better for the United States to destroy the weapons of mass destruction which is [sic] in its possession including poison gas [and] the manufacture of nuclear and biological bombs."[25] He went on to criticize the United States for its military assistance to Israel.

In mid-November Libya sent the secretary general of the United Nations a memorandum that attempted to answer U.S. charges regarding chemical weapons. Libya denied U.S. allegations and reaffirmed that "it has never been its intention to produce any new kind of chemical weapons." After indicating that it was a signatory to the 1925 Protocol, the memorandum reaffirmed Libya's readiness "to take part in any international effort that might ban the production, storage, and use of chemical and biological weapons as well as all other weapons of total annihilation."[26] Consistent with the policy themes mentioned above, this memorandum again linked chemical weapons with others that cause mass destruction, namely, biological weapons and nuclear arms. This was a clever move, because Libya knew that the United States had a stockpile of its own chemical weapons alongside its nuclear arsenal. By continually linking chemical weapons with other major weapons systems, Libya was able to underscore the fact that other powers were vulnerable to criticism about their own military postures.

33

In a defiant gesture, Qadhafi announced in December that the Rabta plant would conduct public "celebrations" marking the beginning of production. "The ambassadors of foreign countries and pressmen will be attending it," he said, "to make the world rest assured about it."[27] He added that any hostile act against a Libyan civilian target would result in strong retaliation.

Later that month JANA reported that physicians, pharmacists, and nurses were staging a sit-in at Rabta to protest what it referred to as President Reagan's threat to bomb the facility.[28] The report indicated that these medical personnel were prepared to defend the facility with their lives.

Summary

The immediate aftermath of the U.S. charge brought forth the policy positions of both Libya and the United States. The Libyans vehemently denied that the Rabta facility was a chemical weapons factory, and they declared that a state of war existed between them and the United States They began to fortify the site, apparently fearing a direct American attack.

The United States intensified its policy of diplomatic pressure on Libya and called for an international conference to discuss the proliferation of chemical weapons. Administration officials refused to rule out an air strike against the Rabta complex. The administration increased efforts to institutionalize antiterrorist policies, giving the Department of State a central role. Foreshadowing events to come, the United States raised sensitive questions with one of its allies, Japan, regarding technical assistance provided to Libya. This set the stage for a major confrontation with the Federal Republic of Germany.

4

The Aftermath of the Charge, 2

International events are multifaceted activities that involve simultaneous developments. The confluence of these developments within a relatively short period of time transforms a "routine" event into a critical international situation. In order to understand such situations, an analyst must disaggregate their chronological evolution with the full knowledge that this disaggregation will not completely capture the true social complexity of the event at any point in time but will ultimately lead to a comprehensive understanding. Because the relationship between West German industrial firms and Libya is a major component of the Rabta situation, I extract it from its social field for close examination. Otherwise, the chronology of this situation might be hopelessly confusing.

This chapter examines West German trade with Libya, which assisted Libya in the creation of what was charged to be a chemical weapons factory. It provides some background information on the Libyan–West German trade connection, then turns to the U.S. accusation that the Bonn government itself was at least partly responsible for the factory's existence. The chapter presents the German government's denial of the American charge and its elaborate justification for that denial. German export control policy is also examined. The chapter concludes with analyses of further assistance Libya received from other nations and of Libyan foreign policy thrusts.

The West German-Libyan Trade Relationship

The West German trade relationship with Libya has deep roots that precede the Rabta episode. This includes, of course, the fact that Germany purchases much of its oil from Libya, not an insignificant consideration. But, as early as 1986, serious questions were raised within the Federal Republic of Germany about relations between various German firms and Libya.

In 1986 *Stern* magazine reported that German engineers and electronics specialists had constructed missiles for Libya under what was labeled "Project Ittissalat."[1] According to documents in possession of the Karlsruhe State Prosecutor's Office, numerous German firms were involved in the project, which may have violated weapons control and foreign trade laws. Once built, the missiles were tested at a range in the Tibesti Desert, and data from the tests were said to have been analyzed on computers belonging to German research institutions. Moreover, parts for the missiles and electronic components had been shipped to Libya from Germany. A German official spokesman reported that the government had "no knowledge" of the situation described in *Stern*.[2] Of course, if a nation is developing chemical weapons, it needs a means of delivering them. Missiles could fulfill such a need.

Also in 1986, the Karlsruhe Prosecutor's Office was reported to have begun investigations of a Karlsruhe firm under Libyan management that was said to have been working since 1985 to supply tanker aircraft to Libya.[3] Subsequently, the Munich Prosecutor's Office announced that it also had begun an investigation of the midair refueling episode.[4] Intec Technical Trade and Logistics Society Limited of Vatterstetten was identified as Libya's general supplier for equipment needed to convert Lockheed Hercules transport planes into midair refueling tankers for Libya's French and Soviet built aircraft—a project that would extend the range of Libya's bombers in the Middle Eastern region.

During a 1987 exchange in the Bundestag, a government official rejected charges that German exports of arms had increased significantly during the Kohl era. The official "promised that Bonn will continue to do everything to prevent illegal actions" in the shipment of arms overseas.[5] But in 1988, *Der Spiegel* charged that German nuclear firms had been breaking international agreements on the trading of uranium for years.[6] A number of firms had made major profits by circumventing the security and trade restrictions of the United States, Australia, and Canada. Indeed, the report pointed out that the federal government itself had consciously been part of the deception when it certified Canadian uranium as "South American material" so that it could be transshipped to the Soviet Union for processing. A longtime scholar of the German nuclear industry, Joachim Radkau of the University of Bielefeld, observed that "West Germany . . . adopted a policy of promoting nuclear exports that ignored, to an extreme degree, the inherent connections between nuclear power and atomic bombs."[7]

Bowing to considerable international pressure, the Bonn government released a report in early 1989 that indicated that since 1980 it had been receiving a flow of warnings from its own embassies and intelligence service and from the United States about possible German participation in Libyan efforts to develop chemical weapons. This report (discussed in detail in Chapter 6) stated that as early as July 1985, the West German embassy in Moscow identified the German chemical firm that was working with Libya to build a chemical weapons plant, and that on 3 March 1986, the US embassy in Bonn informed the German government about the activities of the same firm.[8]

Although it is not the purpose of this study to examine general German export policy, some assessment is necessary in order to get a sense of the context into which the Rabta activities can be placed. Without question, West Germany has followed a probusiness orientation that minimizes government oversight of potential violations of export policies. "The inevitable result," writes Richard Perle, a former member of the Reagan administration, ". . . [is] a deliberate German government policy to subordinate Western security to the commercial interests of German exporters."[9] For export violations to become a criminal offense, the government must prove that they violated international peace, a charge virtually impossible to prove in a court of law. When courts have tried and convicted individuals, the penalties have been minimal. Agencies charged with enforcing export laws have been understaffed. Overall, even though West Germany is a member of the North Atlantic Treaty Organization (NATO) and is thus bound by treaty to engage in strategic cooperation on the proliferation of chemical weapons, it ignored those commitments in order to foster an active export policy that did little to prohibit the sale of security-relevant materials.

As indicated in Chapter 2, West Germany, along with other EC nations, downgraded diplomatic relations with Libya in 1986 because of Libyan support for terrorist activities. In the fall of 1988, the FRG announced it was restoring relations to the ambassadorial level.[10] The Foreign Ministry justified this action by asserting that there had been no terrorist attacks on German territory for the previous two and one-half years. Beyond this, the Foreign Ministry indicated that with a high-level diplomat in Tripoli, it would be

37

easier to maintain the good economic relations that existed between Germany and Libya.

The Public Emergence of the German Connection

U.S. accusations that Libya was building a chemical weapons factory were primarily directed at exerting diplomatic pressure on Libya itself and ceasing its development of the Rabta facility. Even though firms in a number of nations were ultimately shown to be involved, the Reagan administration resorted to quiet diplomatic efforts to convince Libya's suppliers, some of which were identified as U.S. allies, to withdraw from the construction activity. For example, when West German Chancellor Helmut Kohl visited Washington during November 1988, President Reagan and Secretary of State George P. Shultz privately confronted the chancellor with the matter of German participation at Rabta.[11]

These quiet pressures were to no avail, however, and the administration's apparent frustrations were publicly expressed on 31 December 1988, when it announced that West German firms were centrally involved in aiding Libya in the design and construction of the chemical weapons factory.[12] The administration also announced it had identified the West German firm of Imhausen-Chemie as the major player in the supply effort. At the same time, the administration criticized the FRG for its lax export controls and stated its further displeasure about German assistance to Libya in the development of a midair refueling capability for its aircraft.

The next day, the U.S. Department of State released a statement that officially spelled out American concerns regarding the activities of West Germany. That statement deserves to be quoted in its entirety.

> We have discussed with a number of governments, including but not limited to the Federal Republic of Germany, the serious danger posed by Libya's chemical warfare program. We and other governments are seeking to deny Libya the foreign assistance we believe is essential for full development of this capability.
>
> With regard to West Germany, we are confident that it is taking the information we have provided very seriously and is investigating fully. It has, in the past year, vigorously pursued and prosecuted such cases. Stemming from an investigation that began in November 1987, the West German Government and public prosecutors currently are looking into the activities of companies believed to have helped in the construction of chemical warfare facilities in Iraq. Like the United

States, the Federal Republic of Germany is a member of the Australian group which seeks to prevent the proliferation of chemical weapons.

With regard to the Libyan chemical warfare program, we understand that the appropriate German authorities are still conducting their investigations. As with other countries with which we have talked regarding this problem, this is an on-going matter. West Germany has also announced that it is reviewing its export control laws. We understand that an interim report on this subject will be presented to the cabinet soon.

For our part, the United States has provided interested countries information available to us. We believe this information is conclusive with regard to the activities of various foreign firms in the Libyan chemical warfare program. Of course, whether such activities are illegal, and the role of our information on any legal proceedings, depends on the existing national laws affecting such activities. Our dialogue with the West German and other governments on this matter is continuing.[13]

Although some restraint was evident in this statement, press stories painted a considerably different picture. In one story, the administration was reported to have made the following specific charges against the West German chemical firm:

1. Imhausen-Chemie has served as the general contractor for design of the Rabta factory.
2. Imhausen-Chemie has served as the central purchasing agent for Libya in acquiring and assembling construction materials.
3. Imhausen-Chemie shipped chemical weapons processing components to Libya through Hong Kong and Singapore in a complex and deceptive scheme.
4. Imhausen-Chemie oversaw the movement of funds for equipping the Rabta facility through Hong Kong and Swiss banks.
5. Imhausen-Chemie had the technical knowledge to produce pesticides and poison gas.
6. Imhausen-Chemie has consciously followed a policy of concealing its Libyan activities in a carefully planned covert operation.[14]

In addition, Imhausen-Chemie had announced publicly in 1985 that it was having difficulty meeting its financial obligations, making itself ripe for an offer from the Libyan government.

Dr. Jurgen Hippenstiel-Imhausen, president of Imhausen-Chemie, acknowledged that his firm had approached Libya for a contract to manufacture plastic bags, but he said it was not involved in the alleged chemical weapons plant. He stated that Imhausen-

Chemie produced "medical substances and fine chemicals" and supplied them internationally to pharmaceutical houses. He said he "never was in Libya" and did not even know where it was.[15] He went on in stronger terms to deny any connection to the Rabta complex:

> The company had absolutely nothing to do with the allegations . . . concerning the plant presumed to be making chemical weapons in Libya. We don't even have know-how in this area. We have no employees there, no technicians there either. We haven't had people there for years.
>
> The company name has been misused. Everything is based on suspicion and rumors. Libyans don't have money to pay for things like that. We totally deny any involvement in this.[16]

Along with these denials were reports that the Bonn government had begun its own investigation of Imhausen-Chemie. Despite doubts, the Germans indicated that they were taking the U.S. accusations seriously because they did not want to resurrect charges of Naziism and gas warfare against themselves. However, a government spokesperson said that a preliminary finding had revealed nothing to suggest that Imhausen-Chemie was helping Libya manufacture chemical arms.[17] Moreover, Bonn was skeptical of the U.S. aerial reconnaissance reports, which the Germans apparently felt produced ambiguous photographs.

France and Italy also expressed doubts about the aerial photographs, but Britain endorsed American claims that a chemical weapons facility was under construction in Libya. The United States encountered difficulty in gaining international support for its charges because of the belief in Western Europe that the Reagan administration was preparing an attack on Libya. Many nations wanted to distance themselves from such an event should it take place. Since the United States had attacked Libya in 1986 and had recently shot down two Libyan military jets over the Mediterranean, there was a strong feeling that the United States might very well stage a bombing raid on the Rabta complex.

Even stronger denials on behalf of Imhausen-Chemie were made by the West German government. At a press conference on 4 January, Foreign Minister Hans-Dietrich Genscher, responding to U.S. complaints that his government was not moving quickly enough to investigate the alleged activities of Imhausen-Chemie, asserted that the FRG had found no evidence to support either the American charge against the German firm or the fact that Libya was creating a chemical weapons factory at Rabta.[18] The Germans said that they had requested additional materials from the United States, but that those materials had not produced any meaningful evidence. Moreover, West German financial authorities had checked the export ledgers of the firm and had found no evidence of illegal activity.

At the same time, the governing board of Imhausen-Chemie released a statement that denied involvement in the Rabta complex: "Neither Imhausen-Chemie nor any other firm in our group is directly or indirectly in any way involved in the project of this factory in Libya." The statement added that suggestions that a relationship existed between the firm and Libya were "completely groundless."[19]

At this delicate point the government of the FRG and the German public were insulted by the American accusations. Many Germans felt they were publicly accused of activities that, if true, would rekindle recollections of their Nazi past. Yet the government insisted that there was no evidence to support these seemingly bizarre accusations. The Reagan administration was viewed as having precipitously drawn incorrect conclusions from tenuous information. The key German television evening news program asked: "Why the deliberate naming of one German company by the *New York Times*? Was the purpose to prepare the way psychologically for another strike against Qaddafi?"[20]

The irritation with the *New York Times* is of some consequence. To this point (and beyond) the coverage of the Rabta affair by the *New York Times* had been detailed, balanced, and reserved. It had indeed reported on the activities of the Reagan administration, but through its reporter in Bonn, it had also reported quite carefully on German policy and opinion. By its news stories the paper was calling attention, albeit very professionally, to a serious point of friction between the United States and the FRG.

This constant, in-depth coverage caused considerable irritation among the Germans. The Hamburg *Deutsche Presse Agentur (DPA)* reported that Chancellor Helmut Kohl described the "media campaign" regarding alleged German involvement as "not helpful in the matter." Government spokesmen identified an "escalating campaign in the U.S. media" against the FRG. This was described as particularly offensive because no proof of any wrongdoing had been uncovered. If there is any proof, said a government spokesman in a remark directed at the United States, it should "be put on the table now."[21]

Prior to his departure to Washington to discuss the Rabta episode and other matters with U.S. officials, Volker Ruehe, deputy chairman of the Christian Democratic Union/Christian Social Union

(CDU/CSU) Bundestag group, was strongly critical of American policy. He argued that the "shrill tones" emerging from the administration represented a "dangerous mixture" that was resulting in "disturbing trends" that required opposition. He said the FRG was a victim of "cheap propaganda" and "unjustified attacks and campaigns."[22]

To underscore German concern about chemical weaponry, particularly at this time, Foreign Minister Genscher spoke publicly in support of an international convention to ban the production and storage of such weapons.[23] He advocated the establishment of a surprise inspection framework to provide information to the public on chemical warfare agents. At the same time, perhaps foreshadowing events to come, Genscher called for strengthening German export law if present arrangements were proved inadequate.

The remarks by Ruehe and Genscher did little to dissuade the administration from its positions. In the *New York Times* on 6 January, senior Department of State officials again criticized Germany for moving too slowly in its investigations. Acknowledging that criminal activities under current foreign trade law might be difficult to prosecute, U.S. officials nevertheless complained that "we'd like them [the Germans] to be much more up front about it." Part of the reason for the administration's annoyance with the FRG was the fact that the Germans seldom responded to inquiries regarding the export of any security-sensitive products. One U.S. intelligence official was reported to have said that regarding exports the German government had "a sort of see-no-evil mentality."[24]

German spokespersons frequently criticized the United States for not supplying complete information about its charges against Imhausen-Chemie. However, in the *New York Times* story, American officials argued that a considerable amount of information had been transmitted to Bonn, including accurate intelligence reports. Moreover, Britain announced that it had developed independent information about the Rabta complex, and that the information had been shared with other European nations including West Germany. British Foreign Secretary Sir Geoffrey Howe was quoted in the story as saying that "it is information that does show that the plant is very large, and that there can be no doubt it is intended for chemical weapons production."[25]

While West Germany and the United States were in a cycle of charges and denials, two nongovernmental reports seemed to implicate a German firm in the Libyan technology complex. Vienna

Domestic Service reported that German industrial companies had most certainly participated in the construction of the alleged chemical weapons factory, and that information regarding such participation was in the hands of the German government.[26] A few days later Cologne Deutschlandfunk Network reported that Swiss authorities had discovered two front firms in Zurich that appeared to be involved in the Libyan chemical weapons situation.[27] A spokesman for the Swiss foreign ministry indicated that one of the front firms was a subsidiary of Imhausen-Chemie. This firm was identified as IMHICO AG, apparently a contrived name using the parent firm's initials. The other firm was Ihsan Barbouti International (IBI) Engineering. According to a *Die Welt* report, Ihsan Barbouti, an Iraqi with a Jordanian passport, was said to be the pivotal figure in the chemical arms activities.[28] He later emerged as the director of construction at Rabta.

Despite the hints from the press regarding German activities at Rabta, a spokesman for the FRG Finance Ministry said that a three-day investigation of Imhausen-Chemie "yielded no reason for suspicion of a criminal act through illegal exports. Therefore there is no reason to justify the launching of a[n] . . . extended investigation."[29] Other officials reiterated that U.S. charges against German firms were not supported, and that the United States had not furnished hard evidence. The *Frankfurter Allgemeine Zeitung* reported that the German Foreign Ministry said that British information did not produce any evidence that could be used against German firms.[30] Moreover, the FRG asserted that it had no evidence of its own to verify that chemical arms could be produced at Rabta.

In a chilling meeting in Paris between Foreign Minister Genscher and Secretary of State George Shultz, Genscher demanded that Shultz explain the "completely unjustified campaign against the FRG," saying that "the Government will not be silent about attempts that are being made to make Germany the scapegoat."[31] Genscher was supported by Chancellor Kohl, who continued to insist that he had no information regarding U.S. charges against German participation in construction activities at Rabta. In an interview with *Sueddeutscher Rundfunk*, Kohl said it was "simply not conceivable" or "acceptable" that "individuals in the Federal Republic, of German companies, should participate in activities which could in any way endanger peace in parts of the world."[32] Added to this was a strong statement by Dr. Hippenstiel-Imhausen, president of the Imhausen-Chemie firm, who said government findings confirmed "what I have said from the start of this campaign waged against our group of firms—that we have nothing, absolutely nothing, to do with the 'Libya story.'"[33]

By early January 1989, the U.S.-FRG relationship, if judged by press dialogue and official signaling through the press, had reached perhaps its lowest, most bitter point since 1945. On 6 January, the West German government, to underscore its extreme displeasure, renewed its demands for solid evidence from the United States that German firms were involved in the Rabta complex. Complaining about the U.S. media campaign against Germany, Chancellor Helmut Kohl reminded American officials that Bonn had found no evidence of German involvement in the chemical weapons factory project. A spokesman for the Foreign Ministry, Friedhelm Ost, demanded that the United States immediately provide evidence of any German participation at Rabta. He strongly asserted that "in the framework of this examination, no evidence was found that the firm delivered equipment or material for a chemical plant to Libya, either directly or through another country." Moreover, he emphasized that "there was also no evidence that Imhausen-Chemie sent plans for the construction of a chemical plant to Libya, or know-how, in any way whatsoever." He went on in the most vehement terms to state that "not only would the involvement of a German firm in the building of a plant which could produce chemical weapons be against German law, but it would also be against the policy of this Government. . . . There can be no doubt that the German Government would do everything possible to use all measures possible to oppose this."[34]

Despite these strong denials, U.S. officials remained unconvinced. They argued that the FRG had been supplied sufficient information to launch a thorough investigation. Nevertheless, U.S. officials implied that they would provide a more comprehensive briefing for West Germany, and that such a briefing might include the examination of raw intelligence data that to this point the Germans apparently had not seen.[35]

The United States was sensitive to the escalating contentiousness of the situation. A Department of State spokesperson, attempting to calm public debate, was quoted as stating: "I don't think we're in any position of bashing any country. We're working closely with the West German Government and other interested governments on this. We'll continue to bring to their attention relevant information that assists in their ongoing investigations."[36] Nevertheless, the furor persisted.

Reactions in the German press continued to fully support the Bonn government. Many papers were especially critical of U.S. press editorial references to "Auschwitz in the sand."[37] Some asserted that the success of the German chemical industry was a major irritant to the United States, and that German admiration for Soviet leader Mikhail Gorbachev had aroused American distrust for Germans. Munich's *Sueddeutsche Zeitung* pointed out that Germany is the only nation that "has undertaken not to produce chemical weapons and to willingly submit to checks."[38] It also reported that the German Cabinet planned to support stricter regulations on the export of chemical and nuclear materials as well as increase fines for export violations. The *Sued-Kurier* questioned why the United States did not vociferously object to the twenty-year chemical weapons buildup in the Soviet Union.[39] *Frankfurter Allegemeine Zeitung* asserted that "not even a suspicion which would suffice for starting investigations concerning that firm [Imhausen-Chemie] has been corroborated in the FRG."[40] It is interesting to note, however, that as the public debate was building in intensity, FRG Foreign Minister Genscher observed, after listening to U.S. Secretary of State Shultz publicly express his trust in Genscher and Chancellor Kohl at the Paris Chemical Weapons Conference, that the affair between the United States and West Germany was finally closed.[41] Time would show that no judgment could have been more incorrect.

Further Developments in the U.S.-Libyan Confrontation

As the alleged Imhausen-Chemie connection to Libya gained momentum in the press and the U.S.–West German relations deteriorated into increasing harshness, the United States continued to put public pressure on Libya. This was accomplished by a series of public revelations about specific developments regarding the Rabta complex. Such information was probably gained through satellite reconnaissance, and it served to diplomatically pressure not only Libya but the West German government.[42]

On 3 January 1989 the Reagan administration announced that chemicals stored near the Rabta production facility had been relocated from their regular storage sites at the plant.[43] The administration charged that, in effect, Libya had "cleaned up" the site of stored thiodiglycol, a precursor chemical for the manufacture of mustard gas. Such an adjustment would allow Libya to demonstrate that it was not producing weapons at Rabta should an international

45

inspection take place, a possibility that might have emerged from the forthcoming Paris Chemical Weapons Conference. The administration asserted that these activities around the plant justified the U.S. refusal to participate in the onetime inspection that Libya had offered. "Sanitizing" a chemical weapons facility could easily be accomplished.

A day later, William F. Burns, director of the U.S. Arms Control and Disarmament Agency, demanded that Libya destroy the Rabta facility.[44] No international inspection regime, he said, could satisfy U.S. concerns. Recognizing that Libya was not violating international law in building a chemical weapons factory, Mr. Burns nevertheless argued that the UN Charter allows nations to act in their legitimate self-defense should they feel that their security is threatened, thus implying that the U.S. might take military action as a self-defensive measure. Such a position, of course, could have been interpreted in Tripoli as highly threatening, especially since the United States again refused to rule out a military attack on the Libyan plant. Burns stressed that the United States had focused on Libya, despite chemical weapons developments in other nations such as Iraq, because Col. Qadhafi was involved in terrorist undertakings and was an unpredictable international actor. This was the first time during the Libyan episode that the administration publicly used the personal behavioral characteristics of Qadhafi as a possible justification for its international actions.

Searching for diplomatic support for its case against Libya, the United States sought assistance from the Soviet Union, the only other superpower and a possessor of chemical weapons itself.[45] The United States hoped the Soviets would exert pressure on Libya to halt its development of the Rabta facility. The Soviet response, however, was strongly negative. Foreign Minister Eduard A. Shevardnadze publicly challenged the U.S. case against Libya: "I think no government has the right to make such an accusation without proof."[46] Thus, the U.S. attempt to gain Soviet support for its campaign against Libya was unsuccessful.

An odd dimension of U.S. policy during the chemical weapons episode was the fact that the U.S. had not established any direct discussions with Libya, as was indicated by Secretary of State Shultz.[47] While it is true that the United States and Libya had no formal diplomatic relations and that each considered itself to be at war with the other, such a situation has never prevented diplomatic contacts when mutual interests were to be served. Moreover, contact through the United Nations always remained a possibility.

Despite this reality, there were some attempts at direct contact. In late 1988 Saudi Arabia offered to mediate between the United States and Libya, but the United States rejected the Saudi offer. Proposals for mediation from Algeria and Tunisia were also rejected. A Department of State spokesperson reflected the U.S. attitude: "There is nothing for anyone to mediate. What we need is a change in Libyan behavior."[48] Moreover, the United States had sent several messages to Libya through the United Arab Emirates and Belgium, the latter representing U.S. interests in Tripoli. The messages observed quite bluntly that the United States was aware of Libyan activities at Rabta, found them unacceptable, and demanded that Libya dismantle the facility.[49] Libya never responded to the communications.

Other Nations and the Spread of Chemical Weapons in the Middle East

Although the case of Libya represents an important element in understanding the spread of chemical weapons to the third world, the attempt to develop chemical weapons postures by other Middle Eastern nations should not be overlooked. Iran, Iraq, Egypt, and Syria have been described as nations engaged in producing and/or stockpiling chemical weapons. The methods used to engage in this kind of activity involve the purchase or establishment of front companies to be used for clandestine export, the writing of false documents to disguise the end destinations, and the development of elaborate, circuitous shipping routes to avoid detection. Because of the considerable activity in the Middle East regarding chemical weapons, it is not unreasonable to assume that Libya may have been able to utilize regional scientific expertise and to purchase locally the chemical ingredients for manufacturing chemical weapons.

During the early months of 1989, numerous incidents became known regarding the clandestine acquisition of chemicals by Middle Eastern nations. Iran dealt with firms in the United States, Asia, and Western Europe. Alcolac International, a Baltimore chemical manufacturer, pleaded guilty to violating the U.S. Export Administration Act by shipping thiodyglycol, a chemical used to make poison gas, to Chemco GmbH, a West German company under the control of an Iranian diplomat.[50] These chemicals ultimately went to Iran. Other shipments by Alcolac were delivered to Antwerp, Belgium, and Rotterdam, the Netherlands, and were reshipped to Jordan.

Although the ultimate destination was never revealed, Jordan is a major transshipment point for goods going to Iraq.

The Dutch police seized a large shipment (286,000 pounds) of ammonium perchlorate, a chemical used in solid rocket fuel for military missiles, as it was being transported in an elaborate transshipment scheme. The original supplier was Pacific Engineering and Production Co. of Henderson, Nevada.[51] Grindus S.A. of Switzerland imported the chemical and sold it to D.A. Dampf, a West German chemical firm. From there it was loaded onto an Iranian registered ship in Rotterdam, where it was intercepted.

In another example, 60 tons of thionyl chloride, a chemical that can be used to make poison gas or pesticides, was sold to Iran by an Indian trading company, Transpek Private Ltd.[52] A trading firm in Dubai imported the chemical from India and was about to ship it to Iran when it was recalled by the Indian firm.[53] It later became known that India had sold huge quantities of dangerous chemicals to Iran, Iraq, and Egypt over the past two years.[54]

By mid-1989 press reports indicated that a West German firm, Rheineisen Chemical Products of Dusseldorf, had acted as an intermediary between Iran and India.[55] Moreover, Rheineisen was owned by an Iranian woman living in Paris, and the firm employed Iranians in decision-making positions. It was, in effect, a "front company" owned and operated by Iranians to disguise Iranian involvement in the purchasing of restricted chemicals. In addition, the Iranian embassy in Bonn was involved in coordinating the covert purchase of chemicals. The U.S. asked West Germany to expel the Iranian diplomat who oversaw the process, and Iran withdrew the individual at West Germany's request.

It is no exaggeration to state that West Germany was a focal point for the sale, distribution, and shipping of dangerous and restricted chemicals to the Middle East. The German government, eager to support a policy of increasing exports, paid little attention to the effect of its relaxed trade policy on the proliferation of chemical weapons.

Developments in Libya and the Libyan Perspective

During the period of political conflict between West Germany and the United States, the Libyan government astutely positioned itself on the question of chemical weapons. Libyan press reports, officials, and Col. Qadhafi himself never referred to the political storm raging between the United States and its NATO ally. Instead, Libya pursued a multilevel strategy consisting of the following elements: development of a strong internal position within Libyan society and physically around the plant itself; encouragement of support for Libya from Arab nations and the projection of that support into the international community; and linkage of an international ban on chemical weapons with a similar ban on all nuclear weapons. Let us examine each of these policy thrusts in turn.

Development of a strong internal position. Libyan press reports and official statements are frequently characterized by considerable hyperbole. Often accompanying these extreme statements, however, are careful policy choices designed to elicit political support. For example, various groups inside Libyan cities met, presumably under government encouragement, "to discuss the threats directed by the U.S. President against the Libyan Arab People and its civilized achievements that serve man everywhere." Attendees at such meetings echoed the government's positions and asserted "that they are on the stand-by to defend the achievements accomplished by this [Libyan] revolution."[56] At one of these meetings, that of the Zintan Basic Peoples Congress, the group marched to the Rabta facility and staged a sit-in with physicians and nurses at the complex.[57] The activation of citizens groups served to establish a mass emotional foundation of support should it be needed. Moreover, the sit-in at Rabta introduced into the vicinity of the plant unarmed civilians, including medical personnel, who could be used to increase the costs of an air attack on the facility. Few nations would want to be accused of killing large numbers of innocent civilians in a military raid. In order to emphasize the critical character of the situation, the Libyan government declared a state of alert, which it described as a caution against a U.S. or Israeli air attack.[58]

While these activities were in progress, Col. Qadhafi asserted that Libya and the United States should initiate direct negotiations regarding disarmament questions. He called upon the United States to close down its nuclear and chemical weapons plants, arguing that the Libyans "reject being treated differently" than other nations on questions related to weapons.[59]

One effort that apparently did not accomplish its purpose was the Libyan government's invitation to 250 international news agencies, radio representatives, and reporters to visit the Rabta factory and observe its manufacturing of pharmaceuticals and medicines.[60] Guests were also invited to discuss the facility with individuals engaged in the sit-in, and the director of the factory provided a briefing. Some Western journalists reported, however, that the expe-rience was tightly controlled by the Libyan government and did little to clarify the nature of the buildings since they were not allowed inside. Nevertheless, in viewing the exteriors, the visitors indicated that the buildings were guarded by antiaircraft guns.[61] The Libyan government "answered" the concerns by arguing that the journalists were not specialists and therefore not in a position to make an informed judgment about the buildings. With regard to the antiair-craft weapons, the response was that the Libyan people had a right to defend themselves. Neither response was very convincing to Western observers.

More details about this visit were provided by a Reuters corre-spondent in an interview with the *Bangkok Post*.[62] According to the interview, reporters were surprised to see about 200 Thai workers leaving the site at the end of their shift. The presence of these workers was confirmed by the Thai government, even though the plant direc-tor had told the journalists at his briefing that the construction of the complex was solely the responsibility of Libyan workers.

Journalists also complained that the visit to Rabta was timed by the Libyan government to take place at night. Reporters were given a ten minute drive around the facility in total darkness and from a distance of one kilometer, about a half-mile. Libyan guides tried to prevent photographers and film crews from recording images of the site. After their return to Tripoli, the government gave the journalists forty minutes to pack their bags and leave the country.[63] Many of the journalists indicated in their accounts that the heavy security for the factory had convinced them of the validity of U.S. allegations.

In addition, a journalistic source close to several Asian workers reported the following information in the *Bangkok Post*:[64]

1. The project was begun around November 1984.
2. The Rabta complex consisted of ten individual plants with considerable underground facilities.
3. One hundred large tanks, presumably designed to hold chem-icals, were buried underground in the complex.
4. One hundred Libyan troops were guarding the complex, along with the emplacement of antiaircraft weapons.
5. Chemicals were said to be imported from West Germany.
6. The hiring of workers and the installation of equipment was coordinated by an Iraqi citizen with close ties to Col. Qad-hafi. Workers were nationals of Austria, Denmark, Hong Kong, Japan, Thailand, and West Germany.

7. Workers at the site worked six days a week with two hours of overtime each day.
8. The superstructures of the buildings were designed by the Japanese and built with materials imported from Japan. Forty-five Japanese technicians were employed to supervise construction of the buildings.
9. Dump trucks and cranes for use at the site were supplied by Danish firms.
10. Italians were contracted to do the interior decoration.
11. A lathe factory and iron mill were under construction at the complex. Such facilities could be used to manufacture warheads.
12. Security at the complex was very tight. No visitors were allowed into the complex itself, and no blueprints could be removed from the construction site.

In an interview with the press, Dr. Ihsan Barbouti, the construction chief at Rabta, asserted that the plant could not be used to produce poison gas.[65] He said both Libya and the United States were to blame for the public controversy surrounding the Rabta complex, with the United States as the major perpetrator. Barbouti indicated, however, that the Japanese played a "principal part" in constructing the complex. Moreover, he said that equipment was imported from East and West Germany, Denmark, France, Italy, and Yugoslavia. However, it was later revealed that the computer equipment was manufactured in the United States.[66]

Overall, Libya was only partially successful in developing a strong political position regarding the disputed facility. As might be expected, it was easier for the government to mobilize its own citizens than to manipulate the foreign press. The invitation to journalists was a major policy miscalculation, and no favorable publicity for Libya resulted from it. However, Libya's willingness to treat the U.S. accusation with significant internal actions represented an indication of how seriously it viewed the activities surrounding the Rabta complex.

Encouragement of international support for Libya. As a second defensive foreign policy thrust, Libya moved to obtain public support for its actions at Rabta from other nations in the Middle East. Sudanese Prime Minister Sadiq al-Mahdi, for example, criticized the United States for what he referred to as threats against Libya's sovereignty.[67]

Syria's Minister of Health and the Secretary General of the Association of Arab Pharmacists were invited to tour the Rabta complex and to render support to Libya's position. JANA reported that they inspected all buildings in the facility and affirmed Libya's attempt to provide medical security for its people through the under-taking.[68] They also pointed out that Libya's efforts were especially important to the Arab world because they were being done with nonimported materials and substances. "I don't think that there is anything worse," the Syrian Minister of Health stated, "than a threat to a pharmaceutical factory. All the Arabs ... will defend this civilized monument which the great al-Jamahiriyah is building."[69] At the same time the secretary-general of the Arab Pharmacists Association announced that his group had decided to boycott all U.S. medical products.[70]

Working with Libya, Saudi Arabia cautioned against an escala-tion of tension within the Middle East.[71] The Saudis argued that U.S. threats against Libya were harming attempts to establish peace in the region.

Especially strong support for Libya came from Kuwait. The newspaper *Al-Ra'i Al-Amm*, criticizing American charges against Libya, demanded that the United States stop producing and stockpil-ing chemical weapons. An editorial in that paper said, "The Ameri-can threats against Libya have unveiled some awful contradictions in American concepts, because chemical weapons plants do exist in Russia, France, China, Korea, Israel, and West Germany ... and the Libyan plant, if the allegations were true, is no exception."[72] The editorial further criticized the United States for its belief that it had the right of custodianship over small countries.

A Jordanian columnist, Abd al-Rahim Umar, strongly sup-ported the Libyan position. He criticized the United States for acting like a world policeman, for helping Israel "to produce cluster bombs and nerve gas bombs," and for providing technology to Israel to enable it to "manufacture nuclear weapons and to continue to threaten to use them against the Arabs."[73]

Although this international support was not extensive, Libya was able to gather some verbal assistance, extricating itself from an isolated diplomatic position. Yet this was not politically sufficient. Libya itself had to further advance its positions in the international arena.

Linkage of chemical and nuclear weapons. Libya argued its case strongly by attempting to turn U.S. and Israeli chemical and nuclear weapons into a package of concerns that not only would appeal to the Arab world but would be credible at the Paris Chemical Weapons Conference. Although Libya achieved virtually no official support outside of the Middle East, it was quite successful within the Arab world.

One of the most comprehensive statements regarding this linkage was provided by Jadallah Azzuz al-Talhi, secretary for Libya's General People's Committee for Foreign Liaison. After the now customary denial about producing chemical weapons and insistence that Rabta was a pharmaceutical facility, al-Talhi made the following statement.

> The United States knows very well where the chemical and nuclear weapons are in the Middle East. The United States knows that the Zionist state is an arsenal of chemical and nuclear weapons, yet has not raised a single question about it. Furthermore, is it not Washington which gives Israel the aid and the capabilities needed for producing such weapons and is it not the Zionist state which, with U.S. backing and knowledge, refuses to abide by the international laws and treaties concluded in connection with these types of weapons?
>
> The whole world knows that Washington is the party which aids and supports Israel so that it can produce and develop nuclear, chemical, and bacteriological weapons and that there is a U.S.-Israeli military treaty under which the enemy state's capabilities in this connection are developed. We therefore urge the world public to ask the United States the meaning of its artificial uproar against us.[74]

This statement, by interjecting Israel into the chemical weapons episode, links an anti-Israeli position with U.S. nuclear and chemical weapons. Libya persisted in this position, asking why Libya was being singled out for criticism by the United States when Israel, and by implication the United States itself, possessed chemical and nuclear weapons. In the context of Arab politics, this was clearly a credible position.

Libya also made its case to the United Nations. As reported by JANA, Libya's ambassador appealed to the Security Council, arguing that the United States was pursuing a blatantly hostile policy toward Libya.[75] He emphasized that the United States was in effect asking Libya to consent to American hegemony and domination, and he criticized the United States for imposing an economic blockade on Libya. Recalling past military encounters in Libya, he accused the United States of threats, terrorism, and the use of brute force.

More specificity was added to the Libyan position by Sa'd Mustafa Mujbir, secretary of the Arab Libyan Fraternity Bureau. "The present campaign," he stated, "led by President Reagan against

Libya comes in the frame of . . . U.S. logic to try to ban [the acquisition] of high technology" by Libya. He pointed out that "there is still . . . no international legislation banning the creation of firms for the manufacture of chemical armaments," and he emphasized that "the Protocol of 1925 forbade the use . . . [but] not the manufacture of chemical armaments."[76] He argued that Libya refused to allow the United States to become the world's policeman.

Despite the harsh language used to sculpture a policy posture on the Rabta facility, some signs of moderation began to appear. *Al-Ahram*, an Egyptian newspaper, reported that Libya had announced it would not produce or use chemical weapons if the United States committed itself not to attack the complex.[77] It is impossible to verify this report, but such a position seems odd because it accedes to the U.S. demand that Libya halt its chemical weapons activities in return for a resumption of the status quo prior to the U.S. allegations.

There was also a report on Radio Free Lebanon that an emissary of Col. Qadhafi had made a secret visit to Washington, D.C. to consult with U.S. officials.[78] This report is plausible but also unverifiable. If the Libyans were adversely affected by U.S. diplomatic and economic pressure, it is not unreasonable to expect that they might have tried to quietly strike a deal and extricate themselves from a very critical international situation that on balance was not moving in a direction supportive of their interests. They had to know, for example, that the United States was correct about West German involvement at Rabta, no matter how vehemently the Germans denied it. They also probably surmised that it was only a matter of time before U.S. pressure on the FRG would force Bonn to admit and reveal the full extent of German activity in this situation. Such revelations would further ignite the political arena.

Perhaps Qadhafi had these realizations in mind when he expressed a positive appraisal of the new Bush government. "The Bush Administration," he said, "is reasonable and mature; it understands international politics and cannot repeat the ignorance of Reagan."[79] He referred to Mr. Bush as a "non-hostile political personality," and he further described the administration as "wise and learned."[80] In the midst of this dangerous situation, Qadhafi invited the United States and the Soviet Union to explore for oil and gas in Libya and to possibly become involved in water projects.[81]

There was a good deal of credibility in the Libyan international position, especially among third world countries. Even though it insisted that the Rabta complex would produce only medicines, it was correct to point out that no international instrument outlawed the production of chemical weapons. Further, although the United States felt it had a responsibility to halt the proliferation of chemical weapons, it could credibly be asserted that the United States had no right to act as gendarme of the world. Moreover, linking U.S. and other nations' possession of chemical and nuclear weapons with the possibility of Arab states' possession of chemical weapons and insisting that Libya had a right to be treated the same as other nations was a clever juxtaposition. Of course, U.S. policymakers frequently referred to Qadhafi as mentally unbalanced and therefore dangerous, which provided a potential justification for the United States to act on behalf of the international community.

Summary

This chapter illustrated the intense diplomatic conflict between the United States and West Germany regarding German assistance to Libya in its alleged pursuit of a chemical weapons production facility. The U.S. pressure on the FRG took place over several years but escalated to a high point for a three month period from November 1988 through January 1989. During this time, U.S. officials used the press, essentially the *New York Times*, to effectively exert strong public pressure on the Bonn government.

What emerged publicly with regard to Libya, if press reports were accurate, was the realization that it had successfully exploited a broad range of technical resources in the international system. Indeed, Libya had been so successful that a modern chemical production facility was emerging as a fait accompli.

Beyond the construction process itself, Libya moved to defend its actions diplomatically by linking the question of chemical weapons in the third world with the well-known possession of chemical and nuclear arsenals by several major powers. Libya argued effectively that no international instrument forbids the development of a chemical weapons production facility, and that Libya deserved to be treated as a legitimate member of the international system. As long as some nations possessed chemical weapons, and especially the more dangerous nuclear weapons, those nations' arsenals must be considered in any fair discussion of Libya's military posture.

5

The Paris Chemical
Weapons Conference

Recall from Chapter 3 that during the fall of 1988, the United States called for an international conference to address questions related to chemical weapons, especially in the Middle East. The Soviet Union and France supported the U.S. call, but most Middle Eastern nations were unenthusiastic, arguing that the problem was international and not limited solely to a single region. After French President Mitterrand agreed to host the conference, planning proceeded for a meeting in Paris in early January 1989.

In examining the Paris Chemical Weapons Conference, this chapter first briefly explores the international situation just prior to the conference and looks at some preliminary positions. The conference itself is then discussed. And the chapter concludes with an analysis of the aftermath of the conference.

The International Setting

As the key proponent for a conference on chemical weaponry, the United States had assumed a major role in attempting to halt the proliferation of chemical arms. From 1987 to 1989, it had not been successful either in halting the spread or in gaining international support for its positions. However, Great Britain, Australia, Japan, and even West Germany supported the United States in this general aim.

On the eve of the conference, Washington continued to charge Libya of constructing a chemical weapons plant at Rabta.[1] Of course, the Libyans persisted in denying this charge, arguing, as on previous occasions, that the plant was producing only medicinal products. Although the United States had succeeded in alerting the international community to Libya's alleged attempt to acquire a chemical arsenal, it had apparently not succeeded in altering Libya's development plans.

By the same token, U.S. pressure on Bonn to reexamine its export policies and prosecute German firms that had aided Libya appeared to have been unsuccessful. Various investigations by government agencies had not discovered any legal violations. Moreover, German public opinion was incensed at what it viewed as a heavy-handed American effort to embarrass the FRG.

Furthermore, Libya was not the only case of proliferation. Iraq and Iran had acquired chemical weapons, and it became known early in 1989 that a Swiss firm had supplied Egypt with processing equipment that could be used to produce chemical arms.[2] Egypt had had chemical weapons since Nasser's tenure. Syria had been identified in the early 1980s as having a stock of chemical arms.

In addition to their proliferation, chemical weapons had also been used in conflict situations. They had been employed in the Iran-Iraq War and by the Iraqi government against its own population. Such use had taken place with little open concern in the international community.

From the point of view of Washington, the United States stood virtually alone in demanding a halt to the construction at Rabta, in expressing strong concern about chemical weapons proliferation, and in identifying West German commercial activities that contributed to the proliferation problem. The Reagan administration, however, was convinced that it was moving in a proper direction, and it did not relent in its pressures.

Libya too maintained its positions. Its attempt to shift diplomatic attention from itself into the broader international arena involved with chemical and nuclear weapons successfully gained support from third world nations, especially those in the Middle East.

Thus, as the Paris Conference approached, the battle lines were clearly drawn. Some of the major players began publicly discussing the positions they would take at the conference. Soviet Foreign Minister Shevardnadze implied that the Soviet Union would demand proof of American allegations against Libya, while Arab diplomats, and especially Syria, indicated that they intended to link chemical weapons issues with Israel's alleged possession of nuclear weapons.[3] Dealing only with chemical weapons would represent a case of unilateral disarmament for those nations possessing them. As implied by Arab diplomats, it would be unrealistic for a nation to unilaterally disarm itself.

The U.S. position as it entered the conference was more detailed and multifaceted. It consisted of the following objectives and concerns:

1. Strengthen the authority of the UN secretary-general to conduct investigations regarding possible uses of chemical weapons.
2. Adopt new procedures to expedite the investigation of charges regarding the use of chemical weapons.
3. Affirm the threat of economic sanctions against users of chemical weapons.
4. Support UN Charter procedures on carrying out sanctions.
5. Neutralize any attempts to censure the United States for its possession and/or manufacture of new (binary) chemical weapons.
6. Encourage nonsignatories of the 1925 Geneva Protocol to sign.
7. As a result of prior intra-alliance consultations, avoid specifically accusing individual nations of chemical weapons violations.
8. Take decisions at the conference by consensus.[4]

The U.S. position added up to a general condemnation of the use of chemical weapons. It was to be, as one observer put it, a "hortatory exercise—an attempt to administer galvanic shock to the CW [chemical weapons] negotiations."[5] These negotiations had been proceeding for a number of years at the Conference on Disarmament in Geneva. The forty nations in attendance, however, had not reached any agreement on chemical weapons. Thus, the Paris Chemical Weapons Conference could be considered a major public relations effort to focus world attention on the chemical weapons proliferation problem and thereby to exert some pressure on the Geneva negotiators to expedite their attempts to reach an agreement on a chemical weapons convention.

It is important to note the U.S. and French desire not to use the conference to criticize individual nations. This was important because any attempt to criticize Libya would have resulted in the refusal of the Arab states to attend.

A high visibility public relations effort, however, does have its costs. In his fall 1988 speech to the UN, President Reagan indicated that he wanted the Paris Conference to affirm the world's commitment to the 1925 Geneva Protocol on chemical and biological weapons. Such an affirmation would do nothing to eliminate Libya's Rabta facility, the principal focal point of the U.S. chemical weapons proliferation policy. Moreover, the conference contained the risk that the chemical arsenals of the major powers, especially the United States, would be brought clearly to the attention of the world community. The existence and size of these arsenals could then be contrasted with the modest efforts of several Middle Eastern nations. Indeed, the case of Libya could appear unexceptional in light of the activities of other nations. Further, it bears repeating that no international instrument prevents the acquisition of chemical weapons, a position Libya had argued successfully in the past.

The Conference in Paris

From 7 to 11 January 1989, 149 nations met at the headquarters of the UN Educational, Scientific, and Cultural Organization in Paris to consider ways in which the use of chemical weapons might be prohibited. A U.S. Department of State publication proclaimed the conference "a remarkable achievement in that virtually all of the world's nations agreed to put aside their political and ideological differences to condemn the illegal use of chemical weapons."[6] Was it really a "remarkable achievement," and were "political and ideological differences" put aside? Probably not. Indeed, the controversy over the U.S. charges against Libya pervaded the entire conference, even though no specific references to them were made in most speeches or in the final communique.

On the afternoon of the opening day of the conference, U.S. Secretary of State George Shultz, the chief representative of the nation that requested the conference, presented a lengthy formal address.[7] In his speech, Mr. Shultz mentioned no nation by name, but it was clear from his text that major targets were Libya, other Middle Eastern nations, and West Germany.

After briefly reviewing past international experiences with chemical warfare, the American Secretary of State asserted that "the international norms against chemical weapons use have begun to erode in practice." Moreover, he said that "the ability to produce such weapons is rapidly spreading—and with it the technology to produce ballistic missiles as delivery vehicles." Shultz viewed this as something of a crisis situation: "Time is not on our side. Technology is not stagnant."

Shultz was one of the few diplomats at the conference who saw the linkages between biological and chemical weapons. He called attention to what he said were national efforts to develop, produce, and stockpile ever more virulent pathogenic agents. "Isn't it grimly ironic," he asked, "that these new and deadly threats have arisen to

59

haunt us at the very time we have begun to make progress in controlling and reducing nuclear arms?"

Mr. Shultz then linked the use of chemical and biological weapons with the increasing pace of international terrorism. He said the use of such weapons by terrorists would result in dramatic mass media exposure, thereby enhancing terrorist acts. In a thinly veiled reference to Libya, Shultz stated that "some governments which have been known to sponsor terrorism now have sizable chemical weapons capabilities."

In another veiled but easily recognizable reference, Shultz criticized the activities of West German firms with regard to Libya:

There is an urgent need for steps to achieve greater international restraint in the export of chemical weapons-related technologies, chemicals, and weaponry. . . . We should explore possibilities for more effective means to control the transfer of chemical weapons precursors, technology, and weapons without impeding legitimate commerce and peaceful pursuits that will benefit mankind.

References to the export of chemicals and chemical weapons technologies led quite logically to a strong statement on terrorism. "I also urge you," said the secretary of state, "to join me in committing our governments . . . to prevent the spread of chemical weapons to terrorist groups."

In hoping to defuse the expected criticism from Middle Eastern nations that the United States had assumed the self-appointed protectorship role of the developed world, Shultz argued that "chemical weapons proliferation is *not* an issue between the developed and developing world. It is *not* a matter of some nations trying to maintain a monopoly on chemical weapons by making it impossible for other nations to maintain them" (emphasis in original). Shultz urged that the major issue relates to all proliferation and all uses. From the Middle Eastern point of view, this was a weak and ineffective defense, because to verbally assert the meaning of a particular arms configuration without addressing concrete realities would have little if any effect. Indeed, Shultz' articulation of the protectorship issue, the issue of allowing developed nations to maintain chemical and nuclear weapons postures while at the same time denying such capabilities to third world countries, simply aggravated the situation.

After describing the international proliferation of chemical arms as a virtual crisis situation, Shultz encouraged the conferees to support the following three steps immediately:

1. "Every nation must undertake the political commitment to comply with the international norms relating to chemical weapons use."
2. "Nations which have not done so should accede to the 1925 Geneva protocol."
3. "The UN Secretary General's ability to investigate promptly allegations of illegal use of chemical weapons in armed conflict should be reinforced and advanced."

The secretary added a fourth, but less urgent, request that the conference consider procedures for humanitarian aid to the victims of a chemical attack.

Given the contentiousness of the emerging chemical weapons context, especially as it applied to Libya, Shultz' requests for action were mild and easily supportable by the conference. No nation objects to the international norms for chemical weapons use, even though such norms have been violated. Acceding to the 1925 Geneva Protocol raises few problems, and when nations have had concerns, they simply entered reservations to their accessions. Furthermore, 140 of the world's nations were already signatories, and of course, it is well known that this instrument lacks enforcement provisions. The request to enhance the secretary-general's investigative powers regarding the use of chemical weapons had no effect on the process of acquiring chemical arms, and this in no way restricted Libya's activities.

The day after his address to the conference, Secretary of State Shultz presented himself for a press conference in which he provided a bit more detail and clarified some of his remarks. He declared the conference a success because it was raising international consciousness about chemical weaponry.[8] Despite his sensitivity to the question of the Rabta facility, Shultz said the United States did not want to focus primarily on Libya but rather on the general problem of chemical weapons.

The secretary was asked whether the United States, if it was producing new chemical arms, was losing the high moral ground on this issue. Shultz replied that U.S. chemical weapons development was proceeding, but "we are reducing our net stocks as we proceed."[9] He added that the United States had invited inspection of its production facilities and supported a comprehensive ban on all chemical weapons.[10] By implication, Shultz was saying that the United States was a good international citizen because it did not undertake clandestine chemical weapons activities. Shultz was also asked about the role of the chemical industry in the proliferation

61

process. He responded that "the chemical industry will have to accept a degree of openness and inspection that may cause them some heartburn, but they'll have to do it."[11]

The timidness of the U.S. position at the conference did not go unnoticed. Libyan Foreign Minister Jaddallah Azouz al-Talhi asked, "How can any member of the international community proclaim a right it denies others?" He indicated that the United States was pursuing a "discriminatory policy" in denying Libya the ability to possess chemical arms prior to the international outlawing of such weapons. Al-Talhi said, "Agreed international rules must be applied to all parties without discrimination."[12] He also argued for linking a ban of chemical weapons with one on nuclear weapons, and he indicated that Israel had stocks of both nuclear and chemical weapons. Syria and Iraq supported Libya in this linkage.

An important issue at the conference involved export controls on chemicals and chemical processing equipment. Israel argued for such controls, but support among third world nations was not in evidence. Indian Foreign Minister Natwar Singh stated that his nation could not accept such controls because they would favor countries that already had chemical arms stocks, thus restricting trade with nations that might want to import chemicals.[13]

In supporting the linkage between chemical and nuclear weapons, Egyptian Foreign Minister Ahmad Ismat Abd al-Majid called for general disarmament in the Middle Eastern region. "We do not want an arms race which would be destructive to all," he said.[14]

At a press conference in Paris, Israeli Foreign Minister Moshe Arens said that if a chemical weapon pact that called for public exposure of a nation's chemical arsenals was eventually signed, "Israel's response will be positive." Nevertheless, he said, "Israel has taken all the necessary steps to foil a chemical attack."[15]

The Conference Declaration

On 11 January 1989, after all the sparring both at the conference itself and in dealings with the press, the attending nations issued a Final Declaration that was unanimously approved by all nations including Libya. Because the ground rules of the conference, as put forth by France, required decisions to be taken by consensus, it should not be surprising that the Final Declaration was, for the most part, an innocuous document. Nevertheless, getting all the attending nations, which made up most of the world community, to agree on a statement dealing with chemical weapons must be judged as something of a success. The key points can be summarized briefly.

1. The signatories "are determined to prevent any recourse of chemical weapons by completely eliminating them."
2. "They solemnly affirm their commitments not to use chemical weapons and condemn such use."
3. The participating states "support the humanitarian assistance given to the victims affected by chemical weapons."
4. The signatories "solemnly reaffirm the prohibition [of chemical and biological warfare] as established in [the 1925 Geneva Protocol]."
5. "The participating States stress the necessity of concluding, at an early date, a convention on the prohibition of the development, production, stockpiling, and use of all chemical weapons, and on their destruction."
6. The signatories are sensitive to the challenges to scrutiny posed by the spread of chemical weapons. "In this context, they stress the need for the early conclusion and entry into force of the convention, which will be established on a non-discriminatory basis."
7. The participating states "reaffirm their full support for the [UN] Secretary-General in carrying out his responsibilities for investigations in the events of alleged violations of the Geneva Protocol." They call "for early completion of the work undertaken to strengthen the efficiency of existing [investigative] procedures."[16]

Results of the Paris Conference

The Paris Conference was an ambitious, emotional exercise designed to raise international consciousness regarding chemical weapons. If that had been its only aim, the conference could probably be termed successful. However, diplomatic analysts have a right to expect more from a five-day convocation of most of the world's nations. Let us look at some of the specifics as seen from the perspectives of the United States, Libya and other Arab nations, and West Germany.

The United States achieved virtually all the objectives it set for itself as described earlier in this chapter. Under the circumstances, these objectives were quite minimal and general. Most of them had little direct bearing on the Rabta issue, with the exception that the United States supported total and complete chemical disarmament. Secretary of State Shultz could claim that the three items he requested

63

of the conference—compliance with international norms for chemical weapons use, accession to the 1925 Geneva Protocol for those nations that have not yet signed, and the strengthening of the UN secretary-general's investigative powers regarding chemical weapons allegations—were incorporated by the conferees into the Final Declaration. Given the problems at hand, however, these were relatively minor issues that few nations opposed. Nevertheless, if the American objective was indeed consciousness raising, then perhaps the conference could be described as a success.

From the Libyan point of view, the conference was certainly not as damaging as it could have been. No nations were specifically mentioned. Therefore the major international incident at Rabta in which Libya had been involved for the past year and a half was not addressed in the Final Declaration.[17] Moreover, Libya and other Arab nations were provided with a highly publicized worldwide forum from which to charge that the United States, Israel, the Soviet Union, and others already possessed chemical and nuclear weapons and to assert that surely the international community could not demand unilateral chemical disarmament from smaller and more vulnerable Middle Eastern states.[18] This linkage argument was not effectively deflected by non-Middle Eastern states possessing chemical arsenals. However, Arab nations were not successful in incorporating linkage language into the Final Declaration.

Beyond this, the Final Declaration's call for a convention to be established on a nondiscriminatory basis could be considered something of a success for third world nations. While this point should not be overemphasized, the nondiscriminatory concept could prove useful for maintaining the position at the Geneva negotiations that the superpowers should not be accorded special "policing" status over chemical weapons developments in the world.

Libya was probably pleased that the Final Declaration did not deal with questions of verification and enforcement. These are, of course, the key issues in any regime to control chemical weapons. A strong statement on verification and enforcement might have put pressure on Libya to reconsider its Rabta activities.

An additional point that should have pleased Libya was that the entire Final Declaration was use oriented. That is, the document focused almost exclusively on the use of chemical weapons and not on their acquisition. The contentiousness of the Rabta situation rested primarily on questions of acquisition, and therefore Libya's activities escaped scrutiny in the Final Declaration.

It is not surprising that the Final Declaration did not mention controls over the export of chemicals and chemical processing equipment. This issue was so contentious that any attempt to incorporate it into the Final Declaration might have resulted in a breakup of the conference. The next chapter will deal with the extent of German commercial involvement, and Bonn should have been pleased that no language aimed directly at its policies was included in the conference document.

One of the most important results of the conference, and perhaps it can be considered a victory for the United States, was the diplomatic repositioning of chemical weapons issues from an East West perspective to a North-South perspective. The conference, both in its formal sessions and in the press conferences of its attendees, clearly did not conceptualize chemical arms problems as exclusive to the industrialized world, that is, the United States, the Soviet Union, and their associated allies. There was a strong recognition that problems emerging from chemical weapons were primarily third world issues.

By the time the Paris Conference convened, the UN was already establishing new rules and guidelines to be employed by the secretary-general in investigating allegations of chemical weapons use.[19] The Final Declaration's call for strengthening these guidelines effectively supported this worthwhile objective.

The Aftermath of the Paris Conference

A number of developments following the Paris Conference are related to questions of chemical weaponry. Despite the sentiments of the conference's Final Declaration, the proliferation of chemical processing equipment that could be used in weapons production continued. In March 1989 Swiss and U.S. officials charged that Egypt was in the process of improving its capabilities to manufacture poison gas.[20] This was being done with equipment that was purchased from a Zurich firm, Krebs A.G. The equipment was installed at a military manufacturing area in the town Abu Zaabal north of Cairo. The plant itself was being built by Krebs from designs purchased from Stauffer Chemicals, an American firm.[21] The Swiss Foreign Ministry demanded that Krebs disengage from the project because Egypt refused to certify that the plant would not be used for military purposes. The United States charged that the Swiss government had known about these activities for several years but had failed to take expeditious action. The Swiss Foreign Ministry argued that lax export laws prohibited earlier actions. Krebs agreed to sever its connection with the Egyptian project, while the Egyptian government denied that it was producing chemical weapons.[22]

One of the few positive developments that emerged after the conference, even though its roots preceded the conference, was agreement between the United States and the Soviet Union on a cluster of key issues related to a treaty banning chemical weapons.[23] These included a test of inspection procedures and a timetable for eventual destruction of chemical arms. This coincidence of U.S. and Soviet interests can be viewed as an important development that could influence how these superpowers will respond to proliferation problems in the future.

Shortly after the close of the conference, the Bush administration began a comprehensive review of its export policies regarding chemicals and chemical technologies.[24] Several shortcomings had become apparent, and these were similar to those in West German export controls. A U.S. Department of State official was quoted as saying, "I live in fear of the day when the German ambassador may come in here and say that Bonn has found an American company selling chemical weapons materials to the Middle East."[25] The administration indicated the following problems with U.S. export policy:

1. Despite restrictions on the sale of chemicals to Libya, Iran, Iraq, and Syria, U.S. controls on certain critical chemicals do not extend to all Middle Eastern nations.
2. No export controls are in place for the sale of chemical processing equipment and expertise for the manufacturing of chemical arms.
3. Current U.S. laws do not allow for the legal apprehension of individuals who create commercial arrangements overseas for chemicals to be used in Middle Eastern processing plants.[26]

The Bush administration also indicated it would accept legislation imposing economic sanctions on firms that dealt in chemical weapons activities and on nations that employed chemical arms.[27] The Reagan administration had steadfastly refused to support this type of legislation, fearing it would limit the power of the executive branch.

Much of the diplomatic dialogue both before and during the Paris Conference involved issues related to suppliers of chemicals and chemical equipment, that is, private industrial firms. Control of such firms by governments, chiefly through export policies, has proven to be a difficult task. Since 1984 the Australian embassy in Paris has coordinated a group of 21 nations, primarily from Western Europe but including the United States and Australia, which has met twice each year to discuss issues of chemical weapons. As conceived, the Australian Group has been the medium through which governments of the leading industrialized nations of the West share intelligence on chemical weapons proliferation and attempt to inhibit proliferation by developing and harmonizing their export control policies.

At the suggestion of the United States, Australia organized a Government-Industry Conference against Chemical Weapons (GICCW), which was held in Canberra from 18 to 22 September 1989. The rationale underlying the conference was that although diplomatic instruments to control chemical weaponry were essential, such instruments could not be completely effective without the cooperation of the chemical industry. Government and industry representatives from sixty-six countries attended the conference. Libya did not attend. According to one report, 95 percent of the chemical production capacity of the world was represented.[28]

The following chemical industry statement was approved by the conference:

> The world's chemical industries as represented by industry representatives present at the Government-Industry Conference against Chemical Weapons, held in Canberra, from 18–22 September 1989:
>
> Welcome the Government-Industry Conference against Chemical Weapons and the constructive dialogue which had taken place between governments and representatives of the world's chemical industries, and between industrial representatives of different countries.
>
> Express their unequivocal abhorrence of chemical warfare.
>
> Express their willingness to work actively with governments to achieve a global ban on chemical weapons, and their willingness to contribute additional momentum to the general negotiating process.
>
> Affirm their desire to foster international cooperation for the legitimate civil uses of chemical products, their opposition to the diversion of industry's products for the manufacture of chemical weapons.
>
> Declare their support for efforts to conclude and implement the chemical weapons convention at the earliest date. Industry believes that the only solution to the problem of chemical weapons is a global comprehensive and effectively verifiable chemical weapons convention which requires the destruction of all existing stockpiles of, and production facilities for, chemical weapons and which implements measures to assure that their future production does not take place.
>
> Express the strong hope that the negotiating parties in the Confer-

ence on Disarmament in Geneva will resolve urgently the outstanding issues and conclude a chemical weapons convention at the earliest possible date.

State their willingness to continue their dialogue with governments to prepare for the entry into force of an effective chemical weapons convention which protects the free and non-discriminatory exchange of chemicals and transfer of technology for economic development and the willingness to participate in national measures designed to facilitate early implementation of the convention following its conclusion.[29]

This was an important statement and the first of its kind for the world's chemical industry. It pledged the industry to oppose "the diversion of industry's products for the manufacture of chemical weapons," and it stated the industry's willingness to cooperate in the implementation of an eventual chemical weapons convention. In reflecting on this statement, the Australian minister for foreign affairs and trade, Gareth Evans, stated that "this is no slight claim that is being made. This is for all practical purposes, the world's chemical industry that is speaking."[30] Nothing less than this unequivocal declaration would have been acceptable to the international chemical industry community, coming as it did after the revelations made earlier in the year regarding the West German chemical industry (revelations discussed in the next chapter).

A final issue relating to the aftermath of the Paris Conference was a strange item of information apparently leaked to the *New York Times*. Unnamed Bush administration officials were reported to have said Libya was in the process of converting its Rabta facility from chemical weapons to pharmaceutical production.[31] The evidence for this was that Libya was apparently hiring technicians to do refitting work. If this were true, then it would be possible to argue that the Libyan chemical weapons episode had ended, and that U.S. pressure on Libya and the international community had been successful. Unfortunately, this was not to be the case.

Summary

At the initiative of the United States, with the support of France and others, the Paris Chemical Weapons Conference was held in early 1989. The Final Declaration of the conference did not run contrary to the interests of the attending nations. However, considering the problems at hand, especially as they related to Rabta, the document did not deal with the issue of proliferation. If the United

States conceived of the conference as a mechanism to alert the world to general problems of chemical weaponry, the conference was probably a success. If, however, the aim of the conference was to put pressure on Libya to halt its activities at Rabta, the conference must be considered something short of successful.

6

The Explosion of Events in West Germany

As developments in Libya proceeded and the Paris Chemical Weapons Conference unfolded events in the Federal Republic of Germany moved toward a major political explosion. As indicated in the previous chapters, developments regarding the Rabta facility did not occur in sequential fashion. Rather, they overlapped each other and were often intertwined not only in public statements and documents but also in the minds of statesmen. This complexity can only be understood by disaggregating the general event into its component parts and examining those parts microscopically.

The present chapter provides a detailed examination of the West German connection to the construction of the Rabta facility. It explores the initial outlook of the Bonn government to the stimulation of exports and the role of the German press in revealing issues that had to be addressed by federal authorities. Then the chapter moves into debates in the Bundestag over the Libyan affair. The government's report to the Bundestag regarding its knowledge of chemical weapons activities by its firms and the further knowledge it had of Libyan activities is discussed in detail. The central role of the Imhausen-Chemie firm is explained, and several graphic diagrams of Libya's complex business operations are provided.

The Posture of the Bonn Government

Through the conclusion of the Paris Conference, Bonn continued to maintain that it had no knowledge of prosecutable offenses committed by German firms regarding the shipment of chemicals and chemical processing equipment to Libya. German officials professed anger at the harsh treatment the FRG was receiving in the American press. One official called the Libyan coverage a case of "German-bashing."[1] Moreover, the Germans were upset at American insistence that U.S. intelligence was definitive regarding Libya's apparent chemical weapons initiatives. Bonn insisted that it would conduct its own intelligence analysis. Chancellor Kohl was reported to have been so angry with what he viewed as American pressure tactics that he telephoned U.S. Ambassador Richard Burt and complained that the FRG was not a "banana republic" to be pushed around at will by Washington.[2]

It should not be assumed that the BND, the West German intelligence service, was not a major player in the Libyan episode. The BND was fully aware for an extended period of the export of chemical weapons materials to Libya, but it had no effect on German policy. A report on Libya from the BND was transmitted to the chancellery, but Kohl's deputy for intelligence, Waldemar Schreck-enberger, was apparently an incompetent administrator who frequently lost important documents. Indeed, West German observers often referred to the chancellery as "The Bermuda Triangle."[3]

The U.S.-German quarrel must be looked upon as more than a passing squabble. The United States and the FRG are both members of NATO and had developed close strategic cooperation in security matters. The United States had a large contingent of troops and numerous sophisticated weapons systems stationed on German territory. Moreover, for at least a decade, NATO deliberations had called attention to problems of chemical weaponry. These problems had been addressed chiefly in an East-West context, but the mere discussion of them should have served to alert Bonn to the sensitivities of its allies on questions of chemical arms.

Within NATO, West Germany agreed to many alliance statements expressing concern about chemical weapons. For example, the NATO Council meeting of 1983 called for "the prohibition of the development, production, and stockpiling of chemical weapons."[4] Virtually identical statements were agreed upon in subsequent years. Through the 1980s, the alliance consistently took the position that members had a responsibility not to contribute to the proliferation of chemical weapons. Most certainly this included assistance in production.

Part of the irony of the German position is what one German scholar, Frederick-Wilhelm Baer-Kaupert, calls a confusion of the "ethics of motivation" with the "ethics of responsibility." Policymakers must be concerned not only with motivations (for example, the desire to increase German exports) but with certain social responsibilities that flow from those worthy motivations (for example, the proliferation of chemical weapons). Baer-Kaupert maintains

that "to separate these two elements of human behavior is to depreci-
ate man as a social being and to encourage an attitude which is at best
pedantically dogmatic and at worst contemptuous and destructive."[5]
Up to mid-1989, the FRG's Foreign Trade Act focused on goods to
be exported, not on the recipients of those goods. This, of course,
allowed numerous loopholes for the export of chemical weapons
technologies. By the time Rabta-related events in Germany had
reached their climax, a provision in the Foreign Trade Act had been
fully implemented. That provision stated that "controls . . . have to
be configured so that there is as little limitation to the freedom of
economic activity as possible."[6] Unfortunately, this put Bonn in the
awkward position of defending activities of commercial firms that
contributed to the proliferation of chemical armaments.

The West German Press

Immediately after the Paris Chemical Weapons Conference,
general perceptions and events began to change in West Germany.
The stimulus behind this change was the probing attitude of the
German press toward the continuing exposure of pieces of information about chemical developments in Libya. Although it was initially
skeptical regarding U.S. press coverage of German commercial activities in Libya, once those activities became clearer through the acquisition of documented information, the German press moved resolutely to pressure its own government regarding Libyan activities.

Opening the avalanche of activity was what Bonn hoped would
be an innocuous policy shift toward stronger export controls. During
January 1989, the FRG announced it was going to propose stricter
measures for the control of sensitive chemical and nuclear goods. In
an interview with *Die Welt*, Chancellor Kohl argued that tightened
regulations should be looked upon not as an admission of guilt in
the Libyan affair but as an attentive government's "measures for the
future."[7]

The press response to the government's initiative was swift and
critical. *Neue Ruhr-Zeitung* called the new proposal "a late but
necessary decision, which was probably made under the pressure
of U.S. evidence of German deliveries for the construction of the
mysterious chemical plant in Libya." The paper then stated that "it
is incomprehensible why the German investigations . . . have been
so unproductive."[8]

The *Frankfurter Allgemeine* was especially harsh. If it was impossible to legally prove any wrongdoing, then Bonn "missed the point of U.S. accusations." Questioning Kohl's comment on future commercial activities, the newspaper stated:

> If it is correct that no legal regulations were violated, why have the decisions on tightening the foreign trade and military material laws been made now? The tacitly ignored logical connection can only be that Germany's practice in exports and the corresponding laws give rise to complaints. If, in addition, one takes into consideration that 6 months passed between the first hints from Washington and the start of the investigation of Imhausen-Chemie Company, was the rather rude campaign of the U.S. administration not a last necessary means to overcome the dealness of the FRG Government?

The same critical flavor was reflected in comments by the *Sueddeutsche Zeitung* and the *Allgemeine Zeitung*. The *Sueddeutsche Zeitung* questioned whether Bonn would have moved to close export loopholes in the absence of U.S. pressure. The paper maintained that contrary to the chancellor's reflections, it is certainly conceivable that Germans might commit crimes in violation of export laws. The paper argued that the government has a responsibility not only to prosecute crimes by manufacturers of sensitive materials but to try to prevent them. To do this, "one does not need a bureaucracy that paralyses exports." The *Allgemeine Zeitung* charged that Bonn would have been more credible regarding chemical exports if it had acted sooner: "Doubts are in order about whether the measures . . . are sufficient to make an effective contribution to smoke out the international poison kitchens."

Officials Respond

Events in West Germany were moving quite rapidly in mid-January 1989. Nevertheless, Bonn did not institute any emergency measures for Libyan trade. A spokesperson for the Economics Ministry said that although Germany should avoid sensitive exports to Libya, no general freeze on Libyan exports had been instituted.[9]

This reluctance to respond was reinforced by leading politicians who, even at this late date, were willing to maintain Bonn's often stated position on Libya. Hans Stercken, chairman of the Bundestag's Foreign Affairs Committee, told Vienna's *Die Presse* that he had "not been able to detect even the slightest trace of a development in which it [the government] had not acted completely correctly . . . [t]here have not been any such [chemical] exports."[10] Otto Lambsdorff, FDP leader, complained that the United States had made accusations against West Germany without furnishing any proof.[11]

Nevertheless, there were signs that Kohl's government was beginning to sense the seriousness of what was emerging in the nation's press. Hamburg DPA and *Stern* had just published a major story with details about German commercial activities. With this possibly in mind, Foreign Minister Hans-Dietrich Genscher said that if present penalties for Germans involved in the manufacture of chemical weapons were not adequate, they must be made much more severe.[12] The chancellor himself said he was determined to halt *future* exports of militarily useful technologies. He indicated that "reinforced investigations" were continuing, but he again expressed disbelief that any Germans were involved in producing chemical weapons.[13]

The Dam Bursts

Over a year of denial concerning German commercial involvement in Libya simply could not hold up to the flood of detailed information that eventually poured out into the public domain through the press. On 11 January the DPA reported that German customs had confiscated business documents of IBI Engineering in Frankfurt, and that the documents had shown IBI to have coordinated German commercial activities related to the Rabta facility. At the time of the confiscation, that firm was in liquidation, and its director, Ihsan Barbouti, had fled. The DPA also said German officials were working with Belgian customs personnel to investigate the activities of Imhausen-Chemie in Antwerp. Apparently, Imhausen-contracted ships bound for Hong Kong stopped in Antwerp to have the papers covering the destination of their loads changed to Tripoli.[14]

At the same time, *Stern* reported that engineers and construction supervisors were employed through advertisements in the *Kurier* newspaper of Vienna. Their salaries were paid from an account in a branch of the Deutsche Bank in Frankfurt. A day later, government spokesman Friedhelm Ost confirmed that the FRG Intelligence Services had solid information that Libya intended to manufacture chemical arms at the Rabta factory.[15] He said test runs might have already taken place, but that full-scale production had not yet begun. Remarkably, Ost said that the government had been given information in October 1988 on German commercial involvement at Rabta, and that the situation was immediately recognized as serious. He added quickly, however, that this evidence was not usable in court.

The chancellor too began to lay the groundwork for a defense of his government's actions by admitting that there was evidence, probably from the seized IBI Engineering documents, that linked German firms with Libyan chemical activities. He said that this evidence was being "concretely followed up," and that it emerged from "specific documents which may produce convincing proof."[16] While Kohl was softening his stand on German complicity, the Libyan ambassador to the United Nations, Ali Al-Turayki, told Hamburg DPA that Libya had "wide-ranging cooperation with Germany, and a lot of German companies have been involved in a lot of development projects in Libya." He added, however, "I have no information whatever about any sort of German project in connection with the pharmaceutical factory" at Rabta.[17]

In spite of these denials and efforts Hamburg's *Die Welt* described as attempts "to hush everything up,"[18] further specific information regarding commercial activities began to emerge in the German press. *Frankfurter Allgemeine* provided an especially detailed account based upon interviews with German businessmen and the accountant for IBI Frankfurt.[19] According to this report, Ihsan Barbouti orchestrated most if not all of the contracts and purchases related to the construction process. The choice of Barbouti by Libya was an excellent one, because Barbouti was well known in construction circles and his activities in regard to Rabta would therefore raise few questions. Also, Barbouti maintained numerous commercial connections on behalf of Libya.

It was now clear that IBI Engineering had four branch offices, one in West Germany at Frankfurt, two in Switzerland at Zurich and Zug, and one in London. Construction orders came through IBI Zurich and IBI Zug. Apparently Libya paid money into the London branch and perhaps even the two Swiss branches and then transferred these funds to Frankfurt. IBI Frankfurt, through Harry P. Meyer, a Frankfurt tax consultant and accountant, paid the bills, disguising the true purchaser, Libya. IBI Zurich was active in placing orders for equipment. For example, it contracted with a West German firm, John Zink GmbH Construction Technology in Frankfurt, to ship a ground burner for excess gas to Hong Kong. It was presumably reshipped to Libya. The IBI complex on the continent was quite useful for moving around payments and funds, and the existence of branches in Switzerland and West Germany made tracing the movement of monies complicated and difficult.

Acting on behalf of his Libyan employers, Barbouti himself frequently made purchases directly from private firms. Krebs and Kiefer Engineering and Consulting GmbH in Darmstadt was contracted to check structural calculations on the steel construction at Rabta. This firm was concerned essentially with metal fabrication and precision mechanics. Bischoff KG Frankfurt sold drills, cranes, loaders, and fork-stackers directly to Libya. Huennebeck GmbH in Ratengen (FRG) delivered construction scaffolding to Rotterdam and then transshipped it to Rabta. Construction steel was purchased from an East German firm, and machinery for the steel factory came from Japanese and Danish firms.[20]

The fact that the Rabta complex involved various types of industrial facilities further complicated the discovery and tracing process. Purchases for a chemical weapons plant could be ordered for an entirely different kind of factory and simply moved a short distance once they arrived at the Rabta complex. Moreover, it was difficult for authorities to discover the structure of this process because it involved numerous individual firms and several nations. The key, of course, was Barbouti, who had to have an intimate knowledge of the architecture of this elaborate undertaking. The cleverness of the Libyan government should also be noted. It contracted a known construction engineer to orchestrate this process for Libya. Should anything happen, Libya could always deny involvement. None of its government offices were openly involved.

A recognition that the United States may not have acted precipitously and may have been correct all along began to appear in German press reflections. Frankfurt's *Neue Presse* wrote:

> It was not pure wickedness, after all, that caused the United States to scold Bonn because of the chemical weapons plant in Libya. What is coming to light now confirms that the accused companies are not innocent at all. The politicians in Bonn and the journalists who think they know the United States very well should have sensed that Washington would not intervene so massively against the German-Libyan connection without being in possession of evidence.

Westfalenblatt, published in Bielefeld, expressed dismay that Bonn had refused to admit the complicity of German firms, despite burgeoning evidence.

> As recently as 2 days ago, the Government in Bonn called on Washington to mention names. Names have now been specified, and things have turned out to be true which the chancellor had described as

unacceptable: German companies are playing a major role in the production of chemical weapons, have made sizable profits and, in addition to that, have helped one of the leading terrorists in the world to gain possession of terrible weapons of mass destruction.

"One wishes," wrote the *Sueddeutsche Zeitung*, "that the Bonn government would react more calmly and not with so much conviction of having a clear conscience" in the future. The *Frankfurter Rundschau* saw Bonn's actions as damaging the reputation of the FRG.[21]

On 12 January Jozef Gedopt, director of the shipping agency Cross Link in Antwerp, was arrested by Belgian authorities on suspicion of "using false transportation documents and abuse of trust."[22] Mr. Gedopt was accused of facilitating the shipment of goods to the Rabta complex. IBI Engineering had used Cross Link in Antwerp as a transshipment point for goods from Europe to Libya. Changing destinations on documents can be done easily if one has a willing accomplice at a shipping firm.

On 13 January the Offenburg (FRG) Public Prosecutor's Office confirmed that it had instituted an investigation of the Imhausen-Chemie Company in Lahr. The investigation was initiated after disclosures in *Stern* indicated that Imhausen-Chemie may have been involved in the Rabta complex even though the firm had consistently denied involvement. After evaluating the information in *Stern*, the public prosecutor's office said that there were important indications of Imhausen-Chemie's involvement.[23] Despite this, the special state prosecutor's offices for economic crimes in Mannheim and Frankfurt declined to inaugurate investigations on the basis of material available.[24] On 25 January Hamburg DPA reported that the offices of Imhausen-Chemie had been searched by the public prosecutor in Offenburg. Searches of the homes of the top staff personnel of Imhausen were also undertaken.[25]

Stern magazine revealed on 16 January that a subsidiary of the Salzgitter Group, Salzgitter Industriebau GmbH, prepared plans for the construction of a chemical factory in Hong Kong known as Pharma 150.[26] Salzgitter, which is owned by the West German government, said it was paid DM 7 million for design work involving piping and electronics for a pharmaceutical products factory. *Stern* indicated that the Hong Kong destination was only a "cover" for the ultimate destination in Libya. Salzgitter further admitted that Imhausen-Chemie was the commercial firm that contracted its services.

Also on 16 January, the Hamburg DPA reported that two additional firms appeared to be involved in the Rabta complex. The Merck chemical firm in Darmstadt admitted supplying 19 tons of the chemical dichloroethane to Libya. Though Merck said the chemical has multiple uses, one use involves the production of mustard gas. Alfred Tewes GmbH of Frankfurt confirmed to the press that it had supplied ventilation and air extraction equipment to the Pharma 150 project in Hong Kong, and that it knew Hong Kong was not its ultimate destination.[27]

At the end of January, Hamburg DPA reported that a Bavarian firm, Globcsat Company for Applied Satellite Technology, was suspected of violating the weapons control and foreign trade laws by delivering to Libya electronic steering units and testing and measuring systems that could be used in the manufacture of missiles.[28] Degussa AG in Frankfurt was in the process of shipping a large quantity of hexamethylene tetramine to Libya when customs authorities in the port of Bremerhaven seized the shipment since it could have been used for nitramine explosives, underwater projectiles, or missile fuel.[29] One firm, Sartorius Metal Construction in Bensheim, suspended its contract with Libya, allegedly because it found out its products were to be used at the Rabta complex.[30]

Further information regarding the Salzgitter Group appeared in a *Der Spiegel* interview with Ernst Pieper, manager of Salzgitter, who stated that his group had been deceived by the Imhausen-Chemie company. "In 1984 we received an order from Imhausen-Chemie to provide a limited part of the engineering for a chemical plant where primary and intermediate pharmaceutical products are to be produced. We had to hand over these drawings to the German customer [Imhausen] in the FRG. We were told that the plant would be established in Hong Kong." Even though a telex in the Salzgitter files contained the word *Rabta* as early as February 1985, no company officials took any special note of this or raised questions about its meaning. Imhausen provided Salzgitter with plans from French and Italian companies that showed the disposition of electrical equipment and pipelines. According to Pieper, a "hundred German, European, and U.S. enterprises participated in the Pharma 150 project, and so none of the companies knew what was going on."[31] Of course, the two major coordinators of the project, IBI Engineering and Imhausen-Chemie knew very well what was happening. Virtually no information about U.S. firms has been uncovered.

Government Reactions to Revelations

The Bonn government's reaction to six to seven weeks of revelations about the activities of German firms assisting Libya was lame and disorganized. Particularly embarrassing was the knowledge that a state-owned enterprise, Salzgitter, had been a participant in the Rabta effort. In mid-January, official German spokespersons were still insisting that the government had no evidence that could be used in a judicial undertaking.[32] The government's response to press criticism that it did not release information about commercial activities sooner was that it did not want to allow the media to provide an advance warning to the companies involved.[33] The government admitted, however, that it had received intelligence briefings on chemical weapons projects in the Middle East since 1980. Many press reports criticized the government for not taking such briefings seriously.[34] If it had, the embarrassment to West Germany might have been avoided.

Apparently the president of the Federal Intelligence Service (BND), Hans-Georg Wieck, saw the possibility that his unit might be being maneuvered into a position in which it would be blamed for the government's shortcomings in the Libyan affair. He told *Die Welt* that as far back as September 1988, the BND warned the chancellery that a chemical factory was being constructed in Libya and that German businessmen might be involved. To this point the Bonn government had let the impression stand that it had first learned of German involvement at Rabta from Washington.

To relieve some of the pressure on the FRG, German Foreign Minister Genscher proposed to Secretary of State James Baker that the United States and the FRG consult jointly on measures to prevent chemical weapons production in Libya.[35] He further suggested that the European Community undertake joint efforts to halt Libya's quest for chemical weapons. Along these same lines, Bonn called for a worldwide ban on chemical weapons.[36]

These attempts at statesmanship did little to mollify the government's opposition in the Bundestag. An especially harsh debate in which Chancellor Kohl came under strong personal attack took place on 18 January. In a surprise statement, an aide to Mr. Kohl, Chancellery Minister Wolfgang Schauble, acknowledged that the government had long been aware that German firms were involved with the Rabta facility.[37] He insisted, however, that evidence for criminal prosecution was not available. But Norbert Gansel, the weapons expert of the Social Democratic Party, delivered a stunning criticism of the Kohl government.

Gansel argued that Bonn had not recognized the political implications of what was becoming a major international scandal. Speaking directly to Kohl, Gansel said, "You're personally responsible for the fact that German-U.S. relations have been severely damaged and that the world sees Germans calling for a global ban on chemical weapons in public, while you secretly tolerate the production of chemical weapons in crisis areas."[38]

Schauble, again reflecting the government's position, argued that "Independent countries have the duty to do everything to stop this [chemical] threat to nations." Nevertheless, "the experience of the last weeks has shown how limited are the legal possibilities that could have stopped the involvement of German firms in the production of chemical weapons abroad." In the clearest recognition by the government of what was emerging in Libya, Schauble stated that "on the basis of secret service intelligence reports, we must conclude that the plant in Rabta is capable of producing chemical weapons." Moreover, he said, "there are intelligence reports showing the involvement of German firms in the construction of this plant."[39]

This minimal amount of information, however, did not satisfy Mr. Gansel. He charged that the government was controlling information on the Rabta affair, and that only after the press revealed specific items did the government "dribble out" a few facts. On the basis of Gansel's sharp criticisms, the Social Democrats demanded that the government render a full report on the Libyan affair by 15 February. The Bundestag approved.

The Government's Report to the Bundestag

Leading newspapers and magazines dug into the story of German involvement in the Rabta complex with a professional passion. What they reported over several years, as is now known, was essentially accurate. The public accounting of what took place emerged piecemeal in Germany as well as in the United States. Although the Kohl government was especially angry with the *New York Times*, German publications treated German involvement in the Rabta affair far more harshly and provided considerably more detail than the American press.

80

The Explosion of Events in West Germany

The government's Report to the Bundestag, delivered on 15 February 1989, essentially confirmed what had appeared over many months in the public press. The debate had become so contentious in West Germany and emerging questions of the Kohl government's credibility in foreign policy matters were so important that anything less than a full disclosure would probably have failed to satisfy public opinion and might have led to a severe weakening of Germany's international position. Thus, the point had been reached at which it was in the government's interest to set the record straight and, if possible, to portray in the best possible light the government's own rationale for its behavior.

When it appeared, the Kohl government's Report had a dramatic effect. The many months of claims by numerous government officials, including the chancellor himself, that little or no evidence existed of any German involvement with the construction of a chemical weapons factory in Libya were no longer valid. Indeed, despite the government's effort to put the best face on its behavior, the Report was devastating. The document is entitled "Report Submitted by the Government of the Federal Republic of Germany to the German Bundestag on February 15, 1989 concerning Possible Involvement of Germans in the Establishment of a Chemical Weapon Facility in Libya."[40] Although the title refers to "possible involvement," the Report itself acknowledges the involvement of a number of German firms, especially Imhausen-Chemie. Moreover, the tone of the entire document, is cleverly presented to sound as though the government itself initiated an investigation of suspected illegal exports, raided the offices of offending firms, gathered evidence, and led an initiative to convince the international community to outlaw chemical weapons. Indeed, with the exception of a few references to briefings by U.S. officials, a casual reader might easily get the impression that there was no diplomatic activity regarding the Rabta complex save that initiated by West Germany itself.

Of course nothing could be further from the truth. The Kohl government discounted and/or disregarded evidence from a number of allied intelligence services, consistently protected the German commercial community, and produced a report only at the command of the Bundestag. Indeed, in retrospect, bad judgment was clearly in evidence on the part of the German government, because through the many months of official denials of involvement, the credibility of Germany on questions of export of sensitive materials virtually evaporated. Moreover, through its actions, the Kohl government

brought renewed charges from various quarters that it was resurrect-
ing a Nazi past, and this, of course, produced considerable embarrassment among Germans.

The following discussion of the Report itself is divided into
three sections. First, because governments often rely on their own
intelligence services, the information provided for a decade by the
BND is examined. This information was sometimes conflicting. Nevertheless, because of Germany's well-known involvement with poison gas during World Wars I and II, the Germans should have been
hypersensitive to questions of chemical weapons. Second, because
intricate international relationships through diplomatic contacts frequently provide considerable information, the warnings that Germany received from the diplomatic community are examined. Third,
because the government's own Salzgitter firm assisted the Libyans,
it is important to understand the government's justification for Salzgitter's involvement. For details on private firms, the press reports
that have already been examined are quite accurate. Nevertheless,
some use of the government Report is made later in this chapter
when graphics of the commercial arrangements are presented.

BND. As indicated in previous chapters, the Kohl government
became increasingly impatient with U.S. insistence that American
intelligence had provided sufficient information regarding the
involvement of German firms in the Rabta complex to allow action
to be taken by the FRG. The West Germans disputed this, arguing
that they would prefer to depend on the BND, their own intelligence
service. One of the most startling revelations to emerge from the
government's Report was information indicating that the BND had
provided comprehensive, but sometimes contradictory, data on
chemical weapons developments in the Middle East since 1980.[41]
The Report indicates that most of this information was distributed
to the BK-Amt (Federal Chancellery), the AA (Federal Foreign Office), the BMVg (Federal Ministry of Defense), the BMI (Federal
Ministry of the Interior), and sometimes the BMWi (Federal Ministry
of Economics). Although from time to time the distribution list
varied, in almost all instances critical information was routinely sent
to the chancellery, the Foreign Office, and the Ministry of Defense.
Thus, the West German foreign policy community was well informed
regarding chemical weapons developments in the Middle East, and
this information had been provided to decision makers over a period
of almost a decade. The following items of information in the Report
were communicated to the government:

The Explosion of Events in West Germany

22 April 1980
The BND reports that, with the help of unnamed East and West German experts, Libya is developing a plant for the manufacture of chemical warfare agents as well as a system for using them. The BND thinks it is also conceivable that it may be a normal chemical factory. The possibility of the conscious involvement of German companies in the construction of a warfare agents plant was excluded. . . .

12 February 1981
The BND reports that Libya intends to import chemical warfare agents which can be used with long-range artillery, helicopters, and high speed aircraft, as well as with medium-range missiles. The chemicals needed for the production of chemical warfare agents are reportedly to be purchased in Western Europe. . . . It is thought that, in view of the growing amount of evidence, there can be no doubt about the seriousness of Libyan efforts. . . .

22 July 1981
The BND reports that Libya remains committed to the production of chemical warfare agents and is currently endeavoring to purchase the basic chemicals needed for this purpose in Italy and Spain. . . .

15 December 1981
Report by the BND stating that Libya's efforts to achieve its own chemical warfare capability should be taken seriously. Though one could not speak of an actual chemical threat, the ability to use chemical warfare agents might already exist on a small scale. . . .

13 December 1982
The BND reports that it is highly probable that Libya, along with several other states in the Middle East, possesses chemical warfare agents (presumably supplied by the Warsaw Pact) and that a production facility for nerve gases possibly already exists, though it is thought more likely to be still under construction. . . .

22 July 1983
The BND reports that Libya has its own plant for the manufacture of mustard gas which attacks the skin. The plant is said to have started production at the end of 1981. Its location is presumed to be near Abu Khammash. Furthermore, the BND warns that it must be assumed that Libya already possesses effective chemical ammunition.

July 1984
[Although the intelligence information is uncertain, the BND reports] that a former employee of a German company had gone to Libya for

one year and had earned a great deal of money. It is presumed that he had built a plant for the production of mustard gas next to the Abu Khammash chemicals complex. It is reported that this complex contains a chloride electrolysis facility built by a German company according to a standard design and operating on the basis of sea-salt, and that it could produce one of the precursors needed for mustard gas. A memo [on this report] was nevertheless made at the AA . . . which led to top-level consultations on 30 July 1984.

In November 1984 the matter is once again taken up at the AA. This leads to a request for more information from the representative of the BND at the beginning of 1985. It fails to produce any new insights (incidentally, at the time, and later in its report of 13 October 1988) the BND confirmed that contrary to earlier indications no chemical warfare agents were being produced at Abu Khammash. . . .

5 December 1984
The BND reports that a production facility for nerve gases may exist in Libya, though it is thought more likely to be still under construction. . . .

28 January 1986
The BND reports that the plant for the manufacture of mustard gas in Libya is said to have been constructed under the management of a member of a German company identified by name. . . . Precursors which Libya would have to acquire from abroad are thought to have been purchased by bogus Greek, Maltese, and British firms, though these have not yet been identified. . . .

7 February 1986
The BND reports on news from an allied intelligence service according to which 100 tons of sodium fluoride may have been shipped from Zeebrugge to Libya on the Panamanian freighter "Capira" at the beginning of 1985. This is said to involve a German shipping company identified by name. . . .

18 February 1986
The BND reports that Libya possesses chemical warfare agents . . . which it may have produced itself. These agents include mustard gas and possibly sarin, too. The location of the factory remains unclear, but it is thought it could be at Tajura inside or near the Libyan nuclear research center. . . . The BND says it cannot establish for sure whether the 100 tons of sodium fluoride are related to the manufacture of nerve gases. A likely weapons system for the use of chemical warfare agents is thought to be ammunition supplied by a Spanish company in 1980. . . .

The Explosion of Events in West Germany

17 March 1986
The BND reports that the recipient of the 100 tons of sodium fluoride is the Libyan Tajura nuclear research centre where, in the opinion of the allied intelligence service, research work is also carried out on chemical warfare agents. . . .

22 June 1987
Daily briefing by the BND. According to information from an allied intelligence service, a warfare agents factory is about to be completed near Rabta with a production capacity estimated at 1 to 3 tons per day. . . .

2 July 1987
The BND reports that production is expected to begin at Rabta in September 1987. No mention is made of the participation of German companies. . . .

3 August 1987
The BND confirms from its own intelligence (SPOT satellite pictures) that the new industrial plant near Rabta is most likely the new warfare agents factory. . . .

27 August 1987
Daily briefing by the BND. It is reported that Libya possesses specially trained units for chemical warfare. . . . It is also assumed that Libya has the appropriate vehicles for using chemical agents in the air and on the land. . . .

27 January 1988
. . . the BND confirms that its own intelligence and the opinion of allied intelligence services indicate that the object identified near Gharyan (Rabta) is a plant for the production of warfare agents and possibly ammunition. Previous information indicates that the construction of the plant was mainly carried out with the participation of Japanese, Korean, Polish, and GDR citizens but not with companies from the Federal Republic of Germany. . . .

5 May 1988
The BND reports that it is highly likely that a plant for the manufacture of nerve gas is being or has been built in connection with an almost completed industrial plant near Rabta. Companies from the Federal Republic have not so far made an appearance in the business. . . .

15 July 1988
The BND received information from an allied intelligence service

concerning possible supplies from German companies for the construction of a poison gas production plant in Rabta. The firms named are IBI, Pen Tsao, and Imhausen.

12 September 1988
The BND has information showing that the warfare agents plant at Rabta is not yet in operation. More intensive intelligence work reveals the possible involvement of individual citizens of the Federal Republic, who are not named.

30 September 1988
The BND reports that the Libyan plant near Gharyan has been completed for some time. Allied intelligence services point to Japanese suppliers and a Thai company responsible for project implementation. It is said that Germans are to be found among those working on the project, though these are not identified by name. It is reported that even before the project began Imhausen had been delivering unspecified precursors. . . .

13 October 1988
The BND reports that Libya "is very probably about to achieve its long sought-after objective of having its own chemical warfare capability." It says that the work obviously centers on Rabta. The contraction [construction?] work, which has been observed since 1986, is reported to have been almost completed, with the planning and supervision being carried out by Swiss, Austrian, British, and German firms/persons (not identified by name). The BND reports that the construction work for the chemical facilities ("Pharma 150") was organized under Thai management. The supply of precursors from, among others, German firm (identified by name) as early as in 1985 could, it is said, not yet be confirmed, even though this suspicion is based on a source judged to be reliable. . . .

18 October 1988
The BND announces receipt of a report from an allied intelligence on 14 October 1988, stating that in August 1988 staff from the Imhausen company were involved in putting the alleged warfare agents plant into operation and "possibly in the repair of damage to the production facilities, too." The BND adds that Imhausen's involvement has also come to the attention via other channels. It reports that the ZKI [Customs Criminological Institute] has been informed and that the U.S. embassy is expected to approach the responsible agencies of the Federal Government in this matter. . . .

20 October 1988
The Federal Chancellor is briefed for the first time on the information

gathered by the intelligence services in relation to efforts to establish a warfare agents factory. [The] . . . summary [of the situation] also mentions possible involvement of the German company Imhausen. . . .

27 October 1988
The BND comments on previous reports on Rabta and Imhausen's involvement in the alleged warfare agents plant and refers to Imhausen's company offices in Switzerland and Liechtenstein, personal links between Imhausen and Pen Tsao, and Imhausen's business connection's to IBI . . . in Frankfurt. . . .

2 November 1988
The BND makes contact with an informant who, under certain conditions, is prepared to supply business documents of the companies allegedly involved in Rabta.

18 November 1988
The BND reports to the BK-Amt on the particularly important role being played in the Rabta project by Salzgitter AG, which supplied a plan of the plant, and Imhausen Chemie, which has supplied plant components and chemicals. It is also mentioned that an authorized representative of Imhausen, who is not identified by name, has frequently been present at the construction site. . . .

24 November 1988
The BND reports to the Chancellor in response to the evidence presented by the U.S. Administration. Rabta, it says, is intended for the production of chemical warfare agents and corresponding ammunition, but the plant has not yet started production. Until the summer of 1988 the BND had no knowledge of the participation of German companies neither from its own nor from foreign intelligence sources. . . . Since August 1988 there have been, it reports, indications of involvement by the Imhausen group and the supply of unspecified precursors by Imhausen. The BND mentions . . . that plans have been supplied by Salzgitter AG staff . . . and plant components provided by Imhausen. It is explained that deliveries were nominally made to the Pen Tsao company in Hong Kong, which is linked with the Imhausen company. The cargo is reported to have been relabelled . . . [at] sea and delivered to the project in Rabta. . . . The BND repeats that it has evidence of the removal of documents by Imhausen. . . .

4 January 1989
The BND summarizes the information available to date on the plant in Rabta. It says that with the exception of trial runs the plant is not yet operating; operations could begin in April 1989 at the earliest. In the BND's opinion the type of construction and the protective mea-

sures indicate that the plant is designed for the manufacture of warfare agents. . . .

5 January 1989
The BND points out that the Rabta plant still requires technical equipment before it can start operations indicating that it has only been possible to examine and test certain components. The plant control system is not yet available and is to be provided by the GfA [Association for Automation], which belongs to the Imhausen group . . .

9 January 1989
The President of the BND informs the Federal Chancellor on Libya

12 January 1989
The BND reports on the papers received from the ZKI in the week before Christmas. It says that according to the documents the IBI Engineering AG company of Frankfurt arranged the financial transactions and the purchase of small parts and that the Imhausen company and its subsidiaries have played a key role in the planning of all 30 buildings in the "Pharma 150" project and that in the course of construction work several firms belonging to the Imhausen group (i.e. Pen Tsao, Hong Kong) had been involved.

19/25 January 1989
The BND reports on the results of the first examination of the materials confiscated by the ZKI on 14 December, 20 December 1989 [1988?] and 4 January 1989. The documents, it says, reveal business ties between the Imhausen company and IBI and a series of other domestic and foreign firms. The BND notes that the freight papers show that Tripoli is the destination but the freight containers seldom bear labels indicating their contents. Salzgitter Industriebau is mentioned in reports in connection with the plans including those for the water supply system of Rabta.

It is said that construction plans for the metal processing factory reveal that it is a production plant for the manufacture of, amongst other things, tubular components (presumably shells and bombs). The construction plans for "Pharma 150" show security facilities which are superfluous in the case of the production of pharmaceuticals; the plant was also unusually large for two pharmaceutical products. In the plans for "Pharma 150" the names of the firms involved are not entered at the appropriate line in the documents. The joint planning of chemical plants and the metal processing plant as well as security facilities not usually found in a pharmaceutical factory (airtight windows and doors, gas-tight walls between the production and the control unit, burn-off unit, and particularly corrosion-proof lining on pipes, escape routes) make it possible to draw the conclusion that "Pharma 150" is a chemical weapons plant."[42]

This chronology of federal intelligence reports makes is clear that the BND paid close and continuous attention to the emergence of a chemical weapons production facility in Libya. From these reports, released by the Kohl government only when the political pressure became too great, it is also obvious that all the critical components of the Bonn government were well informed about the unfolding progress of construction at Rabta. As is demonstrated in the Report, Bonn had no need for assistance from American or other intelligence services; its own capabilities were quite adequate for monitoring developments in Libya.

Most importantly, the Report reveals that the BND not only was sensitive to Libya's quest for a manufacturing capability in chemical weapons since April 1980 but was aware from this date that both East and West German nationals were involved. This early information was widely distributed within the government to the Federal Chancellery, the Foreign Office, the Ministry of Defense, and the Ministry of the Interior.

The above chronology demonstrates that the BND acquired increasingly detailed information over the course of nine years. Therefore, the argument of the Kohl government that it did not have enough specific information about the activities of Libya and its own firms does not stand up to close scrutiny. Although the information from the BND became more precise over time, this was probably a function of the maturing of the construction enterprise at Rabta. As construction proceeded, more firms quite logically became involved, and more equipment had to be purchased and installed. Thus, the intelligence effort should have gotten easier as construction unfolded.

Nevertheless, the tip-off to the government in 1980 that a chemical weapons factory was under construction and that West Germans might be involved deserved to be considered at that time with the utmost seriousness. The political damage that would result from West German assistance in the proliferation of chemical weapons should have been recognized immediately by political decision makers, especially since on numerous occasions during the 1980s the FRG committed itself to NATO documents against the proliferation of chemical weapons. Of course, all of the details were not available in 1980, but the very nature of the activity of clandestinely building a chemical weapons factory should have alerted the BND and political leaders to the fact that such construction would be masked, and if possible, hidden, by Libya.

It should be kept in mind that this chronology of BND activities is a distillation of BND reports that were circulated to several government agencies. As abbreviated items in this chronology, they represent succinct statements meant to summarize the contents of what surely must have been larger reports from the BND offices. Most certainly, a clandestine effort to construct a chemical weapons factory would have merited considerable attention from an intelligence agency. Thus, the larger reports that were in all likelihood produced regarding this factory should have commanded the attention of Bonn's policymakers. Apparently they did not command attention, a fact that can be attributed to either consummate bad judgment or deliberate inattention. Without question, the BND brought critically important information to the attention of the policy-making community in Bonn. The policymakers had the responsibility to act, yet they did not.

The entry for 20 October 1988 appears to lack credibility. The item indicates that on that date the chancellor was briefed "for the first time" regarding Libyan initiatives in chemical weapons. Given that this date was preceded by eight years of BND reports and briefings on chemical arms in Libya, reports that were circulated to several government agencies and always to the chancellery, it is difficult to imagine how the chancellor could have escaped knowledge about this matter. On this, the Report also conflicts with news accounts of Mr. Kohl telling the press that he first heard of the Rabta activities at a 15 November 1988 meeting in Washington. If the 20 October date is correct, then the chancellery staff must be held accountable for not informing the chancellor of this major foreign policy error. Nevertheless, it is virtually inconceivable that a head of state could remain ignorant of years of information from his own intelligence service about a significant international development.

The BND reports contain many references to private firms. Early in the chronology the firms apparently could not be identified; later they were specified with great precision. The government, of course, produced the Report, and therefore it was the agent that inserted frequent "not identified by name" phrases. Again, credibility is challenged, because natural curiosity would dictate that someone compiling a BND briefing for the chancellery would have asked the name of the German firm involved. It is conceivable that the BND and the chancellery conspired to omit names of commercial firms because each knew how contentious such references might be in any future investigation. Indeed, as far back as 1985 and 1986, specific names of German firms were appearing in secret government documents.

Diplomatic sources of information. Such major international actors as West Germany have well-developed diplomatic networks and capable diplomatic staff. Germany's own diplomats provided important information to Bonn regarding developments in Libya, and this additional information paralleled that generated by the BND. When a nation like Libya is attempting to clandestinely develop a chemical weapons manufacturing capability, informational redundancies are critical to accurate assessment. It should not be surprising, then, that Bonn's diplomatic corps provided policymakers with a considerable amount of information. To understand these contributions, it is critical to extract a focused chronology of diplomatic activities from the main chronology in the government's Report to the Bundestag.

5 July 1985
The German embassy in Moscow reports on information received from a non-Eastern source indicating that the Imhausen Company in Lahr (proprietor Dr. Hippenstiel) has concluded a contract in Hong Kong to provide supplies for a pharmaceutical project. A state-owned German company is said to be involved. The location of the project is unknown.

   In view of the special wishes of the company awarding the contract (glass instead of steel pipes, which implies the production of poison gas) and the secrecy surrounding the location, doubts are said to have arisen among the experts involved as to whether it really is a pharmaceutical project for Hong Kong. It is said that Libya had been mentioned as the true country of destination. In the embassy's opinion it is only conjecture, which it passes on with the request that it be treated with the greatest discretion. . . .

8 July 1985
The AA passes the report on to the BMWi and BND, asking the latter to provide further intelligence if possible.

9 July 1985
The BMWi sends a copy of the embassy report of 5 July 1985 to the BAW [Federal Office of Economics] for examination. Result: Imhausen has not submitted any applications for an export licence, not even for Hong Kong.

19 July 1985
The BND replies to the AA saying that no information is available concerning the embassy report. It is said that though the Imhausen company did have the chemical expertise required to supply any kind of chemical plant and despite the fact that it is also able to supply plants capable of producing warfare agents, this also applies to a whole number of German companies. The assumption that the alterations to the contract (glass instead of steel pipes) would indicate the possibility of warfare agents production is believed to be false: glass pipes are not thought to be evidence of warfare agent production. The BK-Amt is also notified of the BND statement on 23 July 1985. . . .

1 April 1986
The AA passes on to the BMWi a non-paper [unofficial paper] it has received on 25 March 1986 from the US Embassy stating, among other things, that a company was thought to be negotiating with Libya on the sale of NBC [nuclear, biological, and chemical] defence equipment.

27 April 1986
The BMWi informs the BAW. In order to avoid a misinterpretation of the legal position the BAW warns the said company by telephone that it may need to obtain authorization. The company states that conclusion of the contract is still uncertain. . . .

3 November 1986
The BK-Amt informs the AA, BMF and BMWi of the existence of an unofficial paper handed over at the end of October in which the US Administration expresses its growing concern at the proliferation of chemical weapons in the Middle East. Libya is briefly mentioned in the paper in connection with the possible procurement of protective equipment against chemical weapons. . . .

28 October 1987
The German embassy in Tripoli reports to the AA in connection with the Chad/Libya conflict on the following statements by German businessmen: "The Libyan military, they say, are aware that Libya is on the defensive. One is now hoping to have a miracle weapon. This probably refers to the use of poison gas. Preparations are being made in the Sabha region with the assistance of Western companies among others. . . ."

7 January 1988
The German embassy in Tripoli reports to the AA that there is thought to be a Libyan military research facility northwest of Gharyan (Rabta), presumably for research work and the manufacture of NBC

weapons. Participation of German companies is not mentioned. Information passed on to the BND. . . .

26 January 1988
The German embassy in Tripoli reports to the AA on claims to the effect that the military research centre for the production of chemical warfare agents is probably already capable of operating. German companies are also involved, though company names had not been mentioned, it is said. Information passed on to the BND on 27 January 1988.

27 January 1988
The BND comments on the information from the German embassy in Tripoli of 7 January 1988. The BND confirms that its own intelligence and the opinion of allied intelligence services indicate that the object identified near Gharyan is a plant for the production of warfare agents and possibly for ammunition. Previous information indicates that the construction of the plant was mainly carried out with the participation of Japanese, Korean, Polish and GDR citizens but not with companies from the Federal Republic of Germany. . . .

3 February 1988
The German embassy in Tripoli reports that after questioning representatives of German construction firms investigations have shown that no German companies are involved in the construction of the research facility in Gharyan (Rabta). The supply of equipment has mainly been organized via Switzerland, with German intermediaries and German companies being thought to be involved. Passed on to the BND. . . .

18 May 1988
The AA receives a routine level non-paper from the American embassy. It expresses concern over the participation of companies from the Federal Republic of Germany in the supply of chemical facilities to Libya and the re-equipping of Libyan C–130 aircraft to give them mid-air refuelling capability:

"We understand that several firms from the FRG have provided or facilitated Libya's procurement of equipment—such as pumps and chemical processing reactors—for a probably chemical weapons facility. Among the firms involved in this activity are . . . Sihi GmbH and Co. and Imhausen Chemie GmbH.

We also have information that the FRG firm Intec Technical Trade and Logistics Society Limited in Vaterstetten is helping Libya transform C–130 aircraft into refuelling planes which will significantly increase the range of Libyan bombers. Technicians from the FRG are reportedly in Libya working on this project.

The embassy representative is requested to supply more concrete information—if possible within the next few days, but the matter is not specified any further.

25 May 1988

The US paper is passed on with a note from the AA to the BMF, BMWi and BND: The AA asks whether the companies named in the US document have submitted applications for export authorization. Should this not be the case, the AA insists that a foreign trade and payments inspection be considered for the companies concerned. . . .

21 September 1988

The US embassy hands over to the AA a non-paper of 21 September 1988, according to which Libya has developed a chemical weapons production capability with outside help, including Western European companies, and is about to begin mass production. The US Administration appeals for a stop to any assistance to Libya for the development of its own capability to manufacture and use chemical weapons.

Paper passed on by the AA to: BMVg, BND and BMWi, with the latter transmitting the non-paper to the BAW with a request for the matter to be examined. . . .

10 November 1988

The German embassy in Washington cables a report on concerns in the US over Libya's chemical weapons capability and announces a special briefing of the German delegation on the occasion of the Federal Chancellor's visit to Washington on 15 November 1988. . . .

17/18 November 1988

The Federal Chancellor notifies the Federal Cabinet and the Federal Security Council (BSR) of the information received from the US Administration. The Federal Chancellor's statement is recorded in the minutes of the Federal Security Council of 18 November 1988 as follows: "Pictures and documents on the production of chemical weapons in Libya have been presented by the US Government. This information caused him great consternation. A huge arsenal of chemical weapons was being manufactured in production centres in the desert. A considerable part of the equipment was thought to be of German origin and German experts were said to be involved. A problem in this involvement was that civil products manufactured by the chemical industry were sometimes hardly distinguishable from substances destined for chemical weapons. First of all, we had to gain a clear picture of the information available in the US. Then we would have to consider what could be done. If our laws proved to be inadequate, we would have to create new ones. . . ."

The Explosion of Events in West Germany

21 November 1988
The German embassy in Washington reports that the US Department of Defence has confirmed intelligence on the chemical weapons plant and that Head of State Gadhafi reportedly wishes to invite ambassadors and journalists to an opening ceremony at the plant. The AA passes on the cable to BMWi and BMF on 22 November 1988 requesting their comments. . . .

23 November 1988
The BMF receives the cable report of the Washington embassy of 16/17 November 1988. After an assessment of the report it is concluded that further investigations can only be carried out in the cases of Imhausen, IBI and Pen Tsao. On the same day the BMF informs the ZKI by telephone of the cable and asks them to find out whether criminal proceedings can be initiated on the basis of its contents or whether foreign trade and payments inspections should be ordered. The ZKI is of the opinion that the information which has so far become available does not constitute initial grounds for suspicion under Section 34 of the Foreign Trade and Payments Act (AWG). It requests that no decision be made pending the BND briefing scheduled for the same day. . . .

5 December 1988
On the initiative of the AA it is agreed with the Government of the United States that a delegation of American experts should visit the Federal Republic of Germany. In preparation for this meeting the US ambassador hands over at the AA a paper concerning the technology centre and the "Pharma 150" chemical factory in Rabta. The paper contains references to the production of mustard gas and sarin as well as to the participation of the Imhausen and IBI companies. The paper is passed on to the BMWi and BMF. . . .

15 December 1988
The US embassy hands over to the AA and the BMWi a non-paper with an appeal phrased in general terms to counter Libyan efforts to acquire a chemical weapons capability. It does not name any firms. . . .

22 December 1988
Meeting with US delegation at the Federal Foreign Office: participants: AA, BMWi, BMF, ZKI, BND. The US experts present photographic materials on the "Pharma 150" chemical plant to their German colleagues and report on an assembly accident in August 1988. They are convinced that the plant is a chemical weapons production plant. The US experts are unable to provide concrete evidence of the participation of German firms.

They express merely the conviction that the German Imhausen company is responsible for the overall planning.

The US delegation was requested to hand over the written analysis of the plant's production aims as well as the other material available to the United States. Furthermore, the German side requested the US authorities to grant permission for the responsible intelligence analyst to give evidence as a witness to a German public prosecutor or a German judge as and when the need arises. The US delegation agreed to look into the possibility of the provision of documents and witnesses. The US delegation indicated than an answer could be expected by 10 January 1989. . . .

29 December 1988

The German embassy in Tripoli reports on a meeting between the ambassador and the deputy foreign minister requested by the AA. The latter, it is said, confirms Libyan participation in the Paris Conference and the statement contained in the letter to the UN Secretary-General that Libya has absolutely no intention of producing any chemical weapons whatsoever. The Libyan Government requests that the matter be pursued energetically with the United States. . . .

3 January 1989

As instructed, the German ambassador in Tripoli makes a demarche to Head of State Gadhafi with the aim of obtaining Libyan agreement to an international inspection of the Rabta plant. Head of State Gadhafi does not make any concrete promise; he says an answer will be forthcoming. . . .

4 January 1989

The Deputy Libyan Foreign Minister answers the demarche made on 3 January: He says that Libya agrees without reservation to all international mechanisms to which all countries would be subject to the same degree. Libya rejects discriminating measures. . . .

12 January 1989

In Washington a German delegation inquires about the American findings. The US side reports on the storage of precursors in Rabta and links the supply of these products to the Imhausen company. Moreover, it is reported that IBI, Belgian haulage contractors and suppliers from GDR, Great Britain, France, Hungary, Romania, Italy and Japan are involved. Apart from mentioning the names of individual Imhausen staff members the US side also names other German firms.

Both sides agree that Rabta is suited to the production of chemical weapons, that however production has not yet commenced and that Libya is neither capable of repairing damage to the plant nor of completing it without outside assistance. Documents which could have provided useful evidence for further investigations were not presented. . . ."[43]

The information provided by this chronology indicates that Germany's diplomatic posts developed a sensitivity to events in Libya five years later than the BND but well before the public exposure of the issue. The first report, on 5 July 1985, came not from Tripoli, as might have been expected, but from Moscow.[44] Even though the German embassy considered its report "only conjecture," it was remarkably accurate. It established that Imhausen Chemie had contracted to provide a purchaser in Hong Kong with processing supplies for a pharmaceutical project. The embassy expressed its suspicion about the secrecy of the location and the type of equipment being purchased. It also questioned whether the equipment might be destined for use in the "production of poison gas." Libya was suggested as the "true country of destination."

Three days after the receipt of the first report, it was passed on to the Foreign Office, the Ministry of Economics, and the Federal Intelligence Service. The Ministry of Economics, apparently sensing the importance of the report, passed it on a day later to the BAW, the Federal Office of Economics. On 8 July 1985 the Foreign Ministry asked the BND for its interpretation of the report from the Moscow embassy. Curiously, the BND said, "No information is available concerning the embassy report." This was not entirely accurate. Although there is no public evidence that the BND had identified Imhausen by 1985, it did already have five years' worth of data on developments in Libya. Furthermore, it was odd that the Foreign Ministry would make such a request, since BND reports on Libya had routinely been circulated to the Foreign Ministry.

According to the government's Report to the Bundestag, the German embassy in Tripoli began providing information to Bonn in the fall of 1987. Hints of the use of poison gas in the war with Chad and indications that Libya was receiving Western help in producing chemical weapons appeared at that time. By early 1988 the embassy was aware that a military research facility in Rabta that was working on chemical weapons. A few weeks later (26 January 1988), the embassy reported that German firms were involved in the Libyan effort, although a week later the embassy reported no German firms were participating in construction. The embassy's reports were passed on to the BND, and these also served as a redundant source of information that should have strengthened BND perceptions of

Libya's chemical weapons activities. Moreover, although reports from Tripoli to Bonn expressed some confusion about German commercial involvement, there was no question that the embassy in Tripoli was aware that the situation required, at the very least, careful monitoring.

The Report states that the U.S. embassy in Bonn provided information on several occasions about events in Libya. U.S. diplomats appealed for German help in halting Libya's quest for chemical weapons. These appeals were made through non-public diplomatic channels. The German embassy in Washington received briefings from U.S. officials and the U.S. Department of Defense on the Rabta activities. This information too was forwarded to Bonn.

When Kohl and Genscher met with Secretary of State Shultz and CIA Director Webster in Washington in mid-November 1988, U.S. officials thoroughly briefed them on the chemical weapons complex and on German involvement in it. On his return home, Kohl reported on the briefing to the Federal Security Council. The minutes of the meeting reported that "this information caused him great consternation" because photographs documented that "a huge arsenal of chemical weapons was being manufactured in production centres in the desert." With the wealth of data that the BND and the diplomatic community had produced over a long period of time, there was no need for "consternation" on the part of the chancellor. He may very well have expressed consternation, but it was certainly inappropriate. Also, given this information, it is remarkable that various spokespersons for the government continued to maintain that little evidence of German involvement at Rabta existed. This was the public posture of Bonn two and a half months, from mid-November 1988 through January 1989. It is not unreasonable to argue that this position changed only when the Bundestag demanded a full accounting.

Salzgitter Industriebau GmbH (SIG). The involvement in the Rabta factory of the West German government firm Salzgitter was especially embarrassing for Bonn. A separate statement regarding Salzgitter was prepared for the Report to the Bundestag, and it was included as annex 4. Because of its relative brevity, the document is reprinted here in its entirety.

Report on the Sequence of Data Received by the Federal Ministry of Finance on Participation by Salzgitter Industriebau GmbH in the Construction of a Chemical Factory in Libya

13 January 1989
After the Customs Directorate-General of the Federal Ministry of Finance had received only very vague information on possible partici- pation by Salzgitter Industriebau GmBh (SIG), which in the Director- ate-General's opinion did not need to be forwarded to the top level of the Ministry, questioning of the former managing director of IBI in Frankfurt on 12 January 1989 produced for the first time concrete signs of the alleged participation by SIG in planning and executing the "Pharma 150" project in Libya. The Ministry's top level was first informed of this on Friday, 13 January 1989 (Minister Stoltenberg and State Secretary Tietmeyer were in Washington at the time).

16 January 1989
Immediately after returning from Washington, State Secretary Tiet- meyer, acting on behalf of Minister Stoltenberg, requested the Execu- tive Board of Salzgitter AG to present a detailed report. He stated that the company should not just rely on data supplied by its subsid- iary, but also have an internal audit carried out. The Executive Board of Salzgitter AG had already commented on the press reports that had appeared and stated that SIG did not have any contacts with Libya, but had carried out by early 1987 on behalf of Imhausen Chemie GmbH engineering work for a project entitled "Pharma 150" located in Hong Kong.

18 January 1989
The Executive Board of Salzgitter AG communicated a preliminary report, according to which SIG had been awarded by Imhausen Chemie GmbH in 1984 a contract worth approximately DM 7 million on part of the piping and electrical engineering work for a plant designed to manufacture primary and intermediate pharmaceutical products in Hong Kong. As a result of two additional orders in 1985 and 1986, the total volume of the contract was roughly DM 8 million. The planning was largely completed by the end of 1986; some follow- up work was carried out until the spring of 1987.

20 January 1989
The Executive Board of Salzgitter AG submitted a more extensive report, which also contained the results available by then from the internal audit. According to the report, the internal audit of the many documents had not revealed any references to Libya. The SIG management stated that no employee of the company had ever worked at Rabta in Libya or worked on the Rabta project.

24 January 1989
After press reports on more extensive involvement by SIG in the

construction of the Rabta plant appeared on 24 January 1989, the Federal Ministry of Finance again demanded on this date a report from the Executive Board of Salzgitter AG. The same day still, Salzgitter AG reaffirmed to the Ministry and in a press release "that staff of Salzgitter Industriebau GmbH have never been involved in the Libyan Rabta project, nor have they ever been there"; the company stated that Hong Kong had always been the site mentioned for the plant.

25 January 1989
The Federal Ministry of Finance again transmitted to Salzgitter AG Minister Stoltenberg's request that the in house investigations be intensively continued and the in-house questioning of employees also be carried out.

29 January 1989
State Secretary Tietmeyer received a phone call late in the evening from the Chairman of the Executive Board of Salzgitter AG informing him that, in the course of the internal audit, a letter of 25 February 1985 from Imhausen Chemie had been found, attached to which was the copy of a telex written in English, in which the word "rabta" or "rasta" appeared. The Chairman also stated that the plant in Hong Kong had meanwhile been examined by the company's engineers, who had discovered that it did not match the engineering work done by SIG. He added that Salzgitter AG would immediate forward to the Offenburg public prosecutor the letter of 25 February 1985 plus annex.

30 January 1989
Minister Stoltenberg requested that Salzgitter AG submit as quickly as possible a detailed written report on this recent development. By the end of the same day, the Executive Board transmitted its report as well as the letter of 25 February 1985, plus annex, from Imhausen Chemie. Evidently none of the five SIG employees entrusted with the project had underlined or otherwise marked the word "rabta" or "rasta" which appeared in the telex in connection with technical data. The impression gained from the documents was that the employees had overlooked the word or possibly regarded it as the designation of the transformer station. At the time (1985), the word "rabta" had obviously not meant anything to them.

Parallel to these investigations by Salzgitter AG, all documents at the Federal Ministry of Finance concerning SIG were examined, and a statement was obtained from the ministry representative on the SIG Supervisory Board. These investigations did not reveal any information that was at variance with the description submitted by Salzgitter AG and in particular did not produce any indication that Libya was the site of construction.

Although there had been much discussion in the press regarding Salzgitter, it was not until 12 January 1989 that the government felt it had enough "concrete signs of the alleged participation by SIG in planning and executing the 'Pharma 150' project in Libya." It is difficult to comprehend why the government could not have justifiably ordered an investigation of one of its own units at any time.

Nevertheless, as the above report indicates, Salzgitter maintained that since early 1987 it had a contract with Imhausen-Chemie for engineering services for Pharma 150 in Hong Kong. However, later evidence indicated that this contractual work with Imhausen actually dated back to 1984. Salzgitter has insisted that it always believed it was working on a plant under construction in Hong Kong, and that it knew nothing of Rabta, even though the word *Rabta* appears in some documents.

The annex on Salzgitter is sketchy and does not deal with many critical questions about the nature of the contract, the character of the engineering, and the individuals involved at both Salzgitter and Imhausen. The simple assertion that Salzgitter believed its work was for a factory in Hong Kong stretches credibility. At the very least, as indicated by a SIG spokesperson, Salzgitter was deceived by Imhausen-Chemie.

Legislation on foreign trade. It is beyond the scope of this study to explore the many complex dimensions of trade and the restrictions related to the transfer of sensitive materials. Previous chapters have referred to West Germany's lax trade policies and its desire to increase international sales of its products, often without a sensitivity to political ramifications. Yet some reference should be made to legislation changes proposed by the government in its Report to the Bundestag.

In response to the Rabta events, the Kohl administration called for amendments to the Foreign Trade and Payments Act, the Atomic Energy Act, the Foreign Trade and Payments Regulations, the War Weapons Control Act, and the Fiscal Administration Act. In general, these changes were aimed at improving the supervisory and investigational information base, expanding export bans, extending provisions on punishments and fines, and increasing the personnel and equipment available for investigations.[45]

It was also the government's judgment that the War Weapons Control Act had to be substantially strengthened. "Because of the special risks involved in the proliferation of biological and chemical weapons," the Report stated, "any violation of the ban shall attract a term of imprisonment of between 2 and 15 years." The "promotion" of proliferation is banned in the proposal. Under existing laws, the government had to prove that a threat to peace had taken place. In the new proposal, "promoting the production of chemical weapons abroad through West German deliveries of relevant production plant will be punishable also in the absence of any such acute dangers."[46] Thus, the act of promoting proliferation is proposed to be a crime, and judicial authorities will not have to prove that a threat to the peace has occurred.

In a real sense, however, the proposed changes in German legislation came to late. The damage in Libya had been done. The involvement of numerous German firms, organizations, and individuals had been shown, and some faced prosecution. But Libya had constructed a chemical weapons factory, and the Kohl government now accepted this and West German involvement as fact.

The German Government's Justification for Its Actions

The Kohl government, of course, attempted to put in the best possible light its handling of what had become a major international embarrassment. Its actions, or perhaps more accurately nonactions, had contributed to the proliferation of chemical weapons in the highly volatile Middle Eastern region, putting the government in an awkward political situation.

In a statement to the Bundestag on 17 February 1989, Chancellery Minister Wolfgang Schauble provided an overview of the government's Report and attempted to portray Bonn as actively involved in preventing the proliferation of chemical arms.[47] Schauble began his presentation by pointing out that the Report "exposes a large number of documents previously kept secret," and he noted that this was "a unique occurrence in the parliamentary history of our country." He admitted that on the basis of BND information, the government now assumed "that the plant in Rabta is suitable for and meant for the production of chemical weapons." But he based this remark on a BND report of 19–25 January 1989. That report resulted from business documents acquired in a ZKI raid, which showed commercial connections between Imhausen-Chemie and IBI. Schauble admitted that the government had intelligence reports dating back to 1980 on the Rabta complex, but he indicated that they were conflicting and therefore could not constitute a basis for government action.

Although Schauble stated that "the government repeatedly warned German industry against supplying sensitive products from the chemical weapons sector to dubious purchasers," he was quick to point out that investigations by public prosecution authorities are "not the responsibility of the federal government but rather that of the judicial authorities in the individual states." This, of course, was meant to absolve the central government of any judicial responsibility in the case.

Rather than criticizing U.S. behavior in the Libyan matter, as had been the government's previous posture, Schauble argued that "there was an immediate and strong reaction to the American information" about German activity at Rabta. This statement referred to Kohl's meeting with Shultz and Webster in Washington on 15 November 1988 and ignored the many months of previous warnings from "allied intelligence services," the BND, and the diplomatic community.

Schauble admitted that "after-the-fact analysis" conducted in preparing the government's Report demonstrated that "present legislation is not sufficient to provide effective controls on sensitive exports." This judgment was based not on the inherent inadequacy of German export control legislation that many had pointed out over at least the past decade, but rather on "scientific and technical progress," which was "making controls increasingly complicated."

The government also tried to justify its behavior by including in its Report a section entitled "Foreign Policy Implications." This section began with the strong statement that "the Government of the Federal Republic of Germany regards it as an urgent foreign policy task to prevent, in collaboration with its partners and friends, the production of chemical weapons by Libya."[48] This statement, of course, was eminently consistent with commitments that the FRG had made in numerous NATO documents. However, it was especially important because it reflected a policy choice that was not encumbered by a legalistic reliance on the deficiencies of German export legislation. Moreover, the statement implied some kind of cooperative international endeavor to counter Libya's efforts.

Within the European Community, Bonn "demanded urgent treatment of these questions" related to chemical arms and demanded that EC members "launch a joint initiative on the prevention of chemical weapons proliferation."[49] The use of the word *demanded* seemed to imply that the FRG was a lone voice calling for action on proliferation questions. This may have been suitable for internal German politics, but it masked the major damage already done by German exports to Libya.

Again moving away from previous criticisms of the United States, the Report stated that Bonn's proposed legislative and organizational changes regarding export controls had been communicated to the American and Israeli governments, and that those nations had "expressed satisfaction" with the proposals. This is the only place in the Report where Israel is mentioned, and it implied a sensitivity to avoiding what could have become a major confrontation with that Middle Eastern nation. The acquisition of chemical weapons by Libya would strongly influence the balance of military capabilities in the region.

All national governments try to portray their choices and behaviors in the best possible light, and in this regard West Germany is not exceptional. Yet Bonn had a difficult case to make since the admitted assistance to Libya by West German commercial firms contributed substantially to the chemical weapons proliferation problem. Eventually and painfully, the Kohl government came to see what had happened, but its justification rested primarily on an inability to act on conflicting intelligence information and on inadequate export controls.

Schematic Representations of the Libyan Construction Network

On the basis of evidence from the Kohl government's Report, data from investigations, newspaper and magazine accounts, and interviews, it is now possible to compose graphic descriptions of the network assembled to facilitate Libya's construction of a chemical weapons plant at Rabta. It was suggested earlier that over one hundred firms were part of this elaborate scheme, but the graphics here present only a portion of that number. The full list of firms is not publicly available. Nevertheless, for the purposes of this study, the information currently in the public domain nicely illustrates the broad outlines of the network. Further information would simply multiply knowledge of the firms involved.

The two basic pieces of this puzzle are the IBI complex and the Imhausen-Chemie complex. Figure 6.1 represents the IBI complex. Note that the organization exists in three nations: Great Britain,

Figure 6.1.   The IBI Organization

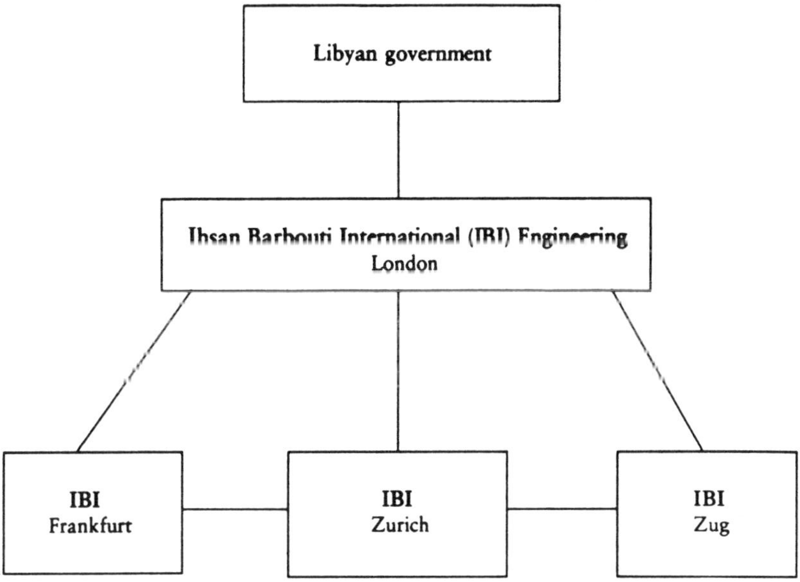

Note: Lines between boxes indicate organizational connections.

West Germany, and Switzerland. The director of IBI Engineering, Ihsan Barbouti, kept his personal office in London, and from there he could maintain easy access to Tripoli.[50]

The Imhausen-Chemie complex, shown in figure 6.2, was much more complicated. Imhausen was a major multinational chemical firm with numerous branches and subsidiaries, which allowed for considerable flexibility in placing orders, transferring funds, and shipping goods. Salzgitter is included in Figure 6.2 because, even though it is a state-owned firm, it had an intimate and long-term relationship with Imhausen.

The Pen Tsao connection is important because it was a shipping outlet for goods from Europe through Hong Kong and on to Libya. Pen Tsao was set up by Imhausen as a dummy corporation with a branch office in Hamburg. Goods could be shipped from any German firm to Pen Tsao/Hamburg thus eliminating the need for an export license. Imhausen transferred control of Pen Tsao to B & M Secretaries in Hong Kong, which was codirected by Daniel P.S. Cheng and his wife Elsa Y. M. Wong. Dee Trading Co. of Hong Kong, which held a large portion of Imhausen-Chemie stock, was also directed by Cheng and Wong. Thus, Imhausen had a very cooperative working relationship with a foreign firm, which for a

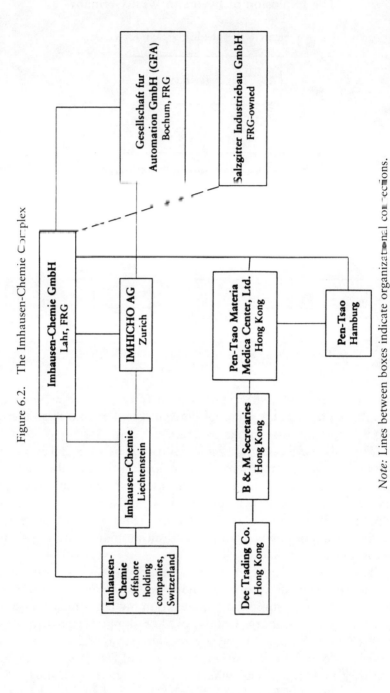

Figure 6.2. The Imhausen-Chemie Complex

Note: Lines between boxes indicate organizational connections.

time was a directly controlled subsidiary. The existence of branches of Imhausen in Switzerland and Liechtenstein also facilitated the transfer of funds and goods. The fact that the Imhausen-Chemie complex was in existence for the better part of a decade or even longer testifies to the care and attention that must have been devoted to keeping it functioning efficiently.

Table 6.1 lists some of the firms involved in providing construction supplies and knowledge to the Rabta undertaking. It lists the firm's name, location, and the known goods sold to Libya. These goods and others moved through four known transshipment points: Antwerp, Belgium; Hong Kong; Rotterdam, the Netherlands; and Singapore. Pen Tsao in Hong Kong and Cross Link in Antwerp were apparently the two most used exit points for cargoes bound for Libya. As indicated in previous discussions, bills of lading were routinely marked for shipment to Pharma 150 in Hong Kong, and then, once the goods arrived at an intermediate destination (for example, Hong Kong or Antwerp), the destination on the bills was simply changed to Libya. It was quite easy, for example, to move goods from West Germany, to Antwerp, to Hong Kong, and then to Libya. Moreover, the sequence of stops could be altered to make investigation difficult, and transshipment points in Singapore and Rotterdam could be used from time to time.

Figure 6.3 assembles these various components to illustrate the complexity of this operation. Central to the operation is Imhausen-Chemie, which is probably the only entity that dealt with every component of this network, even—on occasion and early in the process—with the Libyan government itself. IBI Engineering was the other key player, and it frequently dealt directly with private firms as well as with Imhausen. Salzgitter stands as a more important piece of the network than individual firms, even though it can be classified such. Because Salzgitter provided engineering services over a long period of time, continued contractual relations with Imhausen, and was a state-owned entity, the Kohl government's Report singled that firm out for special treatment. The cooperation of Pen Tsao and Cross Link was also critical to the entire process. Each was depended upon to routinely falsify shipping documents.

Shortcomings in the Information

This schematic information has been developed from open sources and has three shortcomings. First, it is no doubt incomplete. Many more firms were involved than have been illustrated. Second,

Table 6.1   Selected Firms Involved in Providing Construction Supplies and Knowledge to Libya

Firm	Location	Goods/Knowledge Sold
Alexander Wiegand	Klingenberg, FRG	———
Alfred Tewes Klimatechnik GmbH	Frankfurt, FRG	Ventilation and air extraction equipment
Atochem	Fos-sur-Mer, France	Chemicals
Berkefeld-Filter Anlagenbau	Celle, FRG	———
Bischoff KG fork	Frankfurt, FRG	Drills, cranes, loaders, stackers
Bopp and Reuther	Manheim, FRG	———
Brown Boveri-York	Manheim, FRG	———
Calor-Emag	Ratingen, FRG	———
Capsulit	Milan, Italy	———
Chemische Werke Lahr	Lahr, FRG	Chemicals
DeDietrich	France	Appliances and parts
Deutsch Bank	Frankfurt, FRG	Financial matters
Digi Table	Thielen, FRG	———
Eisenwerke Ducker	Laufach, FRG	———
Endress & Hauser	Maulburg, FRG	———
Etamoc	Montceau-les-Mines, France	———
Exner Chemie-Ventile	Neuss, FRG	———
GAB Neumann	Maulburg, FRG	———
GEA Wiegand	Ettlingen, FRG	———

Table 6.1   *(continued)*

Firm	Location	Goods/Knowledge Sold
Globesat Co. for Applied Satellite Technology	Munich, FRG	Electronic steering units, testing and measuring systems
Heinkel Elektro-Aggregate	Hamburg, FRG	———
Hoechst Italia	Rome, Italy	Chemicals
Huennebeck GmbH	Ratengen, FRG	Construction scaffolding and molds
IG Trading	Antwerp, Belgium	———
Imhausen-Chemie	Lahr, FRG	Production plans and chemical-processing equipment
Industrietechnik Kienzler	Vogtsburg-Achkarren, FRG	———
Japan Steel Works	Japan	Lathes and other machinery, desalinization plant
John Zink GmbH Construction Technology	Frankfurt, FRG	Ground burner for excess gas
Kaemmer Ventile	Essen, FRG	———
Kanematsu-Gosho	Tokyo, Japan	Chemicals
Krebs & Kiefer Engineering & Consulting GmbH	Darmstadt, FRG	Checked all structural calculations of steel construction and precision mechanics
Merck	Darmstadt, FRG	Dichloroethane
Phillips Petroleum	Belgium	Thiodiglycol
Preussag AG	Hanover, FRG	Water purification plant
R. Stahl Foerderteknik	Ettlingen, FRG	———

(continued)

Table 6.1 *(continued)*

Firm	Location	Goods/Knowledge Sold
Saeurefabrik	Schweizerhall, Switzerland	Chemicals
Salzgitter Industriebau GmbII	Saltzgitter, FRG	Engineering
Sartorius Mound Construction, Inc.	Hersheim, FRG	electrinics, clearances, and aluminum windows
Schott Glaswerke	Mainz, FRG	———
Siemens	Essen, FRG	Measuring and controlling instruments for chemical plant automation
Sung Fai	Hong Kong	Chemicals
Termoindustriale	Alba, Italy	———
Unielektro	Eschborn, FRG	———
VEB Stahlbau Plauen	German Democratic Republic	Steel construction supplies
Werner Hemmers Elektro-Schaltanlangen	Essen, FRG	———
Wilhelm Pesch Armaturen	Cologne-Godorf	———
———	Thailand	Construction workers
———	Pakistan	Construction workers

Note: Blank spaces indicate data was not available.
Sources: *Business Week*, Hamburg DPA, *Der Spiegel*, *Economist*, *Stern*, Bonn DPA, and *Frankfurter Allgemeine*. The most comprehensive list of firms appeared in *Der Spiegel*, 10 September 1990, 112–18. A translation of this article was published in *JPRS Report: Arms Control*, TAC-90-026 (Washington, D.C.: Joint Publications Research Service), 18 September 1990, 39–43.

no public information exists on the Libyan side of the equation, an important omission. Because of the size of this undertaking, Libya had to have a set of its own organizational complexities. Government procurement agencies and the military establishment had to be involved. Furthermore, there had to be a managerial and coordinating

Figure 6.3. Rabta Construction Activities

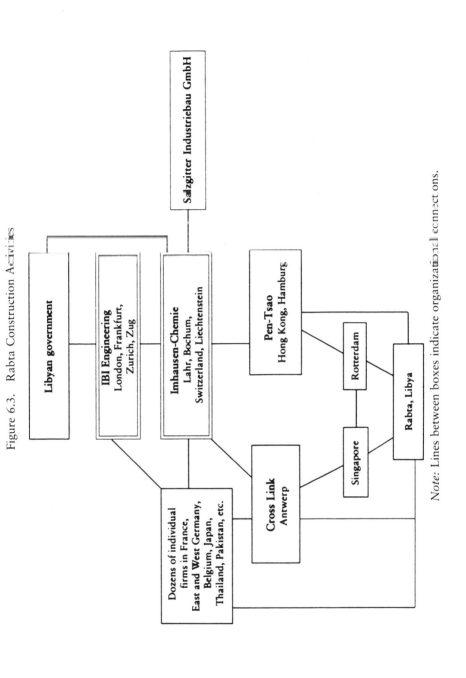

Note: Lines between boxes indicate organizational connections.

structure at Rabta itself. In all likelihood, this information will never be available, but if it were, it would greatly complicate the information in figure 6.3. Third, some of the detailed information may be incorrect, not only because it was developed from open sources, but because verifying it with closed sources is impossible. However, the basic structure of the undertaking is probably accurate as displayed.

Summary

This chapter explored the dramatic evolution of events in West Germany regarding the construction of a chemical weapons factory in Rabta, Libya. Government denials of evidence were first explored, followed by a discussion of the government's admission that Germans were indeed involved in developing such a factory. The comprehensive Report of the Kohl government was examined in detail, and it revealed that as far back as 1980, the government had considerable knowledge of Libya's quest for a chemical arms capability. The graphics presented in this chapter illustrated the complex nature of Libya's attempt to clandestinely develop a chemical weapons facility.

With the complicated nature of this undertaking in mind, it is difficult to understand how Libya could proceed so far in the construction of the plant without detection and without serious complaint from the international community. Indeed, considering the large number of firms involved and the huge sums of money transferred, the entire scheme should have become common knowledge early in its physical development. For allowing the Rabta enterprise to mature into a major international challenge, the Kohl government must take a major share of the blame.

7

Satisfaction and Disenchantment

The Kohl government's Report to the Bundestag, the most comprehensive public document of the entire Libyan chemical arms episode, marked an emotional high point in the evolution of this international situation. This chapter explores the expectations that the events in Germany raised among policymakers concerned with Libya. It also briefly explores Libyan perceptions and provides an update on developments in Libya. To get a sense of the unfolding context of chemical weaponry, the chapter briefly discusses the situation in the Middle East, especially concerning Iraq and the U.S.-Soviet agreement on chemical weapons. The chapter closes with an explanation of the conceptual parameters that shaped this study.

A Sense of Satisfaction

Without question, the United States must have been pleased with the Kohl government's Report, which indicated, as the United States had charged for years, that West German commercial firms bore a major responsibility for assisting Libya to construct a chemical weapons production facility at Rabta. The release of the Report was no doubt viewed by American officials as a vindication of their own extensive activities, which involved private, then public, pressure on the German government, numerous intelligence undertakings, pressure through German and U.S. diplomatic offices, and the broad initiatives of the Paris Chemical Weapons Conference. All of these efforts put considerable strain on the Kohl government and led to a major domestic political crisis for the chancellor.

It should be kept in mind that the attempt to deny Libya a chemical arms capability was a U.S. initiative. Without American pressure, there may not have been an international response to Libya's determined quest. Of course, this can never be known with certainty since it is impossible to predict whether an individual nation or group of nations might have intervened in their own national interests, just as the coalition against Iraq eventually chose a military response over the question of Kuwait. It is probably safe to assume, however, that West Germany, the country with the largest commercial stake in Libya, would not have called a unilateral halt to Tripoli's activities.

From the U.S. point of view, the Kohl government's proposals to tighten export regulations and to increase penalties for violations were most welcome. Lax export policies over many years allowed the Rabta complex to come to, or near to, maturity. In addition, the United States was undoubtedly pleased by German proposals to make assisting in the proliferation of chemical weapons by lending technical expertise a criminal offense.

Perhaps most importantly, the Imhausen-Chemie-IBI Engineering network, constructed with such care over many years, had been destroyed as a result of the Report. Ihsan Barbouti had fled, and the documents that remained in his offices had been confiscated by authorities. Imhausen-Chemie had been publicly disgraced, and several officials were under examination by investigative authorities.

From the German point of view, as well as from the perspective of other nations involved in aiding Libya, the Report signified the end of a three to four year period of intense diplomatic activity. For West Germany, a new page had been turned, and a fresh start appeared possible. The embarrassment of the episode could be forgotten, and new laws could be enacted to prevent any recurrence.

American officials probably expected that the Libyan chemical weapons episode was on its way to solution, and that U.S. pressure had succeeded in achieving its aim. In their view, German legislation would prevent Libya from obtaining raw chemicals and other materials and expertise needed for chemical weapons production. Eventually, Libyan efforts to acquire chemical weapons would grind to a halt or at least become significantly more difficult.

In all likelihood, Libyan decision makers took a decidedly different position. Despite the thrusting of Libya's activities into the public domain, the international pressure, and the well-publicized catharsis in West Germany, Libya still had a factory that was either close to or actually producing chemical weapons. The massive public campaign by the United States had not had any concrete effect on the facility at Rabta. Further acquisition of chemicals and processing equipment might be difficult for Tripoli, but difficulties could eventually be overcome. If necessary, the IBI-Imhausen network could be reconstructed using different principals.

A sound strategy for Libya at this point was to retreat into a quiet, nonhostile, nonthreatening posture. This was apparently done, because for about a year, from February 1989 through February 1990, very little was noted publicly about Libya, and the media turned their attention away from chemical arms. This respite, however, was misleading.

Developments in Libya

The Libyan situation lay dormant for a year, but new hints and reports of activities at Rabta began to emerge in early 1990. For example, *Der Spiegel* reported the BND had evidence that West German companies continued to help Libya develop the Rabta factory.[1]

Again working through reporter Michael Gordon and the *New York Times*, the Bush administration released information from a Defense Intelligence Agency (DIA) report indicating that Libya had begun producing small quantities of mustard gas under a limited production posture and was striving for a full-scale production capacity.[2] The report indicated that small amounts of the nerve gas Sarin were also being produced. The DIA estimated that 30 tons of mustard gas were manufactured during 1989, and that a building had been completed at Rabta to load the gas into plastic containers.

A key and disturbing dimension of the DIA information was an assessment that, although Libya's quest for chemical arms had perhaps been inhibited by the previous three to four years of public evidence, it continued to press ahead with its activities, apparently confident that it could do so without meaningful international hindrance. This assessment was based upon three factors: (1) supervision of activities at Rabta was placed under Libyan military control and Pakistani workers were evicted; (2) Libya was increasing its purchase of precursor chemicals in international markets; and (3) underground storage facilities were being constructed in the Tripoli area, and these would probably be used to store precursor chemicals.[3]

Consistent with positions taken by the Reagan administration, officials in the Bush administration called upon the world community to support "vigorous efforts to stop the operation." The administration indicated there was "a secondary danger" that the products of Rabta would find their way into the hands of terrorists.[4] Also similar to Mr. Reagan's position, President Bush refused to rule out a military attack on the facility.

Still another U.S.-German difference of opinion emerged at this time regarding how to respond to the evidence of continuing chemical weapons activities on the part of Libya. FRG Foreign Minister Genscher proposed that an inspection of the Rabta factory be undertaken by an international team.[5] Such an inspection could verify whether weapons production in fact had ceased. The Bush administration rejected this proposal immediately and strongly, arguing that Libya could easily allow such an inspection and resume production of chemical weapons after the inspectors departed. Instead, U.S. officials insisted that only the permanent dismantling of the Rabta complex would satisfy them.

As the implications of further movement toward a Libyan chemical weapons capability became apparent in Washington, there was a surprising incident that perhaps pleased many in the international community. In mid-March 1990 Bush administration officials revealed that they had learned from Italian diplomats that the Rabta plant was on fire.[6] The Libyan press agency, JANA, confirmed this information. Because of the major efforts of the Americans to stop production at Rabta, the United States was immediately suspected of sabotage. Others suggested that the fire may have resulted from an accident, since it was now widely accepted that Libya did not have sufficient indigenous technical expertise to run the factory on its own.

The Libyans blamed the United States, Israel, and West Germany for the incendiary act. Some Libyans attributed the fire to a terrorist attack, and at least one terrorist organization, representing Libyan army dissidents, claimed responsibility.[7] Libya's ambassador to Italy, Rahman Shalgam, stated that the blaze was apparently set by "a member of the technical staff at the factory." He indicated that the individual would be "executed in the same place where the fire took place."[8]

There were conflicting assessments of the amount of damage resulting from the fire. They ranged from modest damage to very serious, and some U.S. officials stated that the plant was inoperable. However, a French firm asserted that on the basis of reconnaissance from the European satellite SPOT I, the Rabta factory appeared to be intact.[9] Another report said that the main production block had burned, but that the holding tanks that stored chemicals remained undamaged.[10] Yet another expert indicated that the fire at Rabta may have been a hoax instigated by Libya's leader, Moammar Qadhafi.[11]

If the United States had been preparing to attack the Rabta complex out of frustration, the fire, assuming it did result in damage, delayed a U.S. military response. However, if the fire were a hoax, it may have been concocted because Libya believed an American attack was imminent. The Libyan rationale might have been that the United States would have no need to attack a factory that was already damaged and inoperable.

In mid-June 1990 the Bush administration announced that the fire was probably a hoax, and that the Rabta plant was apparently not seriously damaged. Administration spokesperson Marlin Fitzwater was quoted as saying, "It now seems likely that it was a hoax."[12] Supporting this judgment were the CIA, which was said to be "leaning heavily" toward the hoax theory, and U.S. Department of Defense officials who were convinced of a clear act of deception. Some intelligence reports indicated that truckloads of old tires were seen moving toward the factory, and that they may have been used to simulate a blaze. Still another interpretation, according to CIA officials, was that a small fire may have accidentally broken out, and that the Libyans may have ignited tires to exaggerate its effects and to give the impression of serious damage.[13]

Two other developments in Libya merit attention. In March 1990 the U.S. Department of Defense released information that Libya had successfully tested a midair refueling capability for its MIG-23 fighter planes.[14] Although Libya continues to work on the technical aspects of the refueling process, if it is successful, it will create a means to deliver chemical weapons.

In the spring of 1990, Bush administration officials reported that China and Libya were involved in negotiations for the Libyan purchase of chemicals from Chinese firms.[15] U.S. diplomats were instructed to urge China not to sell precursor chemicals to Libya. This effort was apparently successful, because the Bush administration reported later that it had received assurances from the Chinese that they would not sell chemicals for weapons to Libya.[16]

Developments in West Germany

Recall that Dr. Jurgen Hippenstiel-Imhausen, director of Imhausen-Chemie GmbH, insisted in numerous statements to the press that his firm had absolutely no involvement with the development of the Rabta industrial complex. Three months after the Kohl government delivered its Report to the Bundestag, Hippenstiel-Imhausen was arrested by German authorities on the suspicion of violating export laws. The official heading the investigation stated that Hippenstiel was "strongly suspected of having played a significant personal role in the planning and building of a plant designed for the production of chemical weapons in Rabta, Libya."[17]

In March 1990 the German government brought formal charges against Hippenstiel. The government charged that Hippenstiel was guilty of organizing an export process of materials and plans for the Rabta undertaking and/or directly exporting them himself and of failing to pay taxes on the profits made from this venture. At the time these charges were brought, the state prosecutor asserted that the government's investigation "leads to the conclusion that the plant can make not only toxic chemicals but was built and planned solely to produce chemical weapons."[18]

At his trial, which began in June 1990, Hippenstiel confessed that he had indeed assisted Libya since 1984 in secretly building at Rabta a chemical weapons facility valued at DM 255 million ($150 million). However, while admitting involvement in construction and planning, he stated that he did not know that the factory would produce chemical arms. He further admitted that he avoided paying taxes on profits of DM 19.8 million ($11.6 million). Hippenstiel said that in planning the project he suspected his work "would be in conflict with West Germany's export laws," but he proceeded nonetheless because he "didn't want to lose the business."[19] In his testimony, Hippenstiel refused to identify any accomplices, arguing that the full responsibility rested with him. He did indicate, however, that he was first approached by Ihsan Barbouti in the summer of 1984 with a proposal to build a multipurpose chemical plant to produce pharmaceuticals. When Hippenstiel and Barbouti signed a contract on 24 September 1984 in Vienna, a delegation from Libya was present and a member of that delegation also signed the agreement.[20] Hippenstiel learned at that time that the plant was to be built in Libya, with Hong Kong established as a diversionary stop for Imhausen-Chemie shipments. Of course, such diversionary arrangements are not needed for legitimate chemical transactions. On 27 June 1990, Hippenstiel-Imhausen was sentenced to five years in prison for his activities, although under existing German law, he was allowed to retain the profits from this undertaking.[21]

The prosecution of Hippenstiel-Imhausen, however, does not mean that the problem of German exports of sensitive materials has been solved. On the contrary, evidence of German commercial activities in international markets is perhaps even stronger than it was during the 1980s. German firms continue to sell technology and expertise for weapons systems to many countries, especially those in the Middle East. For example, the chemical weapons plant at Samarra, Iraq was constructed essentially by West German firms. Indeed, the FRG government is reportedly investigating several German firms that are assisting Libya in building a second chemical weapons plant underground at the Sabha military base 400 miles south of Tripoli.[22]

Moreover, as of mid-1990, the Kohl government's February 1989 proposal to tighten export legislation had been only partially approved. The maximum punishment for violation of foreign trade and payments laws was increased from three to five years imprisonment, the activities of German nationals abroad were brought under federal authority, and provisions were made for developing an integrated information network on sensitive technologies.[23] Yet, as Der Spiegel reported, when the War Weapons Control Act came up for approval, the maximum sentence was reduced to one year so that it could be committed to probation.[24] Nevertheless, in spite of continuing potential for national embarrassment, the West German commercial community has strongly resisted changes in export laws, and this has been a major factor in preventing the enactment of even more stringent legislation.[25]

The larger German political context may also inhibit legislative action on exports. German reunification is going to be a costly process for a number of years, and the major financial burden will have to be carried by West Germany. In order to generate increased tax revenues in this situation, Bonn will probably have to continue a strong export stimulation policy. Such a policy, of course, could severely undermine efforts by the United States and other nations to prevent the proliferation of chemical weapons.

Other Developments

In an even broader sense, proliferation could be encouraged by developments in Eastern Europe and the Soviet Union. Because these nations no longer appear threatening to Western nations, the United States and other industrial nations are increasing pressures to relax the export of high technology products.[26] A less restrictive atmosphere is emerging in the international community, and this could work to the advantage of Libya and other nations that want to create weapons capabilities by purchasing goods and engineering services in the international marketplace.

The spring 1990 Washington summit at which Presidents Bush

and Gorbachev agreed to begin the cutback of their chemical arsenals should not be interpreted to mean that the problems of chemical weapons have been solved. This is an agreement between only two nations of the international system, and it leaves a general convention on chemical weapons yet to be adopted. Even if the United States and the Soviet Union completely destroy their chemical arms, they still retain significant conventional forces and nuclear weapons. The latter continue to allow Libya and others to insist that they have a right to acquire chemical arms as a measure of deterrence or self-defense against the nuclear powers.

Defining Conceptual Parameters

Most international events are connected to previous happenings and at the same time provide a connecting foundation for future events. Libya's attempt to develop a chemical weapons capability represents a flow of events that challenges an analyst's desire to organize information rationally. No doubt, a thorough chronology, if it could be known, would identify significant pre-1980 Libyan decisional activities that preceded the actual search for equipment and knowledge for the Rabta undertaking. At the other end of the spectrum are future events, as yet unknown, which may intimately connect to Libyan activities during the 1980s.

To achieve an understanding of the clandestine activities of Libya in extracting resources from the international system to construct a chemical weapons factory and accomplish a single case of chemical weapons proliferation, knowledge about a specific set of events is needed. The events discussed in Chapters 2 through 6 can be conceptualized in three distinct phases. Table 7.1 is a skeletal diagram of these phases.

Phases 1 and 3 represent periods of considerable international activity regarding Libya's efforts at Rabta. These two phases are separated by Phase 2, a year-long period of no publicized activity. Phases 1 and 3 have some similarities. The public aspects of each begin with a U.S. charge—in Phase 1 the charge that Libya was constructing a chemical weapons plant at Rabta, and in Phase 3 the charge that Libya had resumed chemical weapons production at the factory. Phase 1 reaches a substantive and cathartic end with the Kohl government Report. For the purposes of this study, Phase 3 ends with the public reports that Libya was seeking to purchase precursor chemicals from China, which was a clear indication that Libya's quest for a chemical weapons capability had not been halted.

Table 7.1 The Three Phases of the Libyan Factory Episode

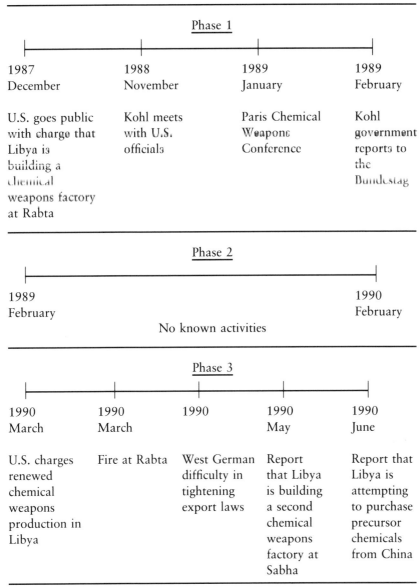

Phase 1

1987 December	1988 November	1989 January	1989 February
U.S. goes public with charge that Libya is building a chemical weapons factory at Rabta	Kohl meets with U.S. officials	Paris Chemical Weapons Conference	Kohl government reports to the Bundestag

Phase 2

1989 February	1990 February

No known activities

Phase 3

1990 March	1990 March	1990	1990 May	1990 June
U.S. charges renewed chemical weapons production in Libya	Fire at Rabta	West German difficulty in tightening export laws	Report that Libya is building a second chemical weapons factory at Sabha	Report that Libya is attempting to purchase precursor chemicals from China

Initially, Phase 1 was conceptualized as a complete set of events with a clear beginning, middle, and end. As indicated earlier in this chapter, the Report to the Bundestag implied a definitive ending of a critical international situation. The Report was thought to have represented the beginning of the attempt to tighten West German export laws, the uncovering and dismantling of the secret network to provide supplies to Libya, and the crippling or ending of Libya's chemical weapons production. This impression was reinforced by the nonevents of Phase 2, which as they extended out from February 1989, seemed to imply that Libya was responding to international pressures by deactivating chemical weapons activities at its Rabta plant. This conclusion was further reinforced by inaccurate press reports that Libya was hiring technical personnel to refit Rabta so that it might produce nonlethal products. After 13 months of "normalcy" in Libya, it would not have been unreasonable to assume that the international system had put the Rabta episode behind it, and that a method of dealing with attempts at chemical weapons proliferation had been found—in essence a method that involved putting vigorous diplomatic pressures on the offending parties to bring about a change in national behavior.

The beginning of Phase 3 provided evidence that, from a non-Libyan point of view, the activities of Phase 1 were a failure. Phase 3 begins with the U.S. charge that Libya had resumed the production of chemical arms. Of course, this also marks the end of Phase 2, the period of inactivity. The fire at Rabta, which attracted considerable media attention, was actually a minor event. Whether it resulted from sabotage, the work of a disgruntled employee, or a planned stunt by Tripoli is inconsequential in view of subsequent developments. Those developments included realizations among members of the international community that West Germany was not getting its export laws in order, that Libya appeared to be expanding its chemical weapons production facilities by building a new factory at Sabha with the probable assistance of West German industrial firms, and that Libya was actively involved in purchasing precursor chemicals from the international marketplace. Phase 3 provides the disconcerting evidence that many years of a broad range of activities aimed at pressuring Libya to cease its quest for chemical weapons did not work. Thus, from an operational point of view, Phase 3 is open-ended, with Libya's chemical weapons activities continuing.

The conceptual parameters, however, are now nicely defined. In looking at Phases 1, 2, and 3, it is likely that continued diplomatic pressures on Libya will have no effect, and evidences of Libyan determination to push ahead are clear. An act of chemical weapons proliferation, messy as it was, has taken place. If the international community desires to halt Libya's progress, additional means, including perhaps military, will have to be employed. Thus, conceptually, this is a case of discovered, clandestine extraction of chemical resources from the international system to create a weapons production facility that the international community, chiefly through the efforts of the United States, unsuccessfully attempted to halt.

The issues that now must be addressed relate to determining why Libya could not be made to comply with presumed international standards on the proliferation of chemical weapons. The following two chapters will look at these issues: Chapter 8 provides an operational assessment of events, and Chapter 9 deals with questions of deception. Chapter 10 provides recommendations to policymakers.

8

An Operational Assessment of the Rabta Episode

With the preceding chapters as a foundation, it is now possible to assess certain operational considerations in the Libyan chemical weapons episode. Of course, this assessment is centered on the case at hand, not on the general issue of chemical weapons within the international system. Nevertheless, the Rabta affair is very much related to the broader issue of chemical weapons proliferation; indeed, it represents a case of proliferation or, from the Libyan point view, of successful acquisition.

This chapter is organized around sets of observations from the United States, Libya, and the Federal Republic of Germany. These observations are conclusions reached on the basis of current evidence.

The United States

The United States apparently viewed the Libyan situation as a test case to prevent the spread of chemical weapons. Thus, it was important to exert enormous pressure on Libya and other elements in the international system to convince Libya to abandon its quest for chemical weapons. The high value that the United States placed on this test case can be measured by American willingness to risk a serious diplomatic rupture with West Germany, a NATO partner. Although, early in the episode the United States was somewhat hesitant to identify the FRG publicly, as Rabta construction proceeded, and as Libya moved toward having a functioning facility, the United States had little choice but to clearly identify West Germany and its commercial firms.

The attempt to halt Libya's quest for chemical weapons was a U.S. initiative. Given the widely recognized need to prevent the proliferation of chemical weapons, it is disappointing that any support the United States received for its initiative was given begrudgingly or with reluctance. Britain was helpful, but it never played an important role. And the German government publicly discounted virtually all U.S. assertions until it had to admit to considerable knowledge.

Part of the difficulty the United States had in making its case against Libya was that the United States offered little hard or documented evidence to the public. Essentially the public U.S. case was based on American verbal assessments of Libya's activities. No sources were ever identified; no photographs were ever presented. Although the United States *said* a factory was under construction at Rabta, failure to publish incriminating photographs seriously jeopardized U.S. credibility. Despite the fact that the CIA apparently shared photographs with the FRG, German officials never indicated any support for their validity. It remains a mystery why the U.S. government never released such photographs if they contributed to the credibility of the U.S. case. However, the work of the Australian Group, largely unpublicized and secret, represented an additional channel of antiproliferation pressure. It is possible that photographs would have undermined or jeopardized the activities of the Australian Group.

The United States failed in its attempt to prevent Libya from acquiring a chemical weapons production facility. Despite a host of diplomatic activities, which included pressures within international organizations and at conferences and extreme pressures on West Germany and Libya, the United States was not able to prevent Libya from developing a chemical weapons plant at Rabta. The United States persisted, at least publicly, for about three years and expended considerable diplomatic capital in its effort. The highest levels of the administration were involved. Although U.S. efforts enhanced sensitivity to chemical weapons proliferation, the United States did not achieve its primary objective with Libya.

U.S. efforts to utilize the press as an instrument of diplomatic pressure were impressive. The administration chose to reveal information through the *New York Times*, which provided accurate reports of Washington's thinking. Although the government of the FRG and the German press expressed danger over *New York Times'* reports, the German press eventually began its own investigations. Had U.S. press accounts on Rabta been less accurate, the German press might have avoided the issue completely. It would not be unreasonable to assert that the *New York Times* stimulated the German press to act, and that without such action, much evidence about Imhausen-Chemie and the German government would never have been brought to light.

U.S. concerns about the proliferation of chemical weapons frequently brought forth counter arguments about the U.S. nuclear and chemical arsenals, and these arguments exposed the weakness in the U.S. position. On this point, the United States found itself between the proverbial rock and a hard place. However, if the United States condemned the proliferation of chemical weapons, it was greeted by Arab arguments that the United States itself had both a chemical and a nuclear arsenal. By what right could the United States deny to others what it already possessed? However, if the United States refused to condemn the spread of chemical weapons, such proliferation could continue without any meaningful challenge.

In addition, the United States had little legal basis to oppose the production of chemical weapons at Rabta. The United States was trying to stop a case of proliferation before a chemical weapons convention had been approved. Although the international community appears to support the nonproliferation of chemical weapons, it is not yet certain how provisions on nonproliferation will eventually, if ever, emerge in convention. Moreover, stripped of its nonessentials, the U.S. position asked Libya, and by implication all other nonnuclear, nonchemical weapons nations, to trust that the United States would act responsibly as a possessor of multiple arsenals. Many nations had accused Libya of supporting numerous acts of terrorism. From the U.S. point of view, then, it was not unreasonable to demand that Libya abandon its chemical weapons activities while the United States continued its own. Of course, as we shall see below, Libya and other Arab nations immediately labeled this as a double standard unworthy of acceptance.

The United States also lost credibility by supporting some Middle Eastern nations that were thought to be seeking chemical weapons postures. Although the United States condemned Libya for seeking a chemical weapons capability, it never publicly criticized Egypt or Israel for apparently making the same quest. Nor did it forcefully criticize Iraq's use of chemical weapons in the Iran-Iraq War or Iraq's acquisition of what was thought to be a reasonably strong chemical weapons posture. Furthermore, no criticisms were made of first world nations that had chemical arsenals. These inconsistencies in U.S. antiproliferation policy undermined the credibility of the U.S. position on Rabta.

Because of the 1986 air attack on Libya, U.S. threats and intimations of another attack were credible not only to Libya but also to other nations. This created an interesting dilemma: The more effective such threats and intimations were with Libya, the more other nations from whom the United States expected some public support backed away from overtly endorsing the U.S. position. No nation wanted to be identified with a U.S. attack on Libya.

However, there was apparently a rather small window of time in which an attack was credible. As the Rabta facility became operational, there was danger that an attack would release noxious chemicals into the atmosphere, and that those chemicals would inflict unintended damage on the towns near Rabta and conceivably on other nations.[1] Deaths of innocent victims of such an attack would make headlines around the world, create negative publicity for the United States, and possibly provide sympathy for Col. Qadhafi and Libya. An act of sabotage would have been a much better way of inhibiting progress at Rabta. Such action could perhaps be more controlled, resulting in little or no loss of life. Available public information does not indicate that the United States attempted sabotage. Libya's apparent official explanation of the fire at Rabta states that a disgruntled employee set it. It will probably never be known exactly how and why this fire originated, but it seems clear that it was not a U.S. act of sabotage.

U.S. policymakers must have felt that their case against West Germany regarding the complicity of its commercial firms in the construction of Rabta was iron clad, and that increasing diplomatic pressure on Germany was bound to result in eventual success. The application of pressure on the Federal Republic of Germany was gradual but persistent. It publicly began when unnamed U.S. officials made gentle charges through the medium of the press, and it proceeded through quite detailed accusations, for example, the identification of Imhausen-Chemie as the major German firm involved at Rabta. During the period of U.S. accusations, German officials offered numerous denials, most of which contained harsh words for the United States. But the United States persisted, which indicated that American policymakers must have had incontrovertible evidence against the Germans.

The United States apparently placed a higher value on halting the proliferation of chemical weapons than on stable relations with its NATO partners. The United States had little overt international support for its antiproliferation activities. In the future, any nation that is willing to choose a strong antiproliferation policy regarding chemical weapons will probably have to confront the fact that such a choice will involve a rank ordering of its international preferences.

127

Given the global extent of the chemical industry, such a rank ordering will probably put the antiproliferation country in conflict with one or more of its friends, allies, or trading partners.

The United States developed a set of stringent export controls to prevent Libya and other nations from acquiring the equipment and precursor chemicals needed to produce chemical weapons, but these controls have been inadequate.[2] A larger, international effort is required, together with a convention banning chemical weapons. But even these efforts are unlikely to eliminate chemical weapons. The major point to be made here is that U.S. export policy by itself cannot accomplish the impossible. The United States used public pressures, bilateral diplomatic communication with the FRG, and even an international conference, along with stringent export measures involving for the most part only two nations, Libya and West Germany. Even with these limited objectives, the United States was not successful. The Rabta facility continues to operate, and Germany has made only modest efforts to tighten its export regulations.

During the Rabta episode, the United States was the only nation that publicly recognized similarities between chemical and biological weapons. This was done chiefly through speeches by Secretary of State George Shultz. Mr. Shultz's objective was no doubt to underscore the seriousness of the situation: as nuclear weapons are brought under control, a new difficulty of chemical and biological weapons emerges. The new reality is much more complex and difficult to control. New processing techniques, such as utilizing genetic engineering to produce novel chemical toxins, are beginning to blur the distinction between biological and chemical weapons, thereby undermining diplomatic distinctions between the two classes of weapons. Thus, the proliferation of chemical weapons capabilities could lead to a proliferation of interest in biological weapons. No other diplomat publicly acknowledged Shultz's concerns.

The Rabta episode demonstrated to the world community that a skillful, clandestine exploitation of international commercial resources in a sensitive field was indeed possible, despite the opposition of one of the superpowers. Libya and West Germany were perhaps the two most unlikely nations to be involved in an act of chemical weapons proliferation, and yet they succeeded. Libya is often judged to be an unstable nation, chiefly because of the behavior of its leader, Moammar Qadhafi. Moreover, Libya lacks a well-developed technological base. Given German involvement with poison gas in World War I and Nazi use of gas chambers to execute Jews during World War II, it would not have been unreasonable to expect that no German business person would risk identification with chemical weapons. That all of this could transpire while one of the superpowers conducted a campaign of public pressure to prevent it from happening stretches the imagination.

The Rabta case might very well be the prototype of a genre of challenge that is likely to confront world leaders in the future. Private commercial firms will cooperate with the clandestine objectives of public authorities in nations seeking to acquire modern weapons systems based contemporary scientific advances. Before a selection of firms is made and a commercial network established, this will require a considerable amount of economic espionage in high technology areas. Already, there is considerable evidence that such espionage is taking place and is likely to increase in the near future.[3] In terms of Middle Eastern politics, economic espionage could exacerbate an already unstable situation.

Libya

As indicated previously in this study, little public information is available regarding the internal decision processes and organizational structures related to Libya's Rabta undertaking. Nevertheless, it is possible to offer several deductive observations about Tripoli's activities.

Libya's decision to build a chemical weapons production facility contained some risk. When initiated in 1980, it was probably viewed as a minimal risk undertaking. But as the project proceeded and became physically visible, Libyan policymakers must have recognized it as an increased risk fraught with future international difficulties. It was clear that the broader community of nations would be unsympathetic to a case of chemical weapons proliferation, but that some support from the Arab world would be forthcoming. Furthermore, Libyan decision makers probably anticipated that if their clandestine activities became known, they would have to deal with a major international incident that would bring their nation under considerable diplomatic and possibly military pressure. Despite these dangers, Libya chose to move ahead with the Rabta project.

Libyan policymakers may have believed success in the situation to be a distinct possibility. The probability of the entire effort becoming known during its early stages was negligible. All the planning, assembling of the network, negotiating of contracts, surveying of land, and beginning of construction were innocuous acts that would raise no suspicions. If the entire effort could be brought to the point of initiating production of chemical weapons, a threshold would be reached in which the costs of destruction by an outside power would be too high since the release of noxious, perhaps lethal, substances would carry considerable political liabilities. Thus, Libya would succeed if it could protect Rabta's exposure until the commencement of production: if the plant was not stopped before production, it would not be stopped after production.

Having made the decision to seek a chemical weapons capability, Libya had to support that decision with the utmost determination. Nothing short of extraordinary, even fanatical, behavior could be tolerated. Thus, Libya moved civilians near the plant to increase the costs of an air attack, provided heavy military fortifications for the plant, and made harsh diplomatic pronouncements, especially at the assembly of the United Nations. Also, the erratic behavior of Col. Qadhafi contributed positively to the aura of doubt regarding precisely what Libya was doing at Rabta.

The public case against Libya's building of a chemical weapons production facility is circumstantial. No outsider is known to have seen chemical weapons being produced at Rabta. Nevertheless, the circumstantial evidence against Libya is quite strong. If Libya were not producing chemical weapons, there would have been no reason for it to oppose international inspections. Moreover, the circumstances under which the foreign press was allowed to view Rabta—from one-half mile away and at night—represented a virtual admission that Libya had something to hide.

The Paris Chemical Weapons Conference gave Libya an excellent forum from which to argue its case. That the superpowers retained chemical weapons while asking Arab states to refrain from acquiring them was attacked as a clear case of selective disarmament that discriminated against a small group of nations. Making this point at Paris amplified its power, and putting it in terms of a north-south issue expanded the range of nations that might be supportive.

Naming several sites Pharma 150 provided an excellent shield for the construction network. The chemical plant, the entire Rabta complex, and the fictitious facility in Hong Kong were all called Pharma 150. Equipment and chemicals could be shipped to Pharma 150 with little risk of discovery, but if some suspicion occurred, they could be rerouted to a different Pharma 150 site. Moreover, the word *pharma* is, of course, a root of the word pharmaceutical, which brings to mind health-aiding drugs and medical assistance.

Locating the chemical weapons plant within a larger, multipurpose civilian enterprise represented skillful siting from which flowed several political advantages. Any attack on the weapons facility risked destroying civilian undertakings and killing innocent people. Goods could be shipped to an innocuous section of the complex then moved within the complex to the weapons plant, further disguising their true destination. Having a cluster of innocent undertakings on a site with a chemical weapons plant introduced considerable confusion in the minds of observers. Even intelligence agencies surveying reconnaissance photographs were probably confused during all but the final stages of construction. Thus, the multipurpose siting gave Libya time to get the plant as close as possible to the production threshold discussed above.

Libya overcame its technical and managerial backwardness to build what the United States charged was the largest chemical weapons plant in the third world. For the right price, virtually any nation can purchase raw chemicals, technical knowledge, and construction management for a clandestine undertaking. One report indicated that Imhausen-Chemie was paid ten times the standard price for equipment.[4] Libya's activities at Rabta represent a clear success in conquering its shortcomings by purchasing equipment and skills.

Libya succeeded in convincing a major West German chemical firm to accept a key role in furnishing chemical processing equipment for Rabta. This success was no doubt related, at least initially, to the financial difficulties of Imhausen-Chemie, which apparently was predisposed to accepting a less than fully legitimate offer. Despite the risks of discovery, which would at least inevitably lead to a major public denunciation, Imhausen-Chemie participated in the project for six years. Once committed to what must have been recognized immediately as a controversial project fraught with risk, Imhausen-Chemie probably would have had a difficult time disengaging from it if it had so desired. Furthermore, from Libya's point of view, Imhausen-Chemie would have been vulnerable to blackmail if the firm had decided to disengage. Thus, after the operation was underway, there were incentives for Imhausen-Chemie to protect the secrecy surrounding Rabta.

Libya recognized that without its own cooperation, it would be virtually impossible to prove that it was building a chemical weapons production facility. By insisting that it was constructing a pharmaceutical factory, for which an international inspection would be unreasonable, Libya prevented the United States from clearly proving its case. This, of course, was also true for other nations in the international community.

Libya's clandestine efforts to become a chemical weapons power escaped general condemnation by the world community. Libya violated no specific international law. As indicated previously, there is no international convention prohibiting the acquisition of chemical weapons. Although, in general, the world community is opposed to the proliferation of chemical weapons, and although this constitutes an informal norm, few nations criticized Libya's activities. This was true even after information generated by West German authorities became public and incriminated numerous German firms. It would not be unreasonable to state that the Rabta episode is a clear example of how to develop a chemical weapons production facility in a world that generally opposes such an undertaking.

West Germany

No public evidence exists that the West German government either provided direct support for or directly facilitated the construction of the Rabta facility. Rather, the available information indicates that the government acquiesced in the long-term activities of numerous German commercial firms. Such firms were allowed to develop commercial ties to Libya with no interference from the government, despite the fact that trade in sensitive materials was taking place and, if discovered, would seriously harm Germany's international reputation.

The government of the FRG resisted U.S. appeals for action to halt assistance to the Libyan chemical weapons plant, claiming the evidence was circumstantial. This of course put the burden of proving the charges on the United States. As indicated elsewhere, however, the United States never stated publicly that it had incontrovertible evidence of Libyan chemical weapons activities. Because of this situation, the German government was able to argue publicly for over a year that confirming evidence was lacking in the case.

The Libyan affair has apparently had only a minimal effect on U.S.–West German relations. U.S. policymakers have become more sensitive to the demonstrated laxity in German export policy, but the broader diplomatic and strategic relationship between the two nations appears unshaken. In part, this may be due to larger U.S. and German interests that transcend the specifics of the Libyan case. However, German export activities throughout the world have stimulated the acquisition of high technology armaments among several nations, influencing a broad range of U.S. foreign policy issues. A wiser course of action for the United States might have been to seek a far more restrictive German export policy in sensitive materials.

Developments in Eastern Europe in the fall of 1989 took official U.S. and international media attention away from the Libyan chemical weapons episode. In particular, the issue of German reunification overwhelmed questions relating to Libya. Just as the FRG was beginning to develop its case against Hippenstiel-Imhausen, and as public pressure was beginning to influence German policy, the events in Eastern Europe commanded the attention of decision makers and the world community. This was unfortunate because Germany was allowed to defer or avoid action on export policies that had broad effects on international politics.

The demands posed by reunification issues may dictate that West Germany loosen rather than tighten export policies related to sensitive materials. It is becoming clear that reunification will be a costly process for many years, indeed far more expensive than originally estimated. Although all West Germans agreed that export controls had to be strengthened to prevent another Libyan affair, the demand for increased tax revenues may force the FRG to encourage expanded high technology exports. If such a development takes place, it will reintroduce German export policy issues to the world community.

Bonn was hypocritical in calling for broad international controls over chemical weapons while allowing its firms to contribute to chemical weapons proliferation. The government, and especially the Foreign Ministry, frequently argued that the Libyan situation would not have moved so far had a chemical weapons convention been in place. But the Germans were well aware that the world community had been trying for years without success to reach agreement on a convention, and that individual nations' policies had to stand as a surrogate for an international instrument. Trying to shift blame for German activities at Rabta to the international level was especially hypocritical.

The Libyan chemical weapons episode undermined years of German efforts to overcome the effects of the Nazi past. Without question, allowing German commercial assistance to Libya for a chemical weapons facility was shortsighted and ill-advised. The German public agreed it was intolerable for their country to be involved in the production of chemical weapons. Many German press reports used the word "shameful" to describe what had happened. Indeed, most non-Germans do not fully appreciate how wrenching this experience was for German politics and the German people.

The West German government remains circumspect about the events surrounding Rabta. Essentially, the government admitted little more than the news media had revealed. The Kohl government gave its Report to the Bundestag only after public pressure and Bundestag inquiries and demands became too great to resist and threatened the government's very existence. It is likely that far more information exists. It should be underscored that to this point only one individual, Jurgen Hippenstiel-Imhausen, has been prosecuted, which indicates that the government prefers not to energetically expose further commercial wrongdoings in the large network of German firms coordinated by Imhausen-Chemie. Indeed, the government became the defender of the commercial community, arguing that it could find no prosecutable offenses. Moreover, it was slow to investigate and even slower to bring charges. To date, however, whatever legal activity has occurred has taken place under the "old" export laws. Success was achieved by the government in the Hippenstiel case, and other cases are pending.

When it was no longer possible to deny German involvement at Rabta, the Kohl government acted as if the affair were a simple administrative matter and not a major political question involving historical sensitivities in the German nation. Letting the issue boil into a major public explosion was a gross political blunder on the part of the Kohl government. Central decision makers had a well-documented record of German activities in Libya since 1980. Therefore they knew the depth of the involvement and the potential for major political damage. Portraying these activities as routine administrative issues contributed to the eventual intensity of the explosion.

The Kohl government knew its assertion that an anti-German campaign was being conducted by the American press was false. Its attempt to transform the U.S. charges of German commercial assistance for chemical weaponry into little more than an anti-German media effort could be described as an example of simple-minded public denial. Since the United States publicly opened the case through the press, it should have struck knowledgeable West German government officials as a highly serious matter. Denying any complicity must be judged either as arrogance, a blunder, or an attempt to intimidate the press into dropping the issue.

*The deception practiced at Imhausen-Chemie had to be exten-
sive and carefully orchestrated.* The firm coordinated many German
activities, and significant numbers of people had to be involved.
Imhausen's behavior must be classified as a case of successful commercial clandestineness. How this large group of people was kept
quiet and/or deceived is a question that remains to be answered.
Those answers will ultimately have to address the individual level
of analysis, because many Germans working at Imhausen had to
support a deception that ran counter to German abhorrence of
chemical weaponry. How this took place within Imhausen-Chemie
would be the subject matter for a major sociopsychological study.

*Imhausen-Chemie, and in particular its chief executive officer
Jurgen Hippenstiel-Imhausen, insulated both Libya and West Germany from further, presumably far more damaging, revelations.* At
his trial, Hippenstiel-Imhausen took sole responsibility for what
happened and implicated no other individuals. Obviously, with over
one hundred firms involved, including the critical IBI Engineering
firm, dozens of key individuals could have been named. The silence
of Hippenstiel-Imhausen blocked further avenues of exploration and
conceivably shielded other persons who contributed to the Rabta
effort. Of particular importance is the protection of Tripoli's administrative modus operandi. Because of the lack of details here, Libya
may have been allowed to maintain the confidentiality of many of
its procedures, thereby inhibiting future tracking of its efforts to
continue chemical weapons developments.

*The international community remains skeptical regarding Ger-
man measures to tighten export laws.* It is discomforting to learn
that although the government of the FRG issued a ban on all German
supplies to the plant at Rabta, German firms may be involved in
Libya's apparent effort to create a second chemical weapons plant
at the non-Rabta site of Sahba. Moreover, German firms, among
others, have sold chemical weapons technologies to Iraq, which has
had a major destabilizing influence in the Middle East. This, coupled
with the sale of nuclear technology to, for example, India, Pakistan,
Argentina, South Africa, Iraq, and Israel, raises questions about the
seriousness of Germany's export-tightening actions.

Conclusions

The observations discussed in this chapter reveal a certain flu-
idity and softness in the Rabta episode. The United States never

publicly offered the hard evidence it claimed to have. Libya success-fully parried U.S. accusations about its activities, and it continues to deny any involvement in chemical weapons production. The govern-ment in Bonn has been significantly less than forthcoming about the involvement of its own commercial firms.

Nevertheless, the "feel" of this episode should not be surpris-ing: any attempt to clandestinely acquire a chemical weapons capa-bility in the contemporary world will be shrouded in secrecy and deception. Much deception can be penetrated with careful research, but future studies of similar activities will need a better knowledge of this concept.

9

Deception, Lies, and Secrecy in an Act of Proliferation

The previous chapters spell out the intricacies of the activities Libya pursued over a number of years to acquire a chemical weapons production facility. A major element of those activities involved strategies of secrecy and deception. This chapter explores the concepts of deception, lies, and secrecy, as a prelude to an examination of military deception. With this as a foundation, the chapter moves on to discuss specific elements of the deception practiced by Libya and West Germany. Corporate deception is examined in the case of Imhausen-Chemie. I conclude the chapter with a reflection on the usefulness of deception, lies, and secrecy, as they relate to the proliferation of chemical weapons.

Machiavelli and Deception

Historically, relations among nations have seldom been characterized as open, forthright, or wholly sincere. Twentieth-century international relations is most certainly no exception to this general rule. The world community has witnessed and continues to witness numerous acts of calculated deception. The Rabta chemical weapons factory is not an isolated case in this regard.

It deserves mentioning that deception is hardly a recent phenomenon. Niccolo Machiavelli, who lived from 1469 to 1527, wrote eloquently about deception in chapter 28 of his classic *The Prince*. That chapter, entitled "How a Prince Should Keep His Word," begins with the following reflection:

> How praiseworthy it is for a prince to keep his word and to live by integrity and not by deceit everyone knows; nevertheless, one sees from the experience of our times that the princes who have accomplished great deeds are those who have cared little for keeping their promises and who have known how to manipulate the minds

of men by shrewdness; and in the end they have surpassed those who laid their foundations upon honesty.[1]

The general rule for Machiavelli's leader might be that a "wise ruler . . . cannot and should not keep his word when such an observance of faith would be to his disadvantage. . . . [If] men were all good, this rule would not be good; but since men are a sorry lot and will not keep their promises to you, you likewise need not keep yours to them." A leader, however, can not allow others to recognize his deceptive nature. Thus, "it is necessary to know how to disguise this nature well and to be a great hypocrite and a liar, and men are so simpleminded and so controlled by their present necessities that one who deceives will always find another who will allow himself to be deceived."[2]

Leaders are in an especially good position to practice deception, because they "have the majesty of the state to defend them." Indeed, leaders ought to capitalize on their buffered positions, because while "everyone sees what you seem to be," very few will ever discover what you really are.[3] As a matter of fact, says Machiavelli, few will actually have the courage to contradict you. Given this situation, it would be foolish not to embody deception in one's behavioral repertoire, since the prince's "methods will always be judged honorable and will be praised by all." Deception is really quite easy, because "ordinary people are always deceived by appearances and by the outcome of a thing; and in the world there is nothing but ordinary people." Therefore, leaders should always have a public posture based on peace and religious faith but should be "entirely opposed" to both in order to preserve the viability of the nation.[4]

Deception and Lying

Deception has been defined in a variety of ways, and most definitions share many common elements. For Mitchell, deception is any phenomenon that fulfills three criteria: "an organism R registers something Y, R believes Y means (or is) X, and it is untrue that X is the case." Mitchell points out that this is a somewhat unusual definition because the deceiver is not mentioned, but he cites an example of what might be termed inadvertent deception: "A straight twig sticking out of a transparent glass of water appears bent to a human observer."[5] Nevertheless, Mitchell recognizes that deception normally involves an interaction between organisms.

For Russow, an operational definition of deception might be a situation in which "the deceiver increases the probability of the occurrence of some desirable action on the part of the deceived by making the deceived believe something which is not so."[6] A similar definition has been advanced by Zuckerman, DePaulo, and Rosenthal: Deception is "an act that is intended to foster in another person a belief or understanding which the deceiver considers false."[7] For political purposes, since we are always dealing with human deceivers, deception involves intentionality as well as the creation of misperception or misbelief in the mind of another human being.

However, deception has deep evolutionary roots in the natural world. Some biologists feel that plants can be deceptive, and most understand that deception, in one form or another, is widespread in the nonhuman animal world. Various organisms frequently engage in mimicry and/or camouflage. Moths, butterflies, fish, reptiles, and primates have all been known to engage in acts of deception. Typically, as Bond and Robinson point out, the capacity for deception and the ability to detect it have evolved through the processes of natural selection. Indeed, deception often results in a selective advantage.[8]

Of course, the focus in this study is on human beings, and we know humans to be thoroughly capable of deception. Bond and Robinson review a broad spectrum of work that illustrates there is a significant genetic basis for human deception.[9] Other studies have shown there is a strong learning component that results in certain facial cues, demeanor, and speech patterns that emerge during acts of deception. The point to be made here is that human nature does indeed allow for deceptive practices.

Nevertheless, all deception is not necessarily intentional, as the example of the twig in the glass illustrates. However, as Bok states, "when we undertake to deceive others intentionally, we communicate messages meant to mislead them, meant to make them believe what we ourselves do not believe."[10] Thus, intentionality is a critical factor since deception can be either intentional or nonintentional. As a result, intentional deception falls into a special category called a lie. Bok defines a lie as "an intentionally deceptive message in the form of a statement."[11] A lie, therefore, is a means to achieve deception.

Effective human choices depend on accurate assessments of reality. Lies can encourage misperceptions, and as a result they can affect choice behavior.[12] The discovery of lies can lead to anger and distrustfulness on the part of the victim of the lie. Lies harm their perpetrators also because the liar eventually loses his/her social trustworthiness.

If one accepts the cynical advice of Machiavelli, lying becomes permissible behavior, at least in matters of statecraft. According to Bok, lying to enemies is often justified in two major ways. First, enemies can be lied to because "they deserve such treatment," that is, "one should treat friends well and enemies badly." Enemies are not trustworthy or truthful, and by implication, they are deserving of untruths. Second, adversaries are "often thought to be outside the 'social contract' and 'do not, or cannot, comply with existing rules. They do not uphold their end of any social arrangements from which they benefit and can therefore not expect the ordinary protections."[13] People who have such personality disorders as paranoia, and who are convinced that others are conspiring against them, may even more easily accept lying as proper behavior.[14] Conspirators, therefore, deserve to be misled.

Yet lying to enemies can be dangerous, because one's friends might also be misled by the lies. This could engender mistrust by friends of the lying party and therefore a diminution of future support. A reputation for dishonesty might be harmful in all one's dealings.

Brooker attempted to test truth as a variable in several long-term simulations. He found that power relationships and the length of the game influenced the degree of honesty exhibited by the players. In a stable power relationship, the hierarchical positions of the players changed very little. A game was "long" if it lasted several playing periods; some individual simulations were conducted for eight weeks. According to type of situation, the basic findings were:

1. "A long game or series of games with stable power relationships. This environment calls for consistency in honesty and/or dishonesty, rather than honesty or dishonesty itself."
2. "A long game or series of games with unstable power relationships. This environment calls for extremely high levels of honesty and dependability."
3. "A short game. This environment calls for thoroughly dishonest behavior and telling whatever lies will be useful."[15]

I return to some reflections on these findings later in this chapter. However, it is important to point out that nations in the international system normally view their behavior in terms of more than eight weeks. Nevertheless, a product of finite length, regardless of its duration, might be viewed as "short," or a strategy of consistent lying might be consciously chosen as a viable long-term strategy.

Secrecy

The concept of deception, often operationalized through lies, carries with it the idea of secrecy. Secrecy is usually required to bring about a convincing act of deception. Bok has some difficulty in offering a precise definition of secrecy. She argues that secrecy contains the idea of something intentionally hidden, that is, the act of purposefully blocking the free flow of information so that others can not possess it or make use of it.[16] Thus, she states, concealment is the defining characteristic of the concept of secrecy. However, although deception almost always involves secrecy, not all secrecy is meant to be deceptive.

Nation states have continuously practiced secrecy. Most affairs of national security, what some call "high politics," involve what statesmen view as justified secrecy. Reserving a state's vital interests often requires elaborate secrecy bolstered by a "noble lie."[17] Many affairs of state are shielded from public view by a policy of secrecy that protects delicate deliberative processes from premature public scrutiny. Most observers would agree that this is a morally legitimate practice as long as the subject matter and judgments of the deliberations become known to a nation's citizenry. Military secrecy is commonly accepted as justified.

Military Deception

A consideration of military deception forms an important element in the traditional "secrets of state." Protecting and enhancing national security chiefly through military means has long been regarded as legitimate state activity, and masking military undertakings from an adversary's view is often looked upon as normal state behavior. The purposeful dissemination of erroneous information about one's military activities, that is, disinformation or lies, is usually justified on the grounds of national security.

"At the root of the rationale for military secrecy," says Bok, "is the imperative of self-preservation. Many religious and philosophical traditions take it to be the most fundamental characteristic of living beings. They hold secrecy (and force, if need be) especially natural and legitimate when undertaken to preserve one's life."[18]

141

The international community appears to tolerate the use of lies to protect military secrets.

Certain psychological factors need to be considered when discussing military deception. For military deception to be effective, it must shape the thoughts of the highest level of opposing decision makers so that they accept disinformation as truth.[19] This requires creative and conscious orchestration of the deception, which requires a deception "story." The story must be directed toward the beliefs the deceiver hopes to create in the adversary's mind. The story, therefore,

> must consequently be feasible, plausible, and in harmony with past operations. It must be realistic both in terms of accomplishment and the enemy's estimate of his opponent's capabilities and intentions. In fact, the deception plan must emerge logically out of the past, must correspond logically with current activities, and proceed logically toward the future. It is therefore vital that the "story" or deception scenario be so designed that when it diverges from reality, as it most assuredly must, the divergence can be explained away in context of what has occurred previously and will happen in the future.[20]

The story or disinformation is often communicated through the press, which is not only an efficient and quick vehicle of information dissemination but also a broad-based media that reaches into all nations. Journalists, however, are frequently aware that governments can use them for less than the most honorable purposes. When journalists become conscious of this, they can become tenacious in pursuing the various elements that contribute to a military deception.[21] Covert manipulations of the press are commonplace, but overt manipulations are unusual, and when they are attempted, they are rarely successful.

Corporate Deception

A business or corporation engages in deception when it acts in illegal (or criminal) ways and then attempts to hide that activity through a policy of secrecy and deception that usually involves the use of lies. This type of corporate behavior is most difficult to uncover because it is frequently organizationally complex—it may involve numerous business entities. When I speak of corporate crime, I mean crime to which several elements within a corporation are a party, and which, if successful, will enhance the financial position of a corporation rather than an individual. Corporate crime involves a set of relationships among many elements within corporations, such as chief executive officers, their immediate subordinates, governing boards, employees, branch offices, other firms, and conceivably government officials. The demands of successful deception in corporate crime are exceedingly intricate.

During the past decade, many writers have pointed out that the culture of corporations can strongly influence a propensity toward crime. Clinard and Yeager state that "a club mentality is bred through overwork, frequent transfers, which inhibit attachment to local communities, and provisions for recreational and educational needs during leisure time. Co-workers and higher-ups become 'significant others' in the individuals' work and social life."[22] According to Jackall, work in this context "creates subtle measures of prestige and an elaborate status hierarchy that, in addition to fostering an intense competition for status, also makes the rules, procedures, social contexts, and protocol of an organization paramount psychological and behavioral guides." As a result, "actual organizational moralities are thus contextual, situational, highly specific, and, most often, unarticulated."[23]

Clinard and Yeager point out that corporate leaders are often insulated from people who disagree with their beliefs. These executives "tend to associate almost exclusively with persons who are pro-business, politically conservative, and generally opposed to government regulation." Indeed, the corporate culture creates "a climate in which there is a lack of consensus about the values society is trying to advance."[24]

Attitudes Toward Government Regulation

In general, as described by Clinard and Yeager, several beliefs seem to be involved to varying degrees in shaping corporate attitudes toward government regulation.[25] Corporate advocates say that the free enterprise system demands a minimal amount of governmental oversight, and that anything more represents an unnecessary interference in commercial activities. Moreover, regulation forces firms to pay compliance costs, thus lowering profits. Regulations are often considered to be too complex and to deal with relatively "unimportant" matters.

Beyond these general attitudes are several more specific items. It is sometimes asserted that corporations do not deliberately violate laws. Infractions are usually the result of mistakes or inattentiveness.

If competing firms violate laws without fear of prosecution, corporations in a related area of business should be able to do likewise since competition requires a level playing field. When violations of law do occur, they usually result from a perceived corporate imperative, such as protecting jobs, maintaining the value of stock, and/or insuring the financial viability of the organization.

To be sure, all these attitudes are not present all the time, nor are they present to the same extent in any individual corporation. Nevertheless, in free enterprise economic systems, all of them appear in some measure to form the basis of corporate attitudes toward government regulations. Firms are often influenced by these attitudes when they shape responses to charges of legal violations.

Individual Morality Within the Corporation

Personal ethics can be strongly affected by group processes, and Irving Janis' work in this regard has influenced analyses in both the corporate and political worlds.[26] Essentially, Janis has argued that since most decisions are made in small groups, there is strong psychological pressure on participants to "go along" with the primary thrust of the group. There are incentives not to adopt a deviant position or reflect an unconventional attitude. Thus, individual ethics is based upon being "the good soldier" who takes an order and does the required job.[27] Jackall maintains that as a result, work can cause "people to bracket, while at work, the moralities that they might hold outside the workplace or that they might adhere to privately and to follow instead the prevailing morality of their particular organizational situation." Thus, "what matters on a day-to-day basis are the moral rules-in-use fashioned within the personal and structural constraints of one's organization."[28]

As Jackall indicates, corporate managers do not normally discuss ethical considerations with each other. Indeed, hierarchical influences usually predominate in superior-subordinate relationships. Quoting a high-level corporate executive, Jackall observes that "what is right in the corporation is what the guy above you wants from you. That's what morality is in the corporation."[29] Even though few individuals would publicly admit to such a blunt formulation, it probably contains considerable truth.

Of course, "what the guy above you wants" emphasizes the hierarchical dimensions of corporate morality. In such a situation, the person at the top of the hierarchical structure sets the ethical tone for the organization and may even dictate specific moral justifications for certain corporate actions. If the chief executive officer (CEO) acts unethically, the communicated values will permeate the corporation, and group dynamics will probably prevent a meaningful counterreaction. If the CEO is consciously pursuing behaviors that he/she knows to be unethical, some form of deception and secrecy is likely to result.

Libya

Given the nature of deception, lies, and secrecy, it is not difficult to understand how a strategy of deception could be justifiably adopted by Libya. Libya considered itself to be circumscribed by enemies within the international system. Few nations endorsed Libya's international behavior, including, of course, the membership of the European Community, which responded harshly to Libya's terrorist activities. The United States, which had been a major object of Arab criticism for decades, stood out as an especially hostile competitor for Libya. After all, the United States had engaged in a direct military attack on Libya, had enacted restrictive trade policies, and for many years had publicly accused Libya of terrorist activities. Thus, in terms of justifying deception by viewing one's nation as surrounded by enemies, Libya certainly qualified.

If Machiavelli's words contain the elements of calculated rationality that observers over the centuries have claimed for them, the initial choice to proceed with a deceptive undertaking to clandestinely construct a chemical weapons production facility might have appeared quite rational to Libyan decision makers. Libya could comfortably call on the "majesty of the state" to defend itself. In modern terminology, the majesty of the state refers to the presumed credibility of the highest level of foreign policy decision making. It is usually assumed that heads of state, foreign ministers, and ambassadors to the United Nations, will not blatantly lie in public. The presumption of credibility is therefore of considerable operational value to a nation that has chosen to engage in a major act of deception.

As controlled by Moammar Qadhafi, the actions the government of Tripoli exercised within Libyan society must be considered coercive. "For coercive governments," writes Bok, "secrecy is essential to every aspect of the exercise of power. These regimes combine control over secrecy with equal control over what becomes public."[30]

A government that exercises secrecy as a normal element of doing business will have no difficulty in pursuing an elaborate foreign policy strategy requiring secrecy and deception. Moreover, within Libyan society, confining access to the Rabta facility by surrounding it with guards and antiaircraft weapons, restricting movement around the facility, and preventing the international press from acquiring information about the activity must have been for the Libyan government a reasonably normal way of conducting business.

Libya's position within the international system and its effort to create the production facility fall into what Brooker has called a long game with stable power relationships. This is a situation in which the hierarchical positions of the players (nations) do not fluctuate greatly. In such an engagement, *consistency* in honesty or dishonesty is more important than the honesty or dishonesty itself.

If one is engaged in an act of deception, the rule to be followed, then, is "Do not deviate one iota from your deception story." Libya's deception story was quite simple: a pharmaceutical factory was being constructed at Rabta; this was an innocent act that did not demand any international attention; and the Libyan government staked its credibility on these assertions. Any deviation from the deception story would open the door to considerable international criticism, and the act really being undertaken was so serious that the international community, and especially the United States, might take military action against Libya. Thus, the story had to be consistently upheld by all Libyan spokespersons, which was effectively accomplished.

As the months wore on, the Rabta episode evolved into an intractable conflict, essentially between Libya and the United States. Such a conflict is one that is apparently unresolvable. But Thorson argues that the word "stubbornness" more accurately describes the quality needed to effectively explain intractability.[31] Stubbornness, the quality of being obstinate and unyielding, is a necessity in advancing a credible deception story. Libya's stubbornness was never bridged, despite the pressures brought to bear on the government.

Stubbornly maintaining the deception story was critical for several additional reasons. Any indication that it might be lying could have forced Libya into a series of admissions that might have been difficult to stop, especially within the give-and-take framework of the United Nations. It would have been just a matter of time, therefore, before the accumulated evidence would have been sufficient (though not absolutely convincing) to justify a military strike against Rabta. Moreover, it was critical for Libya to cross a certain threshold. Once the factory was producing at least a minimal amount of toxic substances, an attack would be risky since the collateral damage done to humans, plants, and animals by the release of the noxious materials would be viewed by the international community as injudicious and perhaps inhumane. Thus, the deception story had to be fiercely maintained over an extended period of time.[32]

The construction network overseen by Ihsan Barbouti, which brought materials, labor, and chemical processing equipment to the Rabta site, was, of course, conducted in complete secrecy until its existence became known. The deception story and Barbouti's tactics carefully took into account the possibility of a revelation at some future point. Using the word-fragment *pharma* to name various sites was an excellent cover that lasted well into the process. Moreover, it created a paper trail with the expression *pharma* on it, an expression that implied the shipment of goods and services to a pharmaceutical site and/or facility.

As described in previous chapters, all of the transactions in Barbouti's network were either accomplished secretly or masked to appear innocent. Libya's deception required this kind of secret behavior if it was to be successful to the point of greatly increasing the costs of attack. Revelation too early in the process would have placed the Rabta facility in jeopardy of an overt attack.

Nevertheless, Libyan officials must have been aware that at some point their deception would be unmasked, as indeed it was by the United States. Precisely when this happened is not clear from the available evidence. West German intelligence was aware as early as 1980. The United States must have been aware well before it made its public charges in late 1987. This knowledge probably came from human intelligence sources as well as from satellite reconnaissance. Once the United States decided to go public, it did so with firm determination, which implies that it had solid knowledge of what was happening at Rabta, and that the secret had become known. In spite of the ensuing diplomatic argument, however, or perhaps because of it, Libya persisted in its deception story.

I asserted in Chapter 8 that Rabta was a risky undertaking for Libya. Libya stood a major chance of having its complex, decade-long effort to construct a chemical weapons production facility physically attacked by a power committed to opposing the further proliferation of chemical weapons. Risky decisions are taken by risk takers, individuals who are willing to tolerate risks. The risk-taking personality is one with strong self-confidence, high competitiveness, and a willingness to break rules. The uncertain outcome of an endeavor can be an incentive for a risk taker to become involved.

Livingstone has observed that "the late Egyptian president Anwar Sadat once described Qadhafi as '100 percent sick and possessed of a demon,'" and a former Sudanese head of state described Qadhafi as having "a split personality—both evil."[33] Whether these amateur appraisals are accurate is for clinical psychologists to ascertain. However, the assertive, aggressive, and norm-challenging behavior of the Libyan head of state is well understood by the international community. These attributes are also characteristics of risk takers. If, indeed, Qadhafi is a risk taker, the Rabta undertaking was a good match for his personality.

By the same token, Ihsan Barbouti played a role that seemed to accord well with risk-taking behavior. Little is known about Barbouti as a person. However, as Libya's key agent in assembling and orchestrating the network, Barbouti had to be aware of the high danger that the complexity of the network might expose his work. There were dozens upon dozens of contacts and firms from which an intentional or unintentional leak could occur. Moreover, as time wore on, Barbouti must have realized that the secrecy and deception could not last. Sooner or later, exposure was a virtual certainty. As an indicator of the nervous sensitivity with which he saw his work, Barbouti hastily fled his offices several months before the story broke publicly. The papers left behind, especially in Zurich, provide an insight into what Barbouti must have considered a high-risk initiative. It is likely that Barbouti had a risk-taking personality, because few individuals could have withstood the stresses of the deception he put into place. As Bok observes, "to live with secrecy day in and day out, to be aware of a threat . . . to oneself from a diminution of secrecy, and to give up ordinary moral restraints in dealing with . . . [clients] is an experience that isolates and transforms" an individual.[34]

Imhausen-Chemie

The behavior of Imhausen-Chemie remains partially concealed from researchers. Although much is known about the firm's external connections with other firms and with Barbouti, there is little knowledge of the decision processes within Imhausen-Chemie. This is primarily because the firm's president, Jurgen Hippenstiel-Imhausen, refused to identify any others who may have been parties to the deception. Nevertheless, some reflections on Imhausen-Chemie's commercial activities are possible.

Most certainly, the corporate culture within West Germany supported vigorous commercial competition with minimal government regulation. The federal export regulations that existed were either underenforced or unenforced. Such a regulatory atmosphere allowed for unconventional and legally borderline undertakings. Given the fact that many German firms were internationally active in selling high technology products that could be related to military activities, Hippenstiel probably felt that the secret and deceptive behavior of his firm had little chance of being discovered.

Furthermore, Hippenstiel sat at the apex of his firm, and therefore the "majesty of hierarchy" reinforced his pursuit of a deceptive strategy. If "what the guy above you wants" defines commercial morality, Hippenstiel was in an excellent position to require subordinates to support his central involvement in the deceptive network. Those who raised objections could be told that their jobs depended on the health of the firm, and that since the firm was in serious financial difficulty, compliance was required to return the firm to profitability and to save jobs. Moreover, since it was the president of the firm who was requiring collusion and/or acquiescence, all blame could easily be shifted to him. Indeed, at his trial, Hippenstiel acknowledged full responsibility for his firm's involvement in a deceptive undertaking that was a national embarrassment to the German people.

To critics of U.S. pressure on the FRG, as well as to those who doubt that Libya was constructing a chemical weapons production facility, it is important to note that Hippenstiel admitted that he was aware he was engaged in a secret effort to plan and construct a chemical factory but said he did not know the factory was to be used to produce chemical weapons. Hippenstiel knew the chemical business, and he should have known where the borders of chemical legality and morality were situated. Secrecy is not required in constructing a pharmaceutical factory. Hippenstiel was involved in a secret project with Libya for at least five years, and he was fully aware of the deceptions in Hong Kong and elsewhere, which were part of Libya's broader and complex deception. That this deception took place, therefore, is not a matter of contention, as Hippenstiel's testimony may illustrate to some. Hippenstiel argued only that he did not know to what use this clandestine undertaking would be put, and this seems implausible.

Why would Hippenstiel place his firm in such jeopardy? After

149

all, as time went on, the spreading of the network must have required more and more attentiveness to maintaining the secrecy that fostered the deception. It is conceivable, and of course this is pure guesswork, that Hippenstiel was a risk taker. In 1984, when Hippenstiel entered the deception with the Libyan government and Ihsan Barbouti, taking a risk in clandestine activity may have seemed like a fair price to pay in order to restore the financial health of Imhausen-Chemie. If, indeed, Hippenstiel was a risk taker, the increasing demands of the deception might have psychologically stimulated him. If he was not a risk taker, perhaps it is best to consider him a victim of bad judgment.

It is often difficult to extricate oneself from an act of deception, and the Rabta episode illustrates this quite well. Once Hippenstiel became a party to the deception, others were likely to be aware of his involvement. Certainly the Libyan government knew of Hippenstiel's important role, and Barbouti knew because he negotiated the deal with Hippenstiel. Hippenstiel negotiated with other suppliers, and therefore they knew of Hippenstiel's involvement. Moreover, competitors in the chemical industry should have had some, even minimal, knowledge of Imhausen-Chemie's activities. Thus, even though Hippenstiel might have wanted to extricate his firm from the network, the deception itself trapped him, because others held over him a tacit threat of exposure. But exposure would not have been a particularly good strategy for the others to follow, because it would have revealed their complicity and the existence of the network. What we have, then, is a set of symbiotic relationships in a deception, and the symbiosis was effective because there was not a single leak from this complexity over a long period of time. The accusations leading to revelations came from outside the network, that is, from the United States.

The Government of the Federal Republic of Germany

Considering the behavior of the government of the Federal Republic of Germany in the context of deception is somewhat awkward because it had a very different role from Libya and Imhausen-Chemie. West Germany, and especially the Kohl government, was not an active player in the effort to emplace a chemical weapons production facility at Rabta. Nevertheless, as indicated at length in previous chapters, West Germany must share some responsibility for the success of the deception. The primary reason for this judgment is based upon what in effect became governmental acquiescence in what were at the time possible violations of German export laws.

It is not unreasonable to assert that the German government acquiesced in the deceptive behavior. As early as 1980 the BND was aware of German commercial activity related to Libya's quest for chemical warfare agents. As the Report to the Bundestag revealed, knowledge of German commercial involvement at Rabta became increasingly detailed and extensive throughout the 1980s. The government's unwillingness to act on this information contributed to the success of the deception. Moreover, while multiple sources of information developed, the government took no action to coordinate this information, which would have provided the comprehensiveness for policymakers to see the extent of what was happening. Even after the United States began to publicly pressure the Kohl government, German authorities moved very slowly to bring legal charges.

The government's major deception was the clear lie that it knew nothing of German commercial involvement in the chemical weapons production facility. The chancellor himself was a party to this. It remains a mystery why the Kohl government made such a strong stand over what it knew to be a false assertion and why it did not easily sense the embarrassing political damage that would ensue when it might eventually have to publicly admit that it knew for years about Libya's chemical activities. This was probably a failure of the internal processes of policy-making. A justification for this mischoice was the government's policy of stimulating exports that produced tax revenues. Clearly, the limits to such a policy were reached with the Rabta episode.

It is relevant to ask to what degree the government was sincere in its prosecution of the various aspects of this case. To this date, only one person, Jurgen Hippenstiel-Imhausen, has been prosecuted. For a secret and deceptive undertaking that involved dozens of firms, it would not be unreasonable to expect that even more indictments would have been issued and more extensive prosecutions undertaken.

The United States

There appears to be little evidence of deceptive U.S. behavior in the Rabta case. The United States never dealt directly with the Libyan criticism that states nations had a right to acquire chemical weapons as long as all nuclear nations did not eliminate their stocks of such weapons. Also, the United States never provided the public with "hard" evidence of chemical weapons activities at Rabta. It is conceivable that such hard evidence never existed beyond textual reports. Satellite photographs of a chemical weapons factory under construction are likely to look like a pharmaceutical factory under construction. Thus, satellite photographs of the Rabta site probably lacked credibility. But these items do not constitute a case for U.S. deception.

However, a television report on the 2 July 1991 broadcast of ABC's *Nightline* program connected Barbouti to an extensive range of commercial activities in the United States during the late 1980s. The IBI complex, according to the report, apparently funded a Boca Raton, Florida chemical processing plant, the byproducts from which could be used to manufacture cyanide. The precursor cyanide may have been shipped to West Germany for processing and then reshipped to Iraq or conceivably Libya.

The *Nightline* broadcast indicated that, despite knowledge of Barbouti's operations in the United States, the Central Intelligence Agency, the Federal Bureau of Investigation, and other units of government, failed to investigate charges from American citizens that illegal, clandestine activities were taking place. An *unsubstantiated* assessment as to why an official investigation never occurred was that Barbouti was in the employ of the Central Intelligence Agency and was supplying information to the CIA on the chemical weapons programs of Libya and Iraq. If this assessment is true, it might explain why the U.S. government failed to provide more detailed public information to support its charges against Libya. Such information might have compromised the U.S. connection with Barbouti.

Conclusion

This chapter examined some theoretical issues of deception, secrecy, and lies. It also looked at the behavior of Libya, Imhausen-Chemie, the Federal Republic of Germany, and the United States, within the context of deception.

What were the results of this deceptive behavior? For Libya, the results were decidedly positive. The Rabta complex is in existence, it is in production, and it does not appear to be in danger of a hostile attack. Imhausen-Chemie, however, has been expelled from the German Chemical Manufacturers Association, and its leader is in jail.

Deception, Lies, and Secrecy

The reputation of the West German government has been significantly hurt, with many nations expressing continuing distrust of German commercial activities in high technology transfer.

The United States has not suffered any major harm from opposing the proliferation of chemical weapons. But why did the United States halt its initiative against the Rabta facility? The disbanding of the clandestine network was a direct result of U.S. antiproliferation efforts, and the United States was a major stimulus in the eventual prosecution of Hippensticl. Nevertheless, Libya possesses a chemical weapons production facility in spite of U.S. efforts. This raises the question of whether the United States has the staying power to pursue a major international objective over the long term.

10

Some Policy-making Considerations

As stated in the introductory chapter, this is a case study of a nation that acquired a major chemical weapons production facility while most of the earth's nations were predisposed to halting the spread of such weapons. The United States stood virtually alone, at least publicly, in demanding that Libya halt its activities and that the Federal Republic of Germany prevent its commercial firms from supplying Libya with equipment and raw chemicals. This "gentleman's solution" did not work.

The present chapter examines in general terms a number of factors statesmen need to take into account in dealing with chemical (and perhaps biological) weapons proliferation. Of course, it should be kept in mind that no act of proliferation will take place in the precise manner of a previous act. Although this chapter is oriented to those who aim at preventing proliferation, it should be recognized that those who seek to acquire a mass destruction weapons capability also learn from previous international experiences. Given the success of the Libyan experience, therefore, future attempts at proliferation are likely to be more sophisticated and more deceptive.

Statesmanship

Able statesmen always seek to determine where they and their nations stand in the evolution of political events. Determining one's location in history provides an advantage to a maneuvering nation. Since the advent of the nuclear era in 1945, we have been living in an age of science in military affairs. For more that forty years, we have witnessed a military science dominated, at least at the mass destruction level, by the discipline of physics. Since the 1970s we have been moving into an age dominated by biochemistry and biotechnology. Although chemical weaponry is certainly not new, new methods and new processes have been developed to aid in the efficient production of chemical weapons. Some of these processes utilize knowledge from biotechnology, and the intellectual relationships between chemistry and biology appear, at least in some areas, to be moving closer. Thus, perceptive statesmen should see themselves as having entered a high technology world in which attentiveness to new developments in science, especially chemistry and biology, will have an increasingly powerful effect on the affairs of state.

This will require that statesmen have some basic knowledge about the world of science. In this regard, the situation is not encouraging. The vast majority of the world's statesmen, including, of course, those from nations in the high technology, industrialized world, continue to have their academic training in law and the standard humanities disciplines. At the present time, there is little hope that this situation will change, which is unfortunate because the pressures from scientific innovation will continue to influence the agendas of international relations. Methods must be found to ensure that traditional specialists in diplomacy have some training in the social, and especially the political, impacts of science and technology. The U.S. Department of State and other foreign ministries should address this issue resolutely and quickly.

Libya

One intriguing question that deserves to be posed is why Libya desired to acquire a chemical weapons production facility. What was Libya's motive? The most obvious answer is we do not know, since Libya continues to deny that it has built anything but a pharmaceutical factory. Nevertheless, policymakers do need to know something about the motives behind an act of chemical weapons proliferation.

Ross sees several broad reasons for arms acquisition by third world nations. These include a sense of insecurity, perceptions of external as well as internal threats, unreliable sources of weapons, vulnerability to arms embargoes, and a desire to develop a weapons production infrastructure.[1] If all or even some of these elements were part of the Libyan rationale for chemical weapons activities, it is not difficult to see Libya's motives. These reasons are especially true for chemical weapons, which are generally considered to be abhorrent, and which are therefore vulnerable to interruption in supplies, equipment, and knowledgeable technical assistance. Also, I do not want to overlook the idea of craziness—in this case Libya's willingness to challenge, with long-term persistence, existing international norms.

Broader motives may also have been involved. Libya may have thought a chemical weapons acquisition strategy would provide entrance into the exclusive club of those who possessed instruments of mass destruction. The previous four decades have demonstrated the significant threat value of such weapons in international affairs. Indeed, Libya may be aiming at establishing regional military superiority, especially with regard to Chad and Niger.

Whatever the motives of Libya's actions, the lessons Libyan policymakers derived from this experience are basically positive. Libya successfully established a chemical weapons production facility. It did so in spite of open U.S. hostility and diplomatic aggressiveness. A clandestine construction network was cleverly created, and it proceeded with its activities for a number of years before it was publicly revealed. By the time the United States reacted, the Rabta facility was either nearing completion, beginning production, or well into the production process. Regardless of the precise status at the time of the U.S. charge, the Libyans had succeeded in their efforts. Despite the verbal defenses that Libya had to enunciate, the physical defenses of Rabta were never breached.

The United States

The Libyan episode provided several important lessons for American policymakers. Among them should be a greater sensitivity to properly timing attempts to halt the spread of chemical weapons. What is the most desirable point at which to intervene in the proliferation process? It would have been far easier to pressure Libya in the early 1980s. By waiting until the late 1980s, the United States was confronted with a Libya quite far along in the process, with supply channels well developed, and with a major investment in the undertaking. Thus, the later in the process, the more vested interests that are involved, and the more difficult it is to acquire support to oppose.[2] Nevertheless, it should be kept in mind that the earlier any punitive action is taken, the more undeveloped and risky is the political case.

The United States also became a victim of two major international developments that drew policymakers' attention away from Libya. When the Kohl government released its Report in February 1989, the disintegration of several communist governments in Eastern Europe was gaining momentum. The profound developments that followed pushed the Libyan episode off the front pages of

European and American newspapers. In the spring of 1990, as the Hippenstiel-Imhausen trial, which demonstrated the severity of what had happened, neared completion, the German public, both East and West, was occupied with the excitement of the unification process. And if this was not enough to reorient the U.S. policy-making community, Iraq's invasion of Kuwait during the summer of 1990, which elicited a massive commitment of U.S. military personnel to Saudi Arabia and the Persian Gulf waters, certainly encouraged the process. The ensuing war completed it. In effect, the international condemnation of the actions of West Germany and others for assisting Libya in acquiring a chemical weapons factory was all but forgotten as a result of these two major developments.

This was unfortunate because the Gulf crisis and war demonstrated the result of unchecked weapons acquisition by Iraq. The apparent U.S. decision to ignore Libyan activities could lead in time to another regional crisis in the Middle East, with Libya as a central actor. Persistence, therefore, is required in both U.S. and West German policy-making communities. If chemical weapons proliferation is undesirable, then the presumed abandonment of active pressure on Libya is, at the very least, unfortunate and ill-advised. The inability to proceed in its effort against Libya could be, of course, a simple measure of U.S. loss of will in the international arena and of America's decline as a superpower. Moreover, the demonstration that the United States does not have the tenacious qualities to pursue a major policy initiative through a variety of "distractions" could encourage additional nations to seek out a chemical weapons posture. In short, an antiproliferation policy directed toward a specific nation should be followed to a successful conclusion, or it should not be initiated in the first place.

U.S. policymakers should have been disappointed at the lack of overt international support for their Libyan initiative. The United States expected support from its NATO allies, but the only enthusiastic support came from Great Britain. The FRG's timidity is well demonstrated by this study. True, the NATO treaty area does not extend to north Africa or most of the Middle East, but this is a bit ambiguous because NATO had pledged itself to prevent the proliferation of chemical weapons, and presumably this referred to areas beyond the borders of the NATO signatories. Indeed, during the Gulf War, a number of NATO nations pledged financial support and/or sent troops and equipment to support the UN coalition against Iraq. Nevertheless, had there not been UN support for this undertaking, it is doubtful whether any NATO nations, again with the probable exception of Great Britain, would have joined forces with the United States.

Given its lead role against Libyan chemical weapons activities, it is not unreasonable to ask whether the United States has become the world's sole enforcer of international morality, at least as regards chemical weapons proliferation. A preliminary answer to this question must be no given the major international interests in a ban on chemical weapons. However, it is one thing to consent to a set of ideas as embodied in a written document, such as a chemical weapons convention, and quite another to take concrete action to prevent the spread of such weapons. Thus, for American policymakers, the lesson seems to be: Don't get out in front of the international community in attempting to halt an act of chemical weapons proliferation. Work to build some kind of consensus; involve the UN or some other international authority as the coordinating arm of the antiproliferation effort.[3] By all means, if you decide to move unilaterally, have the fortitude to stay with the issue or situation until some form of resolution is forthcoming.

Finally, the United States confronted an especially difficult task by attempting to roll back a military posture acquisition process that was well in progress. As Greenwood has argued, it is very difficult, if not often impossible, to constrain the desire of nations to acquire military technologies.[4] This is the case because military technology serves many political purposes, such as projecting an image of strength into the international arena, fostering a feeling of intimidation among potential adversaries, and giving both internal and external observers some evidence of commitment to technological innovations.[5] Since multiple national purposes are served by the acquisition of military technologies, especially in third world countries, it is not surprising that Libya was so unyielding regarding the construction of its Rabta facility. Any future attempts to restrain chemical weapons production facilities will probably confront the same dogged resistance.

Iraq

The case of Iraq is relevant to policy considerations regarding Libya. It is likely that Iraq's successful arms acquisition strategy served as a demonstration for the Libyans. Indeed, the anatomy of Iraqi activities to build a major military force is quite similar to that of Libya's more limited efforts. In legitimate activities over a ten-year period, Iraq purchased a broad range of military equipment from the Soviet Union and numerous western countries, including Great Britain, Italy, France, the Netherlands, the United States, and West Germany.[6] To facilitate their procurement of weapons and militarily relevant technologies, the Iraqis established a set of ostensibly legitimate import-export businesses in Western Europe.[7] Perhaps the strongest demonstration to the Libyans was the ease with which these activities took place. Not only was there no apparent attempt to stop the Iraqis, but arms merchants eagerly offered their wares for sale. Beyond this, of course, was the international community's acquiescence toward Iraq's use of chemical weapons in the war with Iran and against its own citizens.

Libya, therefore, must have been quite surprised to find itself the target of a major U.S. diplomatic effort to halt its construction of a chemical weapons production facility. Not only had Iraq been "allowed" to build a multiplant chemical weapons production posture, but the Iraqis purchased various other weapons without diplomatic interference.

What emerges, therefore, is a gross asymmetry between the U.S. policies regarding Iraq and Libya—that is, harsh opposition to Libya and acquiescence toward Iraq. Policymakers may be quick to defend this asymmetry by arguing that there were "larger" U.S. interests involved with respect to Iraq. Nevertheless, Libya probably interpreted U.S. policy toward Iraq as implied toleration of the construction at Rabta.

The lesson for U.S. decision makers is that policy inconsistencies regarding chemical weapons may have inadvertently encouraged the Libyans to proceed with an ambitious program. In effect, U.S. diplomatic pressure against Libya represented a policy reversal from an existing posture toward Iraq. Libya may have seen what it thought was an opportunity to develop a chemical weapons factory, only to be opposed unexpectedly by the United States.

Export Controls

Third world nations are normally technology deficient. As such, a dependency relationship exists between them and the first world, the technology-rich countries. However, this situation has additional complexities that compound attempts to control the export of sensitive materials. We are living in an era in which exports generate significant private commercial profits and governmental tax revenues. Yet the imperatives of military policy can and do require that certain products be restricted or withdrawn from some trade relationships.

This study has demonstrated that a laxity in the enforcement of laws dealing with restricted materials produced broad-based and lucrative export activities on the part of West German commercial firms vis-à-vis Libya. But even with strict enforcement, policies can fail. The case of supercomputers is illustrative. Both the United States and Japan have restricted the export of computers that can perform an excess of 100 million mathematical calculations per second. From 1984 to 1990, this prevented third world nations such as Libya from acquiring supercomputers to assist in weapons development programs. By mid 1990, however, it was apparent that technological developments were undermining this policy. It is now possible to link together a series of easily obtainable microprocessor chips to do the work of a supercomputer, thereby allowing any nation to construct its own.

In a further refinement of its attempt to control the export of supercomputing capabilities, the Bush administration announced on 7 June 1991 that the United States and Japan will reformulate their export policies to prevent individuals or nations that represent a security threat from obtaining supercomputers. The highest risks are thought to be in the third world, especially among those nations that have not ratified the Nuclear Non-Proliferation Treaty. Export of supercomputers will be allowed to West European countries, but special provisions will be enacted to prevent reexports to high-risk third world nations. Whether this will slow technological developments in Libya remains to be seen.[8]

The United States has taken several steps to control the distribution of dangerous chemicals. On 14 December 1990 the White House announced the Enhanced Proliferation Control Initiative to inhibit the spread of fifty chemicals that could be used to produce chemical weapons.[9] This initiative might be circumvented by new technical developments in biotechnology by which chemicals can be produced. It is unclear whether using the technical capabilities of biotechnology to produce chemicals for weapons falls under the jurisdiction of either the Biological Weapons Convention or the proposed chemical weapons convention. The lack of diplomatic clarity here may very well structure the type of strategy followed by a nation intent upon developing a chemical weapons posture.

On 13 November 1989 the U.S. House of Representatives passed the "Chemical and Biological Warfare Elimination Act," which imposes sanctions against commercial firms that assist in the proliferation of chemical or biological weapons and at the same time establishes sanctions against nations that use or manufacture such weapons in violation of international law.[10] Although this is an ambitious piece of legislation, it is yet to be fully passed and enacted into law. Moreover, the problem of dual-use chemicals remains, and policymakers will be hard pressed to exercise absolute control over their distribution.

Despite U.S. actions to inhibit the transfer of chemical weapons technologies and materials, U.S. policymakers are aware that a single nation cannot control such transfers. Cooperative policies of various kinds are needed, and ways to deal with transgressions and lax enforcement policies must be devised. Had the United States not pressured West Germany, it is doubtful that the flow of technologies and materials to Rabta would have stopped.[11]

A further important consideration for policymakers is how to deal with a NATO alliance associate that, to the detriment of alliance members, refuses to reform its export policies. This is a complex question to which are attached a multitude of considerations. Yet it is in the interests of all alliance members to develop an enforceable policy prior to the emergence of a critical international situation.

As this study illustrates, the Germans are clearly a special case. German commercial firms were not only largely responsible for an act of proliferation in Libya. During the ensuing destabilization of political relationships in the Middle East, they were also major suppliers of knowledge, equipment, and materials to Iraq. Although U.S. leaders no doubt preferred not to deal with the "German question" during the Gulf conflict, American as well as NATO policymakers ought to address Germany's lack of fully committed attentiveness to the export of high technology products. Germany's reluctance to become involved in the Gulf situation could be interpreted as an attempt to keep the door open to future high technology sales.

Unconventional Activities

The Middle East is well known for its unconventional and unpredictable conflict activities. The case of Libya, as well as that of Iraq, illustrates this characteristic well. Given the strained economies of many nations, especially those in third world societies, a strong likelihood exists that many nations will seek a military posture through the cheapest means possible. This, of course, implies that the Middle East may well witness a repetition of the clandestine activities that served Libya so well. Thus, policymakers need to be attentive to the possibility that the lessons demonstrated by the Rabta effort may have been instructive to other nations.

To counteract the continuation of such activities, a number of critical signs need to be carefully monitored. Without question, intelligence activities that alert policymakers to potential problems need to be maintained and increased. Much of this activity must focus on the commercial arena, where the first clues regarding chemical weapons proliferation are likely to emerge. Intelligence should be especially alert to the behavior of chemical firms that are in financial trouble, since such firms would be receptive to lucrative offers from nations that want to clandestinely develop a chemical weapons posture. Intelligence agencies should also assist in guaranteeing that national and international chemical export control procedures are properly monitored by political authorities. This is especially important because it might be in the interest of some nations to encourage lax enforcement.

Commercial monitoring involves intelligence about shipping. Third world nations frequently do not have an indigenous capability to produce precursor chemicals and equipment, which means, of course, that they must import such items. The Libyan success in exploiting shipping channels clearly establishes that shipping should be a major focus of intelligence efforts.

Though many components to manufacture chemical weapons can be legitimately purchased in the open market, smuggling will continue to be a preferred method for acquiring critical, controlled elements for a chemical weapons effort. Presumably, acquiring nuclear weapons materials is more difficult than acquiring the wherewithal for a chemical weapons capability. Nevertheless, Argentina, Brazil, India, Iraq, Israel, and Pakistan have obtained various nuclear commodities through smuggling activities.[12]

If needed items cannot be legally or illegally purchased, they can be stolen. Iraq and Israel have been caught with presumably stolen electronic devices that could be used as triggers for nuclear weapons.[13] Information is especially prone to be stolen, and it has been a classic objective of espionage efforts. Recently, Chinese intelligence agents stole nuclear weapons secrets from the U.S. government's Lawrence Livermore National Laboratory.[14]

Given the momentum of knowledge generation in the industrialized world, especially in the hard sciences, the distances between the first and third worlds on this dimension are growing and will continue to grow. This will make the industrialized nations even more desirable targets for espionage activities. As a result, policymakers will have to develop a far more astute sensitivity toward clandestine efforts to extract information relevant to chemical, biological, and nuclear weapons.

Chemicals vs. Biotechnology

The production of chemical weapons is usually done through well-established, standard technologies and processes. Biotechnology—that is, the manipulation of the genetic structure of living organisms—is normally conceived as a modern high technology that represents state-of-the-art scientific knowledge. Looking at the chemical weapons activities of Libya and Iraq, one can see the enormous politically destabilizing effects of their undertakings. The Gulf War certainly demonstrated this point convincingly. In striving to acquire a chemical weapons posture, they achieved success despite the enormous problems of scale they confronted. For example, chemical weapons factories are large facilities that house large quantities of chemicals and huge pieces of manufacturing equipment. Their output, the weapons themselves, takes up substantial space. The very size of this undertaking makes it vulnerable to satellite and human intelligence. Quite simply, it is very difficult to hide a chemical weapons factory.

However, biotechnology can be used to create a new form of "poor man's atomic bomb" that is not subject to the size vulnerabilities of chemical processing. Production of biological weapons can take place in small laboratories that are easily disguised and not vulnerable to satellite reconnaissance. The biological weapons themselves are small, easily stored and hidden substances that are virtually impossible to detect.[15] Knowledge about biotechnology is transferred from first world to third world scientists through instructional programs and is therefore difficult if not also impossible to monitor or prevent.

Should the avenues to chemical weaponry be blocked, it would not be unreasonable for some nations to turn to the biological discipline for weapons of mass destruction and conceivably terrorism. This would be a long and difficult road because the technology is most sophisticated. But it would be incorrect to argue that such a quest will not happen because of this problem. After all, Libya has

worked for over ten years to develop a chemical weapons factory—
an effort that symbolizes the determination of a political system
intent on developing an effective military posture. The same can be
said for Iraq.

Conclusions

Retention of chemical weapons arsenals by major powers will
certainly not encourage aspiring chemical weapons nations to halt
their quests for such arsenals. Nor is it likely that attempts to selec-
tively apply arms control to individual nations such as Libya will
result in success. As long as major industrialized nations possess
weapons of mass destruction, the rationale for convincing the unarmed not to acquire such weapons will be weak and ineffective.
When ideological considerations are introduced into this equation,
the logic becomes even less convincing.

Furthermore, Iraq's threat to use chemical weapons against
Israel and perhaps other actors in the Middle East demonstrated the
military viability of such weapons. The acquisition of protective
gear by forces in the Gulf War further demonstrated that chemical
weapons have become an element in modern military calculations.
None of this augurs well for a total ban on the possession and/or
use of chemical weapons, at least at the present moment in history.
Of course, some may argue that events in the Middle East demonstrate conclusively that this is the precise moment to consummate a
ban on chemical weapons. Nevertheless, political and military leaders frequently think in practical terms, and unfortunately it is unrealistic to expect such leaders to voluntarily renounce the use of a
weapon a nation is threatening to use against them.

Moreover, the present-day proliferation of chemical weapons
undercuts international efforts to limit or halt research on chemical
weapons and associated vaccines. Indeed, the current spread has
become an incentive to accelerate research on vaccines to be used
for either on troops in the field or on general populations. Leaders
do not want to be accused of sending their military forces into
combat without the vaccines and antidotes necessary should chemical weapons be used against them.

This study of Libyan and international activities can be viewed
as a completed case focusing on the process of clandestinely acquiring a chemical weapons production facility. Obviously, acquisition

is the first and most important step in a long series of efforts to become a chemical weapons power. It is now up to Libya to use Rabta for the manufacture of a chemical weapons arsenal, to develop military doctrines, and to train personnel to use such weapons. These are the successive tasks that must be accomplished if Libya desires to become a credible chemical weapons power.

The United States did not intervene militarily as Libya moved to erect the factory at Rabta. Yet this does not preclude some type of military response, by the United States or another nation, as Libya builds its arsenal. Certainly, the Gulf War has demonstrated the dangers of military overexpansion. However, as indicated previously, the costs of intervention are probably higher now because Libya is likely to struggle with even more determination to maintain a functioning facility.

J. David Singer was surely correct when he argued that "we in academe need to do a better job of helping governments and their leaders get a handle on the causes of war," and that we need to challenge what is really a "good deal of foreign-policy folklore."[16] Singer rightly advocates better scientific training for future foreign policy officials and a greater attentiveness to the results of rigorous research, yet there are additional problems.

At many colleges and universities, courses on conflict and aggression focus much too heavily, and often exclusively, on issues related to nuclear weapons. The community of international relations scholars has developed a good base of knowledge regarding a broad range of concerns related to nuclear conflict, and this knowledge is clearly important in the present era. But we have been curricularly inattentive not only to the rigorous treatment of science and technology in international affairs but to the critical matters of chemical and biological weapons. Chemical and biological weapons are not only weapons of mass destruction that can be utilized openly by governments. They are also weapons that could be used covertly by terrorists. Among some leaders, new properties of these weapons are changing perceptions of their potential usefulness. The general thrust of scientific knowledge is that the shortcomings of chemical and biological weapons are being overcome, making them much more reliable and useful instruments of conflict.

The difficulty here is that it will be many years before our international relations courses routinely include significant components of materials about chemical and biological weapons. Aversion to knowledge from the natural sciences and a desire by many students and professors to think and work at the very highest levels of generalization has resulted in a situation in which the products of our efforts, our students, remain unprepared for the future world of political decision making. Let us hope that this problem can be overcome so that we will be spared an ill-informed adventure down the road.

NOTES

REFERENCES

INDEX

NOTES

1. Introduction

1. Adams 1990; Robinson 1985; Spiers 1989.
2. Although it could be argued that the 1925 Geneva Protocol is an unconditional prohibition, many nations have attached reservations to their accession. Not a few nations have reserved the right to retaliate with chemical weapons against nations that initiate a chemical attack on them.
3. United Nations General Assembly, *Report of the Secretary General on Chemical and Bacteriological (Biological) Weapons and the Effects of Their Possible Use*, A/7575 (New York: United Nations, 1 July 1969), 6; quoted in Spiers 1989, 1.
4. Adams 1990, 5.
5. *Military Chemistry and Chemical Agents*, Department of the Army Technical Manual TM3–215 and the Department of the Air Force Manual AFM255-7, August 1956, 6–7; quoted from Spiers 1989, 1–2.
6. On this point, for example, see Sims 1988; Spiers 1989; Adams 1990; and Geissler 1990.
7. Pirages 1989, 20. See also Pirages 1978; Wiegele 1991. Also useful is the Autumn 1990 special issue of *Science, Technology, and Human Values*, which is devoted to "Technology and the Arms Race."
8. Pirages 1989, 21.
9. Keller 1990.
10. Yehezkel Dror 1980, xiii. This book was originally published in 1971. All quotations are from the reprinted edition. Another book that deals with craziness, but in a different manner, is Kupperman and Kamen 1989.
11. Dror 1980, 63.
12. For a more detailed discussion of this source see Donald and Gerner 1989/90.
13. For a discussion of nuances in the various definitions of crisis see Allison 1971; Brecher 1978; Hermann 1969, 1972;

169

Holsti 1972; Lebow 1981; Oneal 1982; Paige 1968; Snyder and Diesing 1977; and Wiegele et al. 1985.

2. The Development of a Critical International Situation

1. *Chemical and Engineering News*, 24 February 1986, 6.
2. Ember 1986, 8.
3. An exception to this observation is the consistent attention of the *Chemical Weapons Convention Bulletin* published by the Federation of American Scientists.
4. However, public perceptions can change quickly. The Iraqi invasion of Kuwait and the subsequent consideration of Iraq's military capabilities brought the dangers of chemical weapons into sharp public focus.
5. Libyan Sanctions, "President Reagan's Opening Statement, January 7, 1986," *Department of State Bulletin*, March 1986, 36.
6. U.S. Department of State, "Libya under Qadhafi: A Pattern of Aggression," Special Report No. 138, January 1986.
7. "Prohibiting Trade and Certain Transactions Involving Libya," text of Executive Order 12543, 7 January 1986, *Department of State Bulletin*, March 1986, 37–38.
8. "Blocking Libyan Government Property in the United States or Held by U.S. Persons," text of Executive Order 12544, 8 January 1986, *Department of State Bulletin*, March 1986, 38.
9. Libyan Sanctions, "President Reagan's Opening Statement, January 7, 1986," *Department of State Bulletin*, March 1986, 36.
10. *New York Times*, 15 April 1986, 1, 10–11. France denied permission to the United States to overfly its territory.
11. "Export Controls Imposed on Chemical Weapons Substances," *Department of State Bulletin*, October 1987, 49.
12. "White House Statement," *Department of State Bulletin*, October 1986, 37. There was, however, controversy surrounding this statement. See Ember, 1986b, 1987.
13. European Communities, AFP, *Foreign Broadcast Information Service Reports* (=*FBIS Reports*), WEU-86-077, 22 April 1986, B1.

14. European Communities, "EC Ministers Begin Talks on Libya," Paris AFP, *FBIS Reports*, WEU-86-078, 23 April 1986, B1.
15. "EC Arab Envoys Issue Communique on 'Aggression,'" Rome ANSA, *FBIS Reports*, WEU-86-077, 22 April 1986, B2.
16. "Japanese Official Stresses Support for Libya," Tripoli Domestic News Service, *FBIS Reports*, MEA-86-131, 9 July 1986, Q2.
17. Text of Protocol, *League of Nations Treaty Series*, 1929, 94.
18. The text of this convention is in *Arms Control and Disarmament Agreements* (Washington, D.C.: U.S. Arms Control and Disarmament Agency, 1980), 124–31.
19. Adams 1990, 6. See also Geissler 1986, 5–6.
20. Adelman 1987, 21.
21. *New York Times*, 24 December 1987, A1, A6. To my knowledge, no other newspaper carried this story on this date.
22. White and Marsh 1989a.
23. White and Marsh 1989b. Although this article appeared after the U.S. charge, it contains detailed public information about the Libyan facility.

3. The Aftermath of the Charge, 1

1. "U.S. Ban on Medical Supplies Condemned," *FBIS Daily Reports*, NES-88-018, 28 January 1988, 15.
2. Often, the Libyans would not use the term *chemical weapons* in their responses to the United States For example, see "JANA Ridicules U.S. Report on 'Given Weapon,'" *FBIS Daily Reports*, NES-88-181, 19 September 1988, 10.
3. Bremer 1988, 67.
4. Bremer 1988, 67.
5. George Schultz, "Arms Control: Progress and Global Challenges," Current Policy No. 1080, June 1988.
6. *New York Times*, 18 September 1988, 8.
7. *New York Times*, 18 September 1988, 8; *Wall Street Journal*, 19 September 1988, 30.

8. "Government Says No Evidence Found," KYODO, *FBIS Daily Reports*, EAS-88-180, 16 September 1988, 1–2.
9. "Firm's Deny Helm's Charges on Libyan Plant," KYODO, *FBIS Daily Reports*, EAS-89-011, 18 January 1989, 1.
10. *Washington Post*, 15 September 1988.
11. *Washington Post*, 21 September 1988, A23.
12. *New York Times*, 27 September 1988, A1, A10.
13. *New York Times*, 28 September 1988, 4.
14. *New York Times*, 30 September 1988, 6.
15. "Conference on the Use of Chemical Weapons," *Department of State Bulletin*, January 1989, 16.
16. "Conference on the Use of Chemical Weapons," *Department of State Bulletin*, January 1986, 16. See also *Washington Post*, 30 September 1988, A21.
17. Murphy 1988.
18. About this same time, security procedures at U.S. weapons laboratories were brought into public view with the disclosure that Soviet intelligence agents had been admitted to the Los Alamos, Lawrence Livermore, and Sandia National Laboratories. Lax security procedures at these laboratories called into question U.S. desires for stricter foreign government control over the export of chemical processing equipment. See Norman 1988.
19. *Washington Post*, 26 October 1988, A2.
20. *Washington Post*, 19 December 1988, A1, A4.
21. *Washington Post*, 22 December 1988, A1, A7.
22. *Washington Post*, 23 December 1988, A5.
23. *New York Times*, 31 December 1988, 1; *Washington Post*, 31 December 1988, A11. There is some question as to whether *all* traces can actually be removed on short notice.
24. "U.S. Claims on Chemical Weapons Refuted," *FBIS Daily Reports*, NES-88-208, 27 October 1988, 10–11.
25. "Views Chemical Weapons," *FBIS Daily Reports*, NES-88-210, 31 October 1988, 14.
26. "Memorandum Submitted to UN on U.S. Allegations," *FBIS Daily Reports*, NES-88-220, 15 November 1988, 15.
27. "Al-Qadhdhafi Interviewed on Chemical Plant," *FBIS Daily Reports*, NES-88-248, 27 December 1988, 36–37.
28. "Pharmaceutical Plant Workers Stage Protest," *FBIS Daily Reports*, NES-88-001, 3 January 1989. Of course, these individuals could have been ordered to protest, since their

presence would deter an aerial attack by guaranteeing numerous civilian deaths.

4. The Aftermath of the Charge, 2

1. *"Stern* Says German-Built Missiles Sold to Libya," *FBIS Daily Reports*, WEU-86-245, 22 December 1986, J1.
2. "Government Spokesman Comments," *FBIS Daily Reports*, WEU-86-245, 22 December 1986, J1.
3. "Firm Suspected of Supplying Aircraft to Libya," *FBIS Daily Reports*, WEU-86-247, 24 December 1986, J1.
4. *New York Times*, 18 January 1989, 4.
5. "Government to Adhere to Arms Exports Policy," *FBIS Daily Reports*, WEU-87-089, 8 May 1987, J8.
6. "Nuclear Firms Break International Trade Bans," *FBIS Daily Reports*, WEU-88-030, 16 February 1988, 12.
7. Charles 1989.
8. *New York Times*, 16 February 1989, 3.
9. Perle 1989. One informal estimate is that the FRG employed only 3.5 persons to review 200,000 export license applications per year.
10. "Ambassador-Level Relations with Libya Restored," *FBIS Daily Reports*, WEU-88-185, 23 September 1988, 4.
11. *New York Times*, 1 January 1989, 1.
12. *New York Times*, 1 January 1989, 1.
13. "Libyan Chemical Weapons Plant, Statement, January 1, 1989," *Department of State Bulletin*, March 1989, 71.
14. *New York Times*, 1 January 1989, 1, 4. This report also indicated that a French-based firm, De Dietrich, had sold glass-lined cauldrons to Libya, but the company denied any knowledge that they would be used for chemical weapons.
15. *New York Times*, 1 January 1989, 1.
16. *New Tork Times*, 1 January 1989, 4. Later Hippenstiel-Imhausen said that "the Libyans are much too stupid to run a plant like this. All Arabs are lazy and they call in foreign slaves to do the work."
17. *New York Times*, 3 January 1989, 6.
18. *New York Times*, 5 January 1989, 4.
19. *New York Times*, 5 January 1989, 4.

20. *New York Times*, 5 January 1989, 4.
21. "Kohl Discusses 'Media Campaign' against Bonn," *FBIS Daily Reports*, WEU-89-005, 9 January 1989, 22.
22. "CDU-CSU Ruehe on Libya, U.S. Talks, NATO," *FBIS Daily Reports*, WEU-89-003, 5 January 1989, 7.
23. "Genscher Reiterates Support for CW Ban," *FBIS Daily Reports*, WEU-89-004, 6 January 1989.
24. *New York Times*, 6 January 1989, 5.
25. *New York Times*, 6 January 1989, 5.
26. "Companies Help Build Libyan Chemical Factory," *FBIS Daily Reports*, WEU-88-249, 28 December 1988, 6.
27. "German Subsidiary Firms Involved in Libyan Plant," *FBIS Daily Reports*, WEU-89-003, 5 January 1989, 8.
28. "German Subsidiary Firms Involved in Libyan Plant," *FBIS Daily Reports*, WEU-89-003, 5 January 1989, 8.
29. *New York Times*, 6 January 1989, 5.
30. "Ministry Says No Proof of Illegal CW Exports," *FBIS Daily Reports*, WEU-89-005, 9 January 1989, 22.
31. "Genscher Strongly Rejects U.S. Allegations," *FBIS Daily Reports*, WEU-89-005, 9 January 1989, 22.
32. "Kohl Promises 'Severity' on Foreign Projects," *FBIS Daily Reports*, WEU-89-005, 9 January 1989, 23.
33. *New York Times*, 6 January 1989, 5.
34. *New York Times*, 7 January 1989, 4.
35. *New York Times*, 8 January 1989, 1.
36. *New York Times*, 7 January 1989, 4.
37. "Papers View on U.S. Stands," *FBIS Daily Reports*, WEU-89-006, 10 January 1989, 12.
38. "Bonn to Approve Stricter Laws," *FBIS Daily Reports*, WEU-89-006, 10 January 1989, 13.
39. "Press Views CW Conference," *FBIS Daily Reports*, WEU-89-006, 10 January 1989, 14.
40. "Press Views CW Conference," *FBIS Daily Reports*, WEU-89-006, 10 January 1989, 14.
41. "Bonn to Approve Stricter Trade Laws," *FBIS Daily Reports*, WEU-89-006, 10 January 1989, 13.
42. An Austrian press report suggested that two Thai engineers who were employed at the Rabta facility had supplied information to U.S. intelligence services. An additional source might have been Werner Wascher, an Austrian engineer working in Libya. These rumors were unverified, however. See *Vienna Profil*, 23 January 1989, 46.

43. *New York Times*, 4 January 1989, 1.
44. *New York Times*, 5 January 1989, 4.
45. *New York Times*, 6 January 1989, 1.
46. *New York Times*, 7 January 1989, 1.
47. *New York Times*, 6 January 1989, 5.
48. *New York Times*, 7 January 1989, 4. Attempts were also made to link Libya and the United States through private channels of communication. The United States rebuffed all such attempts, probably because of the politically damaging Iran-Contra experience.
49. *New York Times*, 7 January 1989, 1.
50. *New York Times*, 31 January 1989, 1.
51. *New York Times*, 23 March 1989, 4.
52. *New York Times*, 1 July 1989, 1.
53. *New York Times*, 6 July 1989, 5.
54. *New York Times*, 10 July 1989, 1.
55. *New York Times*, 29 June 1989, 3. See also *New York Times*, 27 June 1989, 1; 30 June 1989, 5.
56. "Pan-Arab Congresses Discuss U.S. 'Threats,'" *FBIS Daily Reports*, NES-89-002, 4 January 1989, 9.
57. "Masses March to Al-Rabitak Chemical Plant," *FBIS Daily Reports*, NES-89-004, 6 January 1989, 16.
58. "State of Alert over Fears of Israeli Attack," *FBIS Daily Reports*, NES-89-004, 6 January 1989, 17.
59. "Al-Qadhdhafi Urges Direct Talks with U.S.," *FBIS Daily Reports*, NES-89-005, 9 January 1989, 19.
60. "Foreign Reporters Visit Al-Rabitah Factory," *FBIS Daily Reports*, NES-89-005, 9 January 1989, 23.
61. "JANA Clarifies Details on Al-Rabitah," *FBIS Daily Reports*, NES-89-006, 10 January 1989, 11.
62. "Thai Workers Said Spotted at Al-Rabitak Factory," *FBIS Daily Reports*, NES-89-006, 10 January 1989, 12–13.
63. "Thai Workers Said Spotted at Al-Rabitak Factory," *FBIS Daily Reports*, NES-89-006, 10 January 1989, 13.
64. "Tight Security Reported at Al-Rabitah Plant," *FBIS Daily Reports*, NES-89-008, 12 January 1989, 7.
65. "Construction Chief on Al-Rabitah Complex," *FBIS Daily Reports*, NES-89-012, 19 January 1989, 10.
66. "Lambsdorff Says U.S. Computer in Chemical Plant," *FBIS Daily Reports*, NES-89-023, 6 February 1989, 13.
67. "Premier Condemns U.S. 'Threats' against Libya," *FBIS Daily Reports*, NES-89-001, 3 January 1989, 23.

68. "Syrian Minister of Health Visits Al-Rabitah Factory," *FBIS Daily Reports*, NES-89-003, 5 January 1989, 14.
69. "Comments on Factory Visit," *FBIS Daily Reports*, NES-89-003, 5 January 1989, 15.
70. "Al-Qadhdhafi Meets Syrian Health Minister," *FBIS Daily Reports*, NES-89-002, 4 January 1989, 10.
71. "Reports of Joint Proposal with Libya Denied," *FBIS Daily Reports*, NES-89-005, 9 January 1989, 28.
72. "Paper Criticizes U.S. Accusations over Plant," *FBIS Daily Reports*, NES-89-005, 9 January 1989, 27.
73. "Al-Ray Columnist Urges Solidarity with Libya," *FBIS Daily Reports*, NES-89-002, 4 January 1989, 31.
74. "Al-Talhi Cited on Ties with U.S.," *FBIS Daily Reports* NES-89-003, 5 January 1989, 15.
75. "Delegate Addresses U.N. Security Council," *FBIS Daily Reports*, NES-89-005, 9 January 1989, 23.
76. "Libyan Envoy on U.S. Moves over Chemical Plant," *FBIS Daily Reports*, NES-89-005, 9 January 1989, 12.
77. "Paper Praises Call for U.S. 'Restraint,'" *FBIS Daily Reports*, NES-89-006, 10 January 1989, 7.
78. "Envoy Reportedly Pays 'Secret Visit' to U.S.," *FBIS Daily Reports*, NES-89-122, 27 June 1989, 7.
79. "Al Qadhdhafi Comments on Relations with U.S.," *FBIS Daily Reports*, NES-89-111, 12 June 1989, 8.
80. "Al Qadhdhafi Cited on Relations with U.S.," *FBIS Daily Reports*, NES-89-116, 19 June 1989, 13.
81. "Al Qadhdhafi Comments on Relations with U.S.," *FBIS Daily Reports*, NES-89-111, 12 June 1989, 8.

5. The Paris Chemical Weapons Conference

1. Ember 1989a.
2. Ember 1989b. The United States did little to protest developments in Egypt, possibly because of the close relationship between Washington and Cairo. However, protests about the Libyans had to have been heard in Egypt.
3. *New York Times*, 7 January 1989, 1, 5.
4. *New York Times*, 7 January 1989, 5.
5. Jones 1989.
6. *Update from State*, March–April 1989, 2.
7. The following quotes from Mr. Shultz' address are taken

from "Secretary's Address, January 7, 1989," *Department of State Bulletin*, March 1989, 5–6.

8. Text of news conference, 8 January 1989, *Department of State Bulletin*, March 1989, 9.

9. Text of news conference, 8 January 1989, *Department of State Bulletin*, March 1989, 7.

10. Text of news conference, 8 January 1989, *Department of State Bulletin*, March 1989, 8.

11. Text of news conference, 8 January 1989, *Department of State Bulletin*, March 1989, 7.

12. *New York Times*, 10 January 1989, 6.

13. *New York Times*, 10 January 1989, 6

14. "Al-Majid Interviewed on Chemical Weapons, Peace," *FBIS Daily Reports*, NES-89-009, 13 January 1989, 17.

15. "Discusses Chemical Weapons," *FBIS Daily Reports*, NES-89-006, 10 January 1989, 26.

16. "Final Declaration, January 11, 1989," *Department of State Bulletin*, March 1989, 9.

17. There was also no mention of the use of chemical weapons in the Iran-Iraq war, a case thoroughly documented and photographed for the world community.

18. The Soviet Union announced at the conference that it would begin destroying some of its chemical weapons stocks; see *New York Times*, 9 January 1989, 1; 19 January 1989, 5. The United States had been routinely destroying old stocks for almost a decade; see *New York Times*, 2 September 1989, 8. U.S. diplomats pointed out that the Soviets did not have facilities to destroy their chemical weapons.

19. *New York Times*, 13 January 1989, 4.

20. *New York Times*, 10 March 1989, 1.

21. *New York Times*, 26 March 1989, 8.

22. *New York Times*, 11 March 1989, 5.

23. *New York Times*, 18 July 1989, 1. However, some have charged that the Soviet's were willing to strike a bargain because they perceived that the United States was making considerable progress in the modernization of its chemical arsenal. Presumably, a chemical weapons ban would halt that progress. See Gaffney 1989.

24. *New York Times*, 26 March 1989, 1.

25. *New York Times*, 26 March 1989, 1.

26. *New York Times*, 26 March 1989, 1.

27. *New York Times*, 5 May 1989, 3.

28. Robinson 1989. See also *Los Angeles Times*, 20 September 1989, part 1, p. 1; 21 September 1989, part 1, p. 5; *New York Times*, 18 September 1989, 3.
29. "GICCW—Chemical Industry Supports Weapons Ban," text of statement in *Chemical Weapons Conference*, Embassy of Australia (Washington, D.C., n.d.), 10.
30. "GICCW—Chemical Industry Supports Weapons Ban," text of statement in *Chemical Weapons Conference*, Embassy of Australia (Washington, D.C., n.d.), 10.
31. *New York Times*, 2 March 1989, 4.

6. The Explosion of Events in West Germany

1. *Newsweek*, 10 January 1989, 42.
2. *Newsweek*, 10 January 1989, 42. See also "That German Innocence," *The Economist*, 21 January 1989, 45–46.
3. Birnbaum 1989, 185.
4. "Economic Cooperation and Alliance—Armaments Cooperation—NATO Science Programme," text of statement of 9–10 June 1983, *NATO Final Communiques 1981–1985* (Brussels: NATO Information Service, n.d.), 89.
5. Baer-Kaupert 1985, 18.
6. Brzoska 1989.
7. "Schultz' Note to Kohl," *FBIS Daily Reports*, WEU-89-007, 11 January 1989, 8.
8. For this and the following press responses see "Press Views Stricter Controls," *FBIS Daily Reports*, WEU-89-007, 11 January 1989, 8–9.
9. "Exports to Libya," *FBIS Daily Reports*, WEU-89-007, 11 January 1989, 9.
10. "Expert Rejects Accusations," *FBIS Daily Reports*, WEU-89-008, 12 January 1989, 4.
11. "Lambsdorff on U.S. Relations," *FBIS Daily Reports*, WEU-89-008, 12 January 1989, 5.
12. "Genscher Urges Crackdown," *FBIS Daily Reports*, WEU-89-008, 12 January 1989, 5.
13. "Kohl on EC, U.S. Friendship, Libyan Plant," *FBIS Daily Reports*, WEU-89-008, 12 January 1989, 9.
14. For the DPA report see "Reinforced Inquiry Launched," *FBIS Daily Reports*, WEU-89-008, 12 January 1989, 5.
15. "Ost on Libyan CW Production," *FBIS Daily Reports*, WEU-89-009, 13 January 1989, 7.

16. "Kohl Speaks on Investigations" *FBIS Daily Reports*, WEU-89-009, 13 January 1989, 7.
17. "Libyan Denies FRG Involvement," *FBIS Daily Reports*, WEU-89-009, 13 January 1989, 8.
18. "Daily Analyzes U.S. Relations, *FBIS Daily Reports*, WEU-89-009, 13 January 1989, 9.
19. "Companies Confirm Deliveries," *FBIS Daily Reports*, WEU-89-009, 13 January 1989, 8. Graphics for these and other arrangements are provided later in Chapter 6.
20. An ongoing U.S. Customs Service investigation has revealed that Ihsan Barbouti and his son Haidar operated an oil industry related business in Houston, Texas. The Barbouti's apparently have been successful because they purchased "tens of millions of dollars worth of commercial property" in the area. They are suspected of illegally exporting communications systems for weapons and perhaps even delivering pulse neutron generators to Libya. These generators are used in the oil industry but can be adapted, in combination with other devices, to detonate nuclear weapons. As a result of a customs investigation, $3.8 million of the Barboutis' funds were seized on the suspicion that they had illegally transferred aircraft parts from the United States to Libya. See Jerry Urban, "Local Firm May Be Tied to Libya N-Device Sale," *Houston Chronicle*, 24 December 1990, 1A. Whether the Barbouti enterprise in Houston was involved in Libya's chemical weapons activities is unclear.
21. "Press on Involvement," *FBIS Daily Reports*, WEU-89-009, 13 January 1989, 11.
22. "Belgian Arrested for Involvement," *FBIS Daily Reports*, WEU-89-009, 13 January 1989, 11.
23. "Firm Investigated on Exports," *FBIS Daily Reports*, WEU-89-010, 17 January 1989, 15.
24. "BND Informed Government," *FBIS Daily Reports*, WEU-89-010, 17 January 1989, 16.
25. "Imhausen-Chemie Offices, Staff Homes Searched," *FBIS Daily Reports*, WEU-89-015, 25 January 1989, 5.
26. "Salzgitter Group Involved" and "Company Cited on Libyan Plans," *FBIS Daily Reports*, WEU-89-010, 17 January 1989, 16–17.
27. "Two More Firms Involved," *FBIS Daily Reports*, WEU-89-010, 17 January 1989, 17. In a related development, specifics became known about West German involvement in

179

Notes to Pages 78–82

refitting Libyan transport planes into refueling tankers. Intec Technical Trade and Logistics Society Limited in Vaterstetten near Munich was supervising ten German aircraft engineers in this work. Other German, Italian, Swiss, and Liechtenstein firms were also involved. See "Companies Help Libyan Air Force," *FBIS Daily Reports*, WEU-89-010, 17 January 1989, 17.

28. "Further on Possible Missile Parts Export to Libya," *FBIS Daily Reports*, WEU-89-020, 1 February 1989, 4.
29. "Customs Detains Chemical Shipment to Libya," *FBIS Daily Reports*, WEU-89-022, 3 February 1989, 10.
30. "Company Suspends Al-Rabitah Deliveries," *FBIS Daily Reports*, WEU-89-022, 3 February 1989, 11.
31. "Manager Interviewed on Deception of Company," *FBIS Daily Reports*, NES-89-024, 7 February 1989, 15.
32. "Ost on U.S. CW Reports," *FBIS Daily Reports*, WEU-89-010, 17 January 1989, 14.
33. "Ost on U.S. CW Reports," *FBIS Daily Reports*, WEU-89-010, 17 January 1989, 15.
34. "BND Investigated Firms' Role," *FBIS Daily Reports*, WEU-89-010, 17 January 1989, 15.
35. "Genscher Proposes Talks with U.S., EC, on Libya CW," *FBIS Daily Reports*, WEU-89-018, 30 January 1989, 7.
36. "Government Wants World CW Ban," *FBIS Daily Reports*, WEU-89-023, 6 February 1989, 8.
37. *New York Times*, 19 January 1989, 5.
38. *New York Times*, 19 January 1989, 5.
39. *New York Times*, 19 January 1989, 5.
40. I refer to this document as the Report. As a measure of how seriously the government viewed the contents of a report to its own parliament, this eighty-four-page document was translated into English immediately. The Report is available from the German Information Center in New York City. Stories related to the release of the Report can be found in the *New York Times* (16 February 1989, 3) and *Die Welt* (15 February 1989, 1). Most other German newspapers carried front page stories on 16 February. For Minister of the Chancellery Wolfgang Schaeuble's introduction of the Report to the Bundestag see *FBIS Daily Reports*, WEU-89-032, 17 February 1989, 6–10.
41. Helmut Kohl took office as chancellor on 4 October 1982

180

and therefore was in power during the time when most of the events in this chapter took place.

42. Report, 9–45.
43. Report, 11–41.
44. After the Kohl government issued its Report, additional information about the first diplomatic communication became known. On 17 January 1989, Detlef Lingemann, a diplomat posted at the West German embassy in Moscow in 1985, returned to Bonn and visited the Foreign Ministry to express his outrage at the public confusion the government had allowed to develop regarding the Rabta affair. He pointed out that Bonn's ambassador to Moscow at that time, Joerg Kastel, had fully and explicitly informed the Foreign Ministry about Imhausen-Chemie and its activities regarding the construction of a chemical weapons factory in Libya. This information had been passed on to the chancellory, but no action was taken. See *Der Spiegel*, 11 June 1990, 84–86; reprinted in FBIS *Daily Reports*, WEU-90-114, 13 June 1990, 11–13.
45. Report, 56.
46. Report, 65.
47. "Statement by Chancellery Minister Wolfgang Schauble to the German Bundestag in Bonn, February 17," *Statement and Speeches*, New York: German Information Center, 20 February 1989. The following quotes are from pp. 2–4.
48. Report, 53.
49. Report, 53.
50. Barbouti died in July 1990.

7. Satisfaction and Disenchantment

1. "Aid for Libya in Chemical Weapons Production," *FBIS Daily Reports*, WEU-90-024, 5 February 1990, 15.
2. *New York Times*, 7 March 1990, A1.
3. *New York Times*, 7 March 1990, A5.
4. *Chicago Tribune*, 8 March 1990, sec. 1, p. 3.
5. *New York Times*, 8 March 1990, A6.
6. *New York Times*, 15 March 1990, A1.
7. *Chicago Tribune*, 18 March 1990, sec. 1, p. 3.
8. *Chicago Tribune*, 20 March 1990, sec. 1, p. 12.

9. *Chicago Tribune*, 20 March 1990, sec.1, p. 12.
10. *Newsweek*, 26 March 1990, 27.
11. *Chicago Tribune*, 31 March 1990, sec. 1, p. 4.
12. *New York Times*, 19 June 1990, A4.
13. *New York Times*, 19 June 1990, A4.
14. *New York Times*, 29 March 1990, A5.
15. *New York Times*, 7 June 1990, A8. Czechoslovak President Vaclav Havel revealed in the spring of 1990 that the former communist government in Prague had shipped 1000 tons of the extremely lethal explosive Semtex to Libya. See *New York Times, 25 March 1990, A5.*
16. *New York Times*, 19 June 1990, A4.
17. *New York Times, 11 May 1989.*
18. *New York Times*, 23 March 1990, A5.
19. *New York Times*, 14 June 1990, A7.
20. *Der Spiegel*, 11 June 1990, 84–86; reprinted in *FBIS Daily Reports*, WEU-90-114, 13 June 1990, 12.
21. *New York Times*, 28 June 1990, A4. It should also be noted that the West German Chemical Industry Association expelled the Imhausen-Chemie firm.
22. Lief and Wise 1990, 41. See also Milhollin and Weeks, "Poison Gas Laws: Still Leaking," *New York Times*, 25 March 1990, E19. Moreover, according to West German television reports, Rose GmbH of Stuttgart, Abacus of Ulm, and a Dutch firm were involved in the Sabha construction. Plans supplied for the Rabta facility by Imhausen-Chemie were being used. See "Construction of Second Libyan Gas Plant Reported," *FBIS Reports*, WEU-90-124, 27 June 1990, 14.
23. "Tightening of German Export Controls," press release of the embassy of the Federal Republic of Germany (Washington, D.C., 6 July 1990).
24. "Trade in Nuclear, Chemical, Biological Weapons Banned," *FBIS Daily Reports*, WEU-90-106, 1 June 1990, 11.
25. In the spring of 1991, the upper house of Germany's parliament blocked the approval of revised export controls that would help prevent the manufacture of chemical weapons. The bill was rejected on civil libertarian grounds with the argument that a secret enforcement agency would have to be created. *New York Times*, 23 April 1991, A1.
26. *New York Times*, 8 June 1990, A4.

8. An Operational Assessment of the Rabta Episode

1. For an amplification of this point see Matousek 1990, 30–37.
2. U.S. Department of Commerce, Bureau of Export Administration, *1990 Annual Foreign Policy Report to the Congress* (Washington, D.C., February 1990). See especially pp. 25–29, dealing with Libya, and pp. 31–41, which discuss chemical weapons precursors.
3. See Inman and Burton 1990; Carver 1990.
4. "How Qaddaffi Built His Deadly Chemical Plant," *Business Week*, 23 January 1989, 50–51. However, greed has its costs. See the report of the murdered physicist who was allegedly developing a "supercannon" for Iraq; *New York Times*, 22 April 1990, 1.

9. Deception, Lies, and Secrecy in an Act of Proliferation

1. Machiavelli 1979, 133.
2. Machiavelli 1979, 134.
3. Machiavelli 1979, 135.
4. Machiavelli 1979, 136.
5. Mitchell 1986, 18–19.
6. Russow 1986, 41.
7. Zuckerman, DePaulo, and Rosenthal 1981; cited in Bond and Robinson 1988, 295.
8. Bond and Robinson 1988, 296.
9. Bond and Robinson 1988, 301–3.
10. Bok 1978, 13.
11. Bok 1978, 15.
12. Bok 1978, 19.
13. Bok 1978, 136, 138.
14. Bok 1978, 139.
15. Brooker 1988, 45.
16. Bok 1982, 5–6.
17. Bok 1978, 166–69.
18. Bok 1982, 192.
19. Sexton 1986, 350.
20. Sexton 1986, 352.
21. Cranberg 1987, 15–16.

22. Clinard and Yeager 1980, 63.
23. Jackall 1988, 5–6.
24. Clinard and Yeager 1980, 68.
25. This section on attitudes toward government regulation is based on the information presented in Clinard and Yeager 1980, 68–73.
26. Janis 1983.
27. Clinard and Yeager 1980, 64.
28. Jackall 1988, 6.
29. Jackall 1988, 6.
30. Bok 1982, 176.
31. Thorson 1989, 2–3.
32. The destruction of chemical weapons is so dangerous that the U.S. *planned* destruction of such weapons at Johnson Atoll has generated considerable protests and other vexing problems. This project is already over three years behind schedule. See Lord 1990.
33. Livingstone 1988, 66.
34. Bok 1982, 99.

10. Some Policy-making Considerations

1. Ross 1988.
2. Israel's bombing of an Iraqi nuclear reactor in 1981, well before it became fully operational, certainly caused considerable discussion and criticism. But it was nothing compared to the prolonged argument between the United States and West Germany over Libya.
3. These observations assume that the present political situation will remain largely as it is. If a chemical weapons convention is approved by the international community, that convention will no doubt have an enforcement mechanism to prevent proliferation.
4. Greenwood 1990.
5. Greenwood 1990, 415–17.
6. On 25 August 1990 the *Washington Post* reported that Libya had sent chemical warfare equipment to Iraq after the trade embargo was imposed; cited in U.S. Senate Committee on Governmental Affairs, *Proliferation Watch*, vol. 1, no. 2, August 1990, 4.
7. *New York Times*, 30 October 1990, A6.

8. *New York Times*, 8 June 1991, 17.
9. *New York Times*, 15 December 1990, 5.
10. "Chemical and Biological Warfare Elimination Act," H.R. 3033, 101st Congress, 1st sess., 8 November 1989.
11. Nevertheless, serious questions about German export policies remain. Just days before the outbreak of the Gulf War, the United States presented Bonn with a list of 19 German companies suspected of doing business with Iraq in contravention of the UN sanctions; *International Herald Tribune*, 9 January 1991, 5. *Newsweek* (31 December 1990, 4) reported that German and Jordanian firms were major initiators of sanction-circumventing approaches to the Iraqis.
12. Spector 1990.
13. Spector 1990.
14. *New York Times*, 11 November 1990, A12.
15. For an elaborate discussion of this point see Wiegele 1991, chap. 5.
16. Singer 1990, A52.

REFERENCES

Adams, Valerie. 1990. *Chemical Warfare, Chemical Disarmament*. Bloomington, Ind. Indiana University Press.

Adelman, Kenneth L. 1987. "Arms Control and Openness." *Department of State Bulletin*, May, 19–22.

Allison, G. T. 1971. *Essence of Decision: Explaining the Cuban Missile Crisis*. Boston: Little, Brown.

Baer-Kaupert, Frederick-Wilhelm. 1985. "Peace and the Nuclear Paradox: The Dilemma in the Debate on European Security Policy." *NATO Review*, April, 18.

Birnbaum, Norman. 1989. "Unintelligence." *The Nation*, 13 February, 185.

Bok, Sissela. 1978. *Lying: Moral Choice in Public and Private Life*. New York: Pantheon Books.

———— 1982. *Secrets: On the Ethics of Concealment and Revelation*. New York: Pantheon Books.

Bond, Charles F., and Michael Robinson. 1988. "The Evolution of Deception." *Journal of Nonverbal Behavior* 12 (4): 295–303.

Brecher, M., ed. 1978. *Studies in Crisis Behavior*. New Brunswick, N.J.: Transaction Books.

Bremer, L. Paul III. 1988. "High Technology Terrorism." *Department of State Bulletin*, July, 65–67.

Brooker, Russell G. 1988. "Truth as a Variable: Teaching Political Strategy with Simulation Games." *Simulation and Games* 19 (1): 43–58.

Brzoska, Michael. 1989. "Behind German Export Scandals." *Bulletin of the Atomic Scientist*, July/August, 33.

Carver, George A. Jr. 1990. "Intelligence and Glasnost." *Foreign Affairs* 69 (3): 147–66.

Charles, Dan. 1989. "Exporting Trouble—West Germany's Free-wheeling Nuclear Business." *Bulletin of the Atomic Scientists* 45 (3): 22.

Clinard, Marshall, and Peter C. Yeager. 1980. *Corporate Crime*. New York: The Free Press.

Cranberg, Gilbert. 1987. "Dealing with Disinformation." *Columbia Journalism Review*, January/February, 15–16.

References

Donald, Christopher W., and Deborah J. Gerner. 1989/90. "Foreign Broadcast Information Service *Daily Report*," *Foreign Policy Analysis Notes* 16 (3): 16–19.

Dror, Yehezkel. [1971] 1980. *Crazy States: A Counterconventional Strategic Problem*. Reprint. Millwood, N.Y.: Kraus Reprint.

Ember, Lois R. 1986a. "Worldwide Spread of Chemical Arms Receiving Increased Attention." *Chemical and Engineering News*, 14 April, 8.

———— 1986b. "Battle Looms over Funding of Binary Chemical Weapons." *Chemical and Engineering News*, 11 August, 17–18.

———— 1987. "House Defeats Chemical Arms Amendment." *Chemical and Engineering News*, 1 June, 16.

———— 1989a. "U.S. Assails Libya on Eve of CW Meeting." *Chemical and Engineering News*, 9 January, 5–6.

———— 1989b. "U.S. Vexed by Spread of Chemical Weapons." *Chemical and Engineering News*, 27 March, 23–24.

Gaffney, Frank J. Jr. 1989. "Chemical Warfare: Beware Bush's Perilous Delusions." *Wall Street Journal*, 3 October, A22.

Geissler, Erhard. 1986. *Biological and Toxin Weapons Today*. New York: Oxford University Press.

———— 1990. *Strengthening the Biological Weapons Convention by Confidence Building Measures*. New York: Oxford University Press.

Greenwood, Ted. 1990. "Why Military Technology Is Difficult to Restrain." *Science, Technology, and Human Values* 15 (4): 412–29.

Hermann, C. F. 1969. *Crises in Foreign Policy: A Simulation Analysis*. Indianapolis: Bobbs-Merrill.

———— 1972. *International Crises: Insights from Behavioral Research*. New York: Free Press.

Holsti, O. R. 1972. *Crisis Escalation War*. Montreal: McGill-Queen's University Press.

Inman, B. R., and D. F. Burton, Jr. 1990. "Technology and Competitiveness." *Foreign Affairs* 69 (2): 116–34.

Jackall, Robert. 1988. *Moral Mazes: The World of Corporate Manager*. New York: Oxford University Press.

Janis, Irving. 1983. *Groupthink: Psychological Studies of Policy and Fiascoes*. 2d ed. Boston: Houghton Mifflin.

Jones, David T. 1989. "Eliminating Chemical Weapons: Less than Meets the Eye." *Washington Quarterly* 12 (2): 86.

References

Keller, Kenneth H. 1990. "Science and Technology." *Foreign Affairs* 69 (4): 123–38.

Kupperman, Robert, and Jeff Kamen. 1989. *Final Warning: Averting Disaster in the New Age of Terrorism.* New York: Doubleday.

Lebow, R. N. 1981. *Between Peace and War: The Nature of International Crisis.* Baltimore: Johns Hopkins University Press.

Lief, Louise, and Michael Wise. 1990. "Inside Bonn's Middle East Arms Bazaar." *U.S. News and World Report*, 28 May, 41.

Livingstone, Neil C. 1988. "The Raid on Libya and the Use of Force in Combating Terrorism." In *Beyond the Iran-Contra Crisis: The Shape of Anti-Terrorism Policy in the Post-Reagan Era*, ed. by Neil C. Livingstone and Terrell E. Arnold, 65–84. Lexington, Mass.: Lexington Books.

Lord, Mary. 1990. "Dateline." *U.S. News and World Report*, 12 November, 17.

Machiavelli, Niccolo. 1979. *The Prince.* Reprinted in *The Portable Machiavelli*, ed. by Peter Bondanella and Mark Musa, 133–36. New York: Penguin Books.

Matousek, Jiri. 1990. "The Release in War of Dangerous Forces from Chemical Facilities." In *Environmental Hazards of War: Releasing Dangerous Forces in an Industrialized World*, ed. by Arthur H. Westing, 30–37. Newbury Park, Calif.: Sage Publications.

Mitchell, Robert W. 1986. "A Framework for Discussing Deception." In *Deception: Perspectives on Human and Nonhuman Deceit*, ed. by Robert W. Mitchell and Nicholas S. Thompson, 3–39. Albany: State University of New York Press.

Murphy, Richard W. 1988. "Update on the Situation in the Middle East." *Department of State Bulletin*, December, 44.

Norman, Colin. 1988. "Security at Weapons Labs." *Science*, 21 October, 365.

Oneal, J. R. 1982. *Foreign Policy Making in Times of Crisis.* Columbus: Ohio State University Press.

Paige, G. D. 1968. *The Korean Decision: June 24–30, 1950.* New York: Free Press.

Perle, Richard. 1989. "Selling Security for Deutschmarks." *U.S. News and World Report*, 31 July, 36.

Pirages, Dennis. 1978. *The New Context for International Relations.* North Scituate, Mass.: Duxbury Press.

——— 1989. *Global Technopolitics: The International Politics of Technology and Resources*. Pacific Grove, Calif.: Brooks/Cole Publishing.

Robinson, Julian Perry. 1985. *Chemical Warfare Arms Control*. London and Philadelphia: Taylor and Francis.

——— 1989. "Review: The Canberra Conference." *Chemical Weapons Convention Bulletin*, November, 18.

Ross, Andrew L. 1988. "Arms Acquisition and National Security: The Irony of Military Strength." In *National Security in the Third World: The Management of Internal and External Threats*, ed. by Edward E. Azar and Chung-in Moon, 152-87. Hants, England: Edward Elgar Publishing.

Russow, Lily Marlene. 1986. "Deception: A Philosophical Perspective." In *Deception: Perspectives on Human and Nonhuman Deceit*, ed. by Robert W. Mitchell and Nicholas S. Thompson, 41–51. Albany: State University of New York Press.

Sexton, Donal J. 1986. "The Theory and Psychology of Military Deception." In *Deception: Perspectives on Human and Nonhuman Deceit*, ed. by Robert W. Mitchell and Nicholas S. Thompson, 349–56. Albany: State University of New York Press.

Sims, Nicholas A. 1988. *The Diplomacy of Biological Disarmament: Vicissitudes of a Treaty in Force, 1975–85*. New York: St. Martin's Press.

Singer, J. David. 1990. "Academe Needs to Do a Better Job of Helping Governments and Their Leaders Get a Handle on the Causes of War." *Chronicle of Higher Education*, 14 November, A52.

Snyder, G. H., and P. Diesing. 1977. *Conflict among Nations: Bargaining, Decision Making, and System Structure in International Crisis*. Princeton: Princeton University Press.

Spector, Leonard S. 1990. *Nuclear Exports: The Challenge of Control*. Washington, D.C.: Carnegie Endowment for International Peace.

Spiers, Edward M. 1989. *Chemical Weaponry: A Continuing Challenge*. New York: St. Martin's Press.

Thorson, Stuart J. 1989. "Introduction: Conceptual Issues." In *Intractable Conflicts and Their Transformation*, ed. by Louis Kriesberg, Terrell A. Northrup, and Stuart J. Thorson, 1–10. Syracuse: Syracuse University Press.

White, David, and Peter Marsh. 1989a. "Does He or Doesn't He:

References

Only Qaddafi's Engineers Know." *Financial Times* of London. Reprinted in *World Press Review* (March): 16–17.
——— 1989b. "The New Merchants of Death: Libya's West German Conneciton." *World Press Review* (March): 13–14.
Wiegele, Thomas C. 1991. *Biotechnology and International Relations: The Political Dimensions.* Gainesville: University of Florida Press.
Wiegele, Thomas C., G. Hilton, K. Oots, and S. Kisiel. 1985. *Leaders under Stress: A Psychophysiological Analysis of International Crises.* Durham, N.C.: Duke University Press.
Zuckerman, M., B. M. DePaulo, and R. Rosenthal. 1981. "Verbal and Nonverbal Communication of Deception." In vol. 14 of *Advances in Experimental Psychology*, ed. by L. Berkowitz, 301–3. New York: Academic Press.

Index

Abacus, 182n.22
Adams, Valerie, 2, 19
Adelman, Kenneth, 20
Afghanistan, 13
Al-Ahram, 54
Alcolac International, 47
Alfred Tewes GmbH, 78
Algeria, 47
Allgemeine Zeitung, 73
Andreotti, Giulio, 31
Arab states: and Paris Chemical Weapons
    Conference, 58, 64; support for
    Libya, 17, 51–52, 57. *See also spe-*
    cific countries
Arens, Moshe, 62
Argentina, 135, 162
Arms control, 12, 30
Association of Arab Pharmacists, 51–52
Atomic Energy Act (West Germany), 101
Australia, 36, 56, 67–68. *See also* Austra-
    lian Group
Australian Group, 67, 125
Austria, 86

Baer-Kaupert, Frederick-Wilhelm, 71–72
Baker, James, 79
Bangkok Post, 50–51
Barbouti, Haidar, 179n.20
Barbouti, Ihsan, 43, 51, 75, 76, 118; and
    deception, 147, 148, 150; disappear-
    ance of, 74, 114; U.S. commercial
    activities, 152, 179n.20
Belgium, 47, 96, 107
Biological and Toxin Weapons Conven-
    tion (BWC), 4, 18–19, 20, 160
Biological weapons, 2–4, 18, 19, 128
Biotechnology, 4, 19, 20, 128, 154–55,
    163–64
Bischoff KG Frankfurt, 76
BND (West Germany), 71, 74, 79, 82–91,
    93, 97, 102, 115
Bok, Sissela, 139, 140, 141, 145, 148
Bond, Charles F., 139
Brazil, 162
Bremer, L. Paul, III, 25

Brooker, Russell G., 140, 146
Burns, William F., 46
Burt, Richard, 71
Bush, George, 54, 68, 116; and export
    controls, 66, 160; 1990 summit, 66,
    119–20, Rabta attack threats, 31,
    115. *See also* United States; *U.S.*
    headings
BWC. *See* Biological and Toxin Weapons
    Convention

Canada, 25, 36
CD. *See* Conference on Disarmament
Central Intelligence Agency (CIA) (United
    States), 30, 117, 152
Chad, 21, 92, 97, 156; and Libya, 21, 92,
    97, 156
Chemco GmbH, 47
Chemical and Biological Warfare Elimina-
    tion Act (United States), 160–61
Chemical weapons: definitions of, 2–3,
    19; new biotechnology, 4, 19, 20,
    128, 154–55, 160, 163–64; public
    opinion, 12–13, 170n.4. *See also*
    specific topics
Chemical weapons conventions: Confer-
    ence on Disarmament negotiations,
    4; lack of, 2, 4, 54–55, 59, 132,
    169n.2; and new biotechnology, 4,
    19, 160; Paris Conference call for,
    63, 64; "rolling text," 4; West Ger-
    man support, 42, 80, 133. *See also*
    Geneva Protocol (1925)
Cheng, Daniel P. S., 105
China, 117, 162
CIA. *See* Central Intelligence Agency
    (United States)
Clinard, Marshall, 143
COCOM. *See* Coordinating Committee
    for Export Controls
Cologne Deutschlandfunk Network, 43
Conference on Disarmament (CD), 4, 13,
    58
Convention on The Prohibition of the De-
    velopment, Production, and Stockpil-

193

Index

ing of Bacteriological (Biological) and
Toxin Weapons and on Their De-
struction. *See* Biological and Toxin
Weapons Convention

Coordinating Committee for Export Controls (COCOM), 27

Corporate deception, 142–45, 149. *See
also* Deception

"Crazy states," 5–6, 155

Cross Link, 77, 107

Czechoslovakia, 182n.15

D. A. Dampf, 48

Deception, 137–49; Johansen-Chemik,
135, 148–50; Libya's use of, 145–
48; monitoring, 161–63

De Dietrich, 170n.14

Dee Trading Co., 105

Defense Department (United States), 117

Defense Intelligence Agency (DIA) (United
States), 115

Degussa AG, 78

Delivery systems, 36, 117

Democratic Republic of Germany. *See*
East Germany

Denmark, 51, 76

DePaulo, B. M., 139

Deutsche Presse Agentur (DPA), 41, 74,
77, 78

DIA. *See* Defense Intelligence Agency
(United States)

DPA. See Deutsche Presse Agentur

Dror, Yehezkel, 5

Eastern Europe, 133, 156–57

East Germany, 51, 76, 85, 89, 93

EC. *See* European Community

Economic espionage, 129

Egypt, 65–66, 176n.2; chemical weapons
possession, 13, 47, 48, 57, 126,
176n.2

Enhanced Proliferation Control Initiative,
160

European Community (EC), 16–17, 79,
103–4

Evans, Gareth, 68

Executive Order 12543, 14

Export controls: and German reunification, 119; Paris Chemical Weapons
Conference discussion, 62, 64–65,
66–67; policy-making, 159–61;
United States, 16, 47, 66, 128, 160–
61. *See also* West German export
controls

Federal Bureau of Investigation (FBI),
152

Federal Republic of Germany. *See* West
Germany

Fiscal Administration Act (West Germany), 101

Fitzwater, Marlin, 117

Foreign Trade and Payments Act (West
Germany), 72, 95, 101

Foreign Trade and Payments Regulations
(West Germany), 101

France, 13, 40; and Paris Chemical Weapons Conference, 29, 58, 62; supplier
firms, 51, 70, 96, 170n.14

Frankfurter Allgemeine Zeitung, 43, 45,
72–73, 75

Frankfurter Rundschau, 77

Gansel, Norbert, 79–80

Gedopf, Jozef, 77

Geissler, Erhard, 19

Genetic engineering, 4, 19, 128

Geneva Protocol (1925), 17–19, 33, 54,
169n.2; and Paris Chemical Weapons Conference, 28, 58, 61, 63, 64

Genscher, Hans-Dietrich, 79, 98, 116; on
export controls, 42, 74; responses to
U.S. charges, 40–41, 43, 45

German Chemical Manufacturers Association, 152

German reunification, 119, 133, 157

GICCW. *See* Government-Industry Conference against Chemical Weapons

Global technopolitics, 4–5

Globesat Company for Applied Satellite
Technology, 78

Gorbachev, Mikhail, 45, 66, 119–20

Gordon, Michael R., 21–22, 115

Government-Industry Conference against
Chemical Weapons (GICCW), 67–68

Great Britain. *See* United Kingdom

Greenwood, Ted, 158

Grindus, S. A., 48

Gulf Crisis (1990–91), 157–58, 163, 164,
165, 170n.4, 184n.6, 185n.11

Havel, Vaclav, 182n.15

Hippenstiel-Imhausen, Jurgen, 39–40, 43–
44, 173n.16; prosecution of, 117–
18, 133, 134, 135, 148–49, 151; use
of deception, 148–50

Hong Kong, 87, 88, 91, 99, 100, 101,
105, 118, 130

Howe, Geoffrey, 42

Index

Huennebeck GmbH, 76
Hungary, 96

IBI Engineering. *See* Ihsan Barbouti International Engineering
IG/T. *See* Inter-Departmental Group on Terrorism (United States)
Ihsan Barbouti International Engineering (IBI), 43, 74, 75, 77, 78, 114, 135; Report, 87, 88, 95, 96; schema, 104–5, 105 (figure), 107; U.S. commercial activities, 152, 179n.20
Imhausen-Chemie, 38, 42; deception by, 131, 135, 148–50; denials by, 39–41, 43 44, 117; disgrace of, 114, 117–18, 152, 182n.21; Report, 81, 87, 88, 91, 93, 95, 96, 99, 100, 101, 181n.44; and Salzgitter Group, 77, 78, 99, 101, 105; schema, 104, 105, 106 (figure), 107
IMHICO AG, 43
India, 48, 62, 135, 162
Intec Technical Trade and Logistics Society Limited of Vatterstetten, 36, 93, 179–80n.27
Inter-Departmental Group on Terrorism (IG/T) (United States), 25
International relations: "crazy states," 5–6, 155; deception, 137–43; statesmanship, 154–55
Iran, 21, 47, 48, 175n.48. *See also* Iran-Iraq War
Iran-Contra scandal, 175n.48
Iran-Iraq War, 12–13, 16, 28, 57, 126, 177n.17
Iraq: arms acquisition, 8, 158–59, 161, 185n.11; chemical weapons possession, 12–13, 47, 48, 57, 119, 126, 135, 164, 184n.6; Israeli nuclear reactor bombing, 184n.2; nuclear technology, 135, 162; support for Libya, 62. *See also* Gulf Crisis (1990–91)
Israel, 30, 62, 184n.2; U.S. assistance, 32, 33, 52, 53. *See also* Israeli nuclear and chemical weapons possession
Israeli nuclear and chemical weapons possession, 13, 62, 135, 162; Libyan linkage strategy, 32, 33, 52, 53, 57, 64, 126
Italy, 40, 51, 78, 83, 96, 180n.27

Jackall, Robert, 144
Jamahiriyah News Agency of Libya (JANA), 24, 34, 51–52, 53, 116

JANA. *See* Jamahiriyah News Agency of Libya
Janis, Irving, 144
Japan, 17, 25, 56, 160; supplier firms, 26–27, 30, 51, 76, 85, 86, 93, 96
Japan Steel Works. *See* Nihon Seikojo
John Zink GmbH Construction Technology, 75
Jordan, 47, 48, 185n.11

Kastel, Joerg, 181n.44
Kiefer Engineering and Consulting, 76
Kohl, Helmut, 38, 79–80, 98, 180–81n.41; deception by, 134, 151; and export controls, 36, 72, 119; protestations by, 41, 43, 44, 71, 75, 134. *See also* West German headings
Korea, 85, 93
Krebs, A. G., 65–66, 76
Kuwait, 52. *See also* Gulf Crisis (1990–91)

Lambsdorff, Otto, 73–74
Laos, 13
Libya, 13, 122; and Biological and Toxin Weapons Convention, 18; and Chad, 21, 92, 97, 156; coercive regime, 145–46. *See also* Libyyan responses to U.S. charges; Rabta complex; U.S. factory construction charges; U.S.-Libyan relations
Libyan responses to U.S. charges, 48–55; compromise rumors, 54; and damage threshold, 130, 147, 184n.32; and deception, 146–47; denial, 6, 32, 33, 171n.2; international inspection offers, 31–32, 49–51, 130, 172n.23; international support, 51–52, 57; and Paris Chemical Weapons Conference, 56, 64; superpower weapons linkage strategy, 32, 33, 49, 52–55, 62, 64, 126, 151–52; and U.S. embargo, 24–25
Liechtenstein, 87, 107, 180n.27
Lingemann, Detlef, 181n.44
Livingstone, Neil C., 148

Machiavelli, Niccolo, 137–38, 140, 145
al-Mahdi, Sadiq, 51
al-Majid, Ahmad Ismat Abd, 62
Merck, 78
Meyer, Harry P., 75
Middle East, 161–62. *See also* Arab states; Israel

Military deception, 141–42
Ministry of International Trade and In-
dustry (MITI) (Japan), 26–27
Mitchell, Robert W., 138
MITI. *See* Ministry of International Trade
and Industry (Japan)
Mitterrand, François, 29
Mujbir, Sa'd Mustafa, 53–54
Murphy, Richard W., 29–30
Mustard gas, 13

NATO. *See* North Atlantic Treaty Organi-
zation
Nerve gas, 13
Netherlands, 48, 107, 182n.22
Neue Presse, 76
Neues Deutschland, 77
New York Times, 21, 41, 42, 68, 80, 115,
125
Nidal, Abu, 14
Niger, 156
Nightline (ABC), 152
Nihon Seikojo (Japan Steel Works), 26–
27
North Atlantic Treaty Organization
(NATO), 31, 37, 71, 103, 127–28,
157, 161
North Vietnam, 13
Nuclear Non-Proliferation Treaty, 160
Nuclear weapons, 3, 13, 25; Israeli pos-
session, 13, 32, 33, 53, 57, 62, 64;
Libyan linkage strategy, 32, 33, 49,
52–55, 62, 64, 126, 151–52. *See
also* Arms control

Oakley, Phyllis, 31–32
Ost, Friedhelm, 44, 74–75

Pacific Engineering and Production Co.,
48
Pakistan, 135, 162
Paris Chemical Weapons Conference, 2,
28, 29, 56–69, 177n.17; aftermath,
65–68; final declaration, 62–63; international context, 56–59; Libyan
superpower weapons linkage strategy, 52–53, 130; U.S. position, 57–
62, 63–64; U.S. proposals, 28–29,
56
Pen Tsao, 87, 88, 95, 105, 107
Perle, Richard, 37
Persian Gulf states, 28. *See also* Arab
states; *specific countries*
Pieper, Ernst, 78

Pirages, Dennis, 4–5
Poland, 93
Press: and deception, 142, 146; and Eastern European events, 156–57; Libyan, 24, 34, 49; Libyan inspection
invitation, 49–51, 130; U.S. charges
coverage, 1–2, 41, 42, 44, 125–26.
See also West German press
Presse, Die, 73
Prince, The (Machiavelli), 137–38
Project Ittissalat, 36
Proliferation, 21, 47–48, 57, 65; commercial monitoring, 161–63; and Gulf
crisis, 157, 163; and dual-use tech-
nology, 128, 163–64; policy-making,
154–66; precursor availability, 3, 20,
26, 29, 161; public opinion, 12, 17;
third world motivations, 155–56,
158. *See also* Export controls; Paris
Chemical Weapons Conference; Sup-
plier firms; U.S. factory construction
charges; U.S. proliferation policies;
Use of chemical weapons in conflicts
Protocol for the Prohibition of the Use in
War of Asphyxiating, Poisonous or
Other Gases, and of Bacteriological
Methods of Warfare. *See* Geneva
Protocol (1925)

Qadhafi, Moammar, 31, 54, 96, 116,
145–46; instability charges, 55, 128,
130, 148; and terrorism, 14, 46; and
U.S. factory construction charges, 33,
34, 48–49; on U.S.-Libyan disarmament negotiations, 49

Rabta complex, 8, 21–22; civilian presence, 34, 49, 130, 131, 172–73n.28;
deception, 145–48; defense arrangements for, 31, 50, 130; fire (1990),
116–17, 122, 127; international activity phases, 120–23, 121 (table);
international inspection proposals,
31–32, 49–51, 96, 116, 130,
172n.23; Israeli attack threats, 49;
Libyan motivations, 155–56; Libyan
policy, 129–32, 145; location, 21;
risky nature of, 129, 147–48, 150;
Der Spiegel description, 22–23; supplier network schema, 104–12, 105
(figure), 106 (figure), 108–10 (table),
111 (figure); underground storage
facilities, 23, 115. *See also* Libyan responses to U.S. charges; U.S. factory

construction charges; West German involvement

Radio Free Lebanon, 54

Radkau, Joachim, 36–37

Al-Ra'i Al-Amm, 52

Reagan, Ronald, 16, 28, 29, 38, 58, 66. *See also* United States; *U.S. headings*

Redman, Charles E., 28

"Report Submitted by the Government of the Federal Republic of Germany to the German Bundestag on February 15, 1989 concerning Possible Involvement of Germans in the Establishment of a Chemical Weapons Facility in Libya." *See* West German Government Report

Rheincisen Chemical Products, 48

Robinson, Michael, 139

"Rolling text," 4

Romania, 96

Rose GmbH, 182n.22

Rosenthal, R., 139

Ross, Andrew L., 155

Ruehe, Volker, 41–42

Russow, Lily-Marlene, 139

Sabha plant, 119, 122, 135, 182n.22

Sadat, Anwar, 148

Salzgitter Industriebau GmbH (SIG), 77, 78, 79; Report, 87, 88, 98–101, 107; schema, 105, 107

Sartorius Metal Construction, 78

Saudi Arabia, 47, 52

Schauble, Wolfgang, 79, 80, 102–3

Schreckenberger, Waldemar, 71

Secrecy, 141. *See also* Deception

Shalgam, Rahman, 116

Shevardnadze, Eduard, 28, 46, 57

Shultz, George, 25–26, 27, 46, 128; and Paris Chemical Weapons Conference, 59–62, 63–64; and West Germany, 38, 43, 45, 98, 103

SIG. *See* Salzgitter Industriebau GmbH

Sihi GmbH and Co., 93

Simpson, Natasha, 14

Singapore, 107

Singer, J. David, 165

Singh, Natwar, 62

South Africa, 135

Soviet Union, 18, 26, 28, 54; chemical weapons possession, 13, 20, 45, 64, 177n.18; support for Libya, 31, 46, 57; U.S. chemical weapons agreement, 66, 119–20

Spain, 83

Spiegel, Der, (West Germany), 22–23, 36, 78, 115, 119

Spiers, Edward M., 3

State behavior. *See* International relations

Statesmanship, 154–55

Stauffer Chemicals, 65

Stercken, Hans, 73

Stern, 36, 74, 77

Stoltenberg, 99, 100

Sudan, 51

Sueddeutscher Rundfunk, 43

Sueddeutsche Zeitung, 45, 73, 77

Sued Kurier, 45

Supplier firms, 29, 30, 31, 47, 48, 51, 117; schema for Rabta complex, 104–12. *See also* Export controls; Japan; Proliferation; West German involvement

Surprise inspection network proposals, 42

Switzerland, 43, 48, 57, 65–66, 75; supplier firms, 86, 87, 93, 107, 180n.27

Syria, 47, 51–52, 57, 62

Tabun, 13

al-Talhi, Jadallah Azzuz, 53, 62

Technology: global technopolitics, 4–5; terrorist use of, 25; third world deficiencies, 5, 159. *See also specific topics*

Terrorism, 14, 15, 25, 116; and U.S.-Libyan relations, 13–14, 20, 46, 145

Thailand, 50, 86

Thorson, Stuart J., 146

Tietmeyer, 99, 100

Toshiba Corporation, 26

Toxins, 4, 18, 19

Transpek Private Ltd., 48

Tunisia, 47

Umar, Abd al-Rahim, 52

United Arab Emirates, 47

United Kingdom, 25, 31, 42, 56; supplier firms, 86, 96; support for United States, 125, 157

United Nations, 2, 12–13, 25–26; investigate powers, 61, 63, 64, 65; Libyan complaints, 53, 130

United States: assistance to Israel, 32, 33, 52; and Biological and Toxin Weapons Convention, 18; draft treaty, 4; and Egypt, 176n.2; export firms, 47, 48, 51; nuclear weapons possession, 32, 33, 49, 52–55, 62, 64; Rabta complex attack threats, 31–32, 34, 172–73n.28; Soviet chemical weapons agreement, 66, 119–20. *See also* Paris Chemical Weapons Conference; U.S. factory construction charges; *U.S. headings; U.S. headings under other subjects;* West German involvement

U.S. Arms Control and Disarmament Agency, 20, 46

U.S. chemical weapons possession, 13, 16, 20; Bush Gorbachev agreement (1990), 66, 119–20; Libyan linkage strategy, 32, 33, 49, 52–53, 62, 64, 126; old stock destruction, 177n.18, 184n.32; and Paris Chemical Weapons Conference, 59–62, 64

U.S. Congress, 16, 160–61

Use of chemical weapons in conflicts: Chad, 21, 92, 97; Iran-Iraq War, 12–13, 16, 28, 57, 126, 177n.17

U.S. Export Administration Act, 47

U.S. factory construction charges, 30, 56, 68, 124–29; destruction demands, 46; DIA information, 115; diplomatic contact attempts, 46–47, 54, 175n.48; diplomatic pressure, 25–26, 27–30, 45–46, 125; evidence for, 6, 40, 45, 125, 130, 131, 135–36, 147, 152, 174n.42; foreign supplier suspicions, 2, 26–27, 30; international support, 125, 157; Japanese supplier firms, 26–27; *New York Times* article, 21–22; renewed charges (1990), 115–16, 122; and U.S. policy towards Iraq, 159. *See also* Libyan responses to U.S. charges; Rabta complex; West German involvement

U.S.-Libyan relations, 54; and terrorism, 13–14, 20, 46, 145; U.S. air raid (1986), 15, 20, 29–30, 31, 40, 126–27, 145; U.S. embargo, 14–15, 20, 24–25, 145. *See also* U.S. factory construction charges

U.S. proliferation policies, 1–2, 25–26, 29–30, 124; charges against Egypt, 65–66; export controls, 16, 47, 66, 128, 160–61; Paris Chemical Weapons Conference, 59–62; policy-making, 156–58, 159, 184n.3; Redman statement, 27–28; timing, 156; and U.S. security procedures, 162, 172n.18

U.S. Rabta attack threats, 31, 46, 115, 116–17, 165; and civilian presence, 34, 49, 130, 131, 172–73n.28; and damage threshold, 130, 147, 184n.32; and deception, 146–47; international opinion, 40, 126–27

Verification and enforcement, 64

Vienna Domestic Service, 42–43

Vietnam War, 13

War Weapons Control Act (West Germany), 101–2, 119

Wascher, Werner, 174n.42

Webster, 98, 103

Webster, William H., 58

Welt, Die, 43, 72, 75, 79

Western European restrictions on Libyan, 36; [illegible] supplier firms, 36, 45, 47. *See also specific countries*

Westfalenblatt, 76–77

West German Chemical Industry Association, 182n.21

West German export controls: initial laxness, 36, 37, 38, 72, 149, 160, 173n.9; lack of implementation, 119, 122, 128, 133, 135, 185n.11; strengthening proposals, 42, 45, 73, 74, 101–2, 182n.25. *See also* West German involvement

West German Government Report, 37, 80–102, 151, 180n.40; BND information, 82–91, 93, 97; diplomatic sources, 91–98, 181n.44; as end of situation, 121–22; Libyan responses, 114–15; public pressure for, 134; Salzgitter Industriebau GmbH, 87, 88, 98–101, 107; U.S. responses, 113–14. *See also* West German export controls

West German involvement, 132–35; blackmail vulnerability, 131; BND information on, 71, 74, 79, 82–91, 93, 97, 102, 115, 147, 151; continuation of, 118–19, 122; and deception, 134, 150–51, 152–53; diplomatic relations, 37–38; early speculations, 28; evidence for, 42, 82; and German history, 40, 41, 45, 128–29, 133–34; nongovernmental reports, 42–43; other Middle East chemical weapons, 47, 48, 135; Paris Chemical Weapons Conference discussion, 60; public emergence, 38–45, 74–78, 179–80n.27; Sabha plant, 119, 122, 135, 182n.22;

schema, 104–12; U.S. briefing, 44, 98, 103; U.S. media coverage, 1–2, 41, 42, 44, 125–26; U.S. policy, 124, 127–28, 161; U.S.-West German consultation proposal, 79; and U.S.-West German relations, 41–42, 43, 44–45, 57, 70–71, 132–33, 134; Western European reactions, 40; West German inspection request, 96; West German investigations, 35–37; West German justifications, 102–4. *See also* West German export controls; West German Government Report; West German press; West German protestations

West German press: investigation by, 6–7, 22–23, 36, 41, 43, 72–73, 74, 75, 76–77, 78, 80, 125–26; support for government, 41, 45; and West German Government Report, 180n.40

West German protestations, 57, 125; Imhausen-Chemie denials, 39–40, 43–44, 173n.16; lack of evidence, 40, 40–41, 42, 43, 44, 73–74, 79, 132; and Paris Chemical Weapons Conference, 70–71; West German press support, 41, 45

West Germany, 18, 25, 56. *See also West German headings*

WHO. *See* World Health Organization

Wieck, Hans-Georg, 79

Wong, Elsa Y. M., 105

World Health Organization (WHO), 24

Yeager, Peter C., 143

Yemen civil war, 13

Yugoslavia, 51

Zintan Basic Peoples Congress, 49

Zuckerman, M., 139

THOMAS C. WIEGELE
(1932–1991)

In the midst of working on the copyedited version of this book, Thomas C. Wiegele died unexpectedly. His death was especially untimely in that he had just retired from full time teaching and was planning to spend more time on his first love, photography, and to do more traveling and writing.

As a former colleague of his at Northern Illinois University, I know that Dr. Wiegele will be remembered fondly by all the people he knew professionally and personally. His record of professional accomplishments is long and distinguished, spanning teaching, research, and administration. He was a professor of political science and a Presidential Research Professor at NIU, a founding member and executive director (1981–91) of the Association for Politics and the Life Sciences, and editor (1981–91) of the journal *Politics and the Life Sciences*. He was also one of the first persons in the country to work in the new field of biosocial research. As director of the Program for Biosocial Research at NIU, Dr. Weigele was a leader of innovative research in his tireless quest to bridge the gap between biology and politics.

As the prime mover in establishing a graduate field in biopolitics in the Department of Political Science at Northern Illinois University, Dr. Wiegele had a tremendous impact on many graduate students from various disciplines. His dedication to the graduate program— through curricular initiatives, internships, and research contributions—will long be remembered by those colleagues and students whose lives he touched over the last two decades. He leaves them with this legacy: an increased sensitivity to the complexities of the world and the challenge to step beyond the safety and comfort of "conventional wisdom."

Dr. Wiegele wrote several books, including *Biotechnology and International Relations: The Political Dimensions*, 1991; *Leaders under Stress: A Psychophysiological Analysis of International Crises*, 1985 (coauthored with G. Hilton, K. Oots, and S. Kisiel); *Biology and the Social Sciences: An Emerging Revolution*, 1982; and *Biopolitics: Search for a More Human Political Science*, 1979. He published articles in various journals such as *Political Psychology, Presidential Studies Quarterly, Issues in Science and Technology, International Political Science Review,* and *International Studies Quarterly.*

This book is a cogent reflection of Dr. Wiegele's interest in clarifying the political implications of the rapid advances in the biological sciences. More than any of his previous books, Dr. Wiegele was looking forward to the publication of *The Clandestine Building of Libya's Chemical Weapons Factory: A Study in International Collusion.* It is sad that he did not live to see the product of his work. However, he would have been gratified to know that, thanks to his carefully maintained research files and the collaborative efforts of Miriam Levitt, Carolyn Cradduck, and James Schubert, the publisher's production deadline was met without compromising the book's integrity.

He would be rightfully proud of this work. As with his other writings, the book is a thoughtful and balanced analysis of a complex issue. His careful and thorough scholarship reflects his philosophy that anything worth doing will not be easy. Hopefully, the book will have the impact on scholars and international policymakers that he anticipated.

Dr. Wiegele will be sorely missed by his friends, colleagues, students, and others who respected him for his high personal and professional standards. His legacy will be a better understanding of the need for a flexible, future-oriented perspective that transcends conventional disciplinary boundaries. For that the world will be a better place.

Robert H. Blank
University of Canterbury